Understanding Chaucer's Intellectual and Interpretative World

Front cover art by GRETCHEN DE GRASSE

Understanding Chaucer's Intellectual and Interpretative World
Nominalist Fiction

Edward E. Foster

Studies in British Literature
Volume 41

The Edwin Mellen Press
Lewiston•Queenston•Lampeter

Library of Congress Cataloging-in-Publication Data

Foster, Edward E.
   Understanding Chaucer's intellectual and interpretative world : nominalist fiction / Edward E. Foster.
      p. cm. -- (Studies in British literature ; v. 41)
   Includes bibliographical references and index.
   ISBN 0-7734-7972-4
   1. Chaucer, Geoffrey, d. 1400--Philosophy. 2. Narrative poetry, English (Middle)--History and criticism. 3. Philosophy, Medieval, in literature. 4. Nominalism in literature. 5. Narration (Rhetoric) 6. Rhetoric, Medieval. I. Title. II. Series.
PR1875.P5F67   1999
821'.1--dc21   99-24666
                                                                                                              CIP

```
This is volume 41 in the continuing series
Studies in British Literature
Volume 41  ISBN 0-7734-7972-4
SBL Series  ISBN 0-88946-917-X
```

A CIP catalog record for this book is available from the British Library.

Copyright © 1999 Edward E. Foster

All rights reserved. For information contact

        The Edwin Mellen Press   The Edwin Mellen Press
                Box 450   Box 67
            Lewiston, New York   Queenston, Ontario
            USA 14092-0450   CANADA L0S 1L0

                      The Edwin Mellen Press, Ltd.
                      Lampeter, Ceredigion, Wales
                    UNITED KINGDOM SA48 8LT

                    Printed in the United States of America

For Jan, John, and James

TABLE OF CONTENTS

Foreword	i
Preface	iii
Acknowledgements	vii
Chapter I: A General Prologue	1
Chapter II: The Interpretation of Dreams	25
Chapter III: The Approximation of Truth	61
Chapter IV: Gentilesse	91
Chapter V: The Limitations of Teachers	129
Chapter VI: The Tellable Truth	157
Chapter VII: Paradigm Lost—*Troilus and Criseyde*	185
Chapter VIII: Epilogue	203
Notes	207
Bibliography	219
Index	231

Foreword

To paraphrase Talbot Donaldson, when I undertook this project, I had no idea how much commentary I would not be able to read. The volume of Chaucer criticism is so great that, with the best will and the most scrupulous conscience, it would not be possible to read, assimilate, and integrate all that exists. If I had tried to, this book would have become an annotated bibliography, and incomplete at that. What I have tried to do is absorb as much as I could, acknowledge those sources which were most influential in shaping my views, and indicate a reasonable amount of related or corroborating material in notes, in bibliography, and, where appropriate, in my text. I have tried to make use of existing scholarship without letting it clog the progress of my own argument. I have conceived of the overwhelming mass of Chaucer criticism as arrayed in four concentric circles. The innermost circle is comprised of those few studies which are truly the intellectual ancestors of my book.[1] The next circle includes all of those studies which have affected my general argument tangentially or specific parts of my argument directly. The third circle encompasses works that I have, at some time, read or consulted but are only broadly contextual rather than influential in my thinking. The outermost circle is all, everything that has been written about Chaucer; it finds its proper and accessible home in the Bibliography of the Modern Language Association. For the sake of intellectual honesty and expository clarity, I have explicitly cited only studies from the first two circles.

Indeed, the very mass of Chaucer criticism provides extrinsic support for my thesis and intrinsic guidelines for my procedures. That there should be so much Chaucer criticism is in itself a sign of the elusiveness and inexhaustibility of the poet. Nor is the fact that much of it is both very good and contradictory surprising. Virtually none of my specific interpretations has not been argued before in some form, but originality in every individual interpretation is not my central goal. I want to provide a different angle of vision that will, I hope, illuminate Chaucer's fictional corpus in a broader way. My central view is that Chaucer invites interpretation because he is himself so interested in the process of interpretation itself—of fiction, of the world, and of the relationship between the two.[2]

I am grateful to all those who have commented on Chaucer and I wish that I could have taken all of them into account. But, rest assured, the very contributions of these predecessors are the necessary foundation for my assay of Chaucer's analogy between the interpretation of fiction and the interpretation of reality. I am grateful to them all, even those whose names and contributions I have not been able to integrate specifically.

Preface

Literary criticism can offer two quite different pleasures. One comes from the criticism that makes us see a work entirely differently, because it offers a new critical approach, or grounds its view in contextual material we didn't know. The other sort of pleasure is quite the opposite; we find ourselves greeting it like an old friend—"Hello, I know you." It isn't that we have in fact read these ideas before, but rather that they strike us with a sense of familiarity: yes, that's exactly how I've responded to that passage or work or author, but I'd never articulated my response to myself as clearly and explicitly as this writer has. So, in reading *Understanding Chaucer's Intellectual and Interpretative World*, I found I was doubling my pleasure, for the ideas had that quality of immediate recognition, as if I knew them as I did their author, Ed Foster.

Partly the familiarity of the ideas comes from their similarity to my own understanding of Shakespeare. Norman Rabkin has said of Shakespeare that he gives us an image of life so complex that in experiencing his plays, we "re-experience ... the unresolvable complexity of life as life presents itself to the fullest human consciousness." For me, that re-experiencing comes in the struggle to make sense of Shakespeare's characters and their world, a struggle that reflects our struggle to make sense of our own world and the people who fill it. So I was delighted to have Foster reveal the same in Chaucer, that "the interpretation of Chaucer's texts is a metaphor for the interpretation of the very world that gives rise to the necessity of textual interpretation."

Probably I should have expected to find Foster's reading of Chaucer familiar in this way, since that reading exhibits qualities that I associate with Ed—comon sense and generosity. I first met Ed when I was a new Ph.D. starting a sabbatical replacement position at Whitman College, where he was then Dean of Faculty. No one can do such a job, especially if they do it well, without annoying this professor, and antagonizing that one, even making enemies, but the longer I spend in the profession, the more respect I have for the job Ed was doing at Whitman while I was there. The common sense I could see in the way he balanced the competing agendas inevitable on any campus, while there on a temporary appointment. I'm sorry that my time at Whitman ended before Ed returned to teaching, for this is one of those books that is the fruit of years of teaching and scholarship, and working alongside Ed as he developed it would have been fascinating and stimulating.

Here, I see his generosity particularly in his willingness to consider any and all possible interpretations, and to reject only their claims to exclusive authority, finding rather that it is exactly the existence of a multiplicity of interpretations that is the essence of Chaucer. Many readers who argue Chaucer's undecideability in the end want to pin him down to their particular notion of undecideability, whereas Foster allows questions to remain open. He is not the first to ground his approach in nominalism, but is unusual in not applying nominalism as a rigid framework for interpretation, but merely as the way of thinking available at the time that most closely resembled Chaucer's own as a "maker of fictions rather than a maker of propositions."

The common sense I find especially in Foster's decision to emphasize his engagement with Chaucer's texts, rather than with other critics. Too often reading recent criticism becomes an exercise that Spenser, Chaucer's greatest fan, would have recognized. Like Una, we find ourselves riding behind our guide through the interpretive woods. Our guide meticulously names and characterizes each tree we pass, and yet somehow we find ourselves at the mouth of Errour's cave, wondering whether the darkness within hides a dragon, or merely emptiness.

Foster instead takes care to chart his path through the woods before he enters, in an opening chapter which does locate his approach in relation to other recent studies. Once he begins his journey through Chaucer's texts, he sticks to his chosen path, reading each work as sensitively and comprehensively as he can; indeed, the proper metaphor here might be flying over the woods, rather than riding through them, because Foster is very much concerned to see not the individual trees, but the shape and character of the whole forest. Still, though the focus stays consistently on Chaucer's works, the notes make clear the breadth and depth of Foster's reading of others' interpretations, which constantly inform his own. The style of the book may remind one of the best criticism of a time before theory took hold of the profession, yet the book's central concern with Chaucer's indeterminacy or "undecideability" is very much of the moment. At the same time, indeterminacy is given historical viability in the nominalist emphasis on individual experience and distrust of abstraction and universals.

Foster's approach can be appreciated by looking at his discussion of the "Prioress's Tale", where he has fully incorporated recent examinations of the tale's anti-Semitism, though he mentions them only in the notes. The Prioress may have her aristocratic pretensions, but she intends to tell a simple didactic tale of spiritual import; Foster shows us, however, the dangers of such spiritual simplicity, that "can generate a sanguinary vision of the universe in which we must work out our salvation." Without, as he says, trying to make Chaucer politically correct, Foster suggests that the tale makes use of the culture's identification of Jews as symbols of the physical and spiritual dangers Christians faced, but also reveals the violence which those same Christians were capable of in their vengeful justice.

This book manages to make us sense the unity in Chaucer's work without reducing that unity to a simple formula. From the dream visions through *The Canterbury Tales* to *Troilus and Criseyde*, though it takes many and varied forms, Chaucer's central project is the representation in his own fiction of the effort to interpret what Foster calls the struggle to understand, though the limitations on human knowing mean that any understandings they achieve must ultimately be partial. The "Knight's Tale", for instance, is told in a way that questions its idealism, yet the realism and cynicism of the "Miller's Tale" is not the answer, either, nor is some arithmetical midpoint between the two. Rather, we find ourselves floating between the two, as the best they can give us is "an approximation of truth." We must be content with that approximation, for the conventional Christianity of the "Man of Law's Tale" or the "Retraction" provides only an apparent resolution. For Foster, moments like these, or the end of *Troilus*, give us a perspective which is true on its own plane of existence, but finally solves or explains nothing for human beings living out their lives "suspended between time and eternity." The interpretation of Chaucer is a game, but a game to be played in earnest, Ed Foster tells us, and we can play with confidence and delight if we take him for our coach.

Peter Greenfield   University of Puget Sound

Acknowledgements

I would like to thank Tiffany Meyers for assistance in preparing the Bibliography, James Kennedy Foster for proofreading the quotations from Middle English and assisting in the preparation of the Index, and especially Gretchen de Grasse for her abstract graphic rendering "The House of Tidings" on the front cover. Throughout, Ms. Patricia Schultz of the Edwin Mellen Press was helpful in devising the format. Most profoundly I am grateful to my Chaucer students, especially the class of Spring 1996, for their patience as I tried out many of these ideas.

On a more practical level, I am grateful to Whitman College for providing time, in the form of a sabbatical leave, and money, in the form of generous support for preparation of the manuscript.

Chapter I: A General Prologue

There is a powerful impulse in literary criticism to explain, to gloss, to pin down, even when attempting to deal with chaotic visions of the world or with recalcitrant literary techniques like irony and paradox. Chaucer's fictions, however, do not solve the world or definitively explicate the human condition, nor do his fictional techniques encapsulate a satisfied spiritual or secular vision of the way things are. This is not to say that Chaucer rejected God, faith, or the accepted truths of Christianity, although there is little doubt that he played with some of them, teased and toyed with our capacity to comprehend them. Nor is it to say that we live in an impenetrably opaque world. Chaucer's fiction is intrinsically mysterious, but not terminally frustrating because, as I hope to show, this is exactly the tantalizing view of the world that Chaucer, throughout his career, assayed to represent.

The situation is analogous, although the methods are radically different, to the problem that we face with any of the greatest Shakespeare plays: anything we say of any substance is open to sensible contradiction; any interpretive thesis must expect to be confronted with oblique truths which, although they do not invalidate one's first thesis, assert themselves from the wealth of textual evidence in various persuasive ways. The result is not confusion, but the revelation of a world that is too complex and various to fit our categories of thought. Chaucer does much the same thing, but in Chaucer not only is the vision of the world too ample for propositional containment; the very process of our struggle to understand is woven into the fabric of narrative techniques. Indeed, the techniques themselves are an emblem of the human predicament in elucidating the human condition.

Lest my discussion become so abstract as to evade comprehension or curiosity, let me attend to some familiar, and I believe astute, characterizations of Chaucerian fiction, Chaucerian belief, and the Chaucerian enterprise.[1] The problem, broadly conceived, is: what do we know when we know Chaucer. Many critics have, in various ways, dealing with the corpus in whole or in part, come to the opinion that Chaucer's fictions, in one way or another, are not "finished." One might say that they are unfinished either in fact, like the *Canterbury Tales*, or in resolution, like *Troilus and Criseyde*. Perhaps, the best example of the matter is the *House of Fame* in which the narrative may literally be unfinished and the view of the world is indeterminate.[2] The conundrum may be articulated in several ways. Chaucer's poems are unfinished but conclusive or inconclusive but complete, or incomplete but resolved as long as we do not take resolved to be synonymous with solved.

An eagle's eye view of some of Chaucer's poems may be clarifying. *The House of Fame* endeavors to instruct the narrator but the poem breaks off before the appearance of "the man of great authority." *The Parliament of Fowls* does not resolve the mating of the eagles. The *Book of the Duchess* does not leave us with any confidence as to what or whether the narrator has learned. The *Canterbury Tales* is missing a lot of tales (no matter which plan for the journey we accept), intrudes a narrator who was not at the Tabard, and ends with a "Retraction" that ostensibly subverts many of the narrated tales, as well as others of Chaucer's works. Even within individual tales, the Knight seems to be vainly struggling to find a shape for an unruly world, the Clerk's allegory seems to be more than he or we can handle, the Franklin's concluding question may not have a legitimate answer, and the highly sophisticated tale of the Nun's Priest may simply dissolve into a platitude. Finally, in *Troilus and Criseyde*, over 8,000 lines of perplexity and agony are tidied up in 84 lines of celestial perspective. Now, it is true that all of these "problems" have solutions in a mountain of Chaucer criticism; indeed each has many solutions. Nevertheless, the accumulation of similar cruxes throughout the length of Chaucer's writing career may suggest a commonalty, a recurrent even persistent preoccupation, that pervades the canon and leads to a question about what Chaucer's work, comprehensively considered, is about. What, through this accumulation of perhaps individually solvable issues, does Chaucer mean or mean to mean?

The problem, if indeed it is one, is compounded by the apparent confusion, within and across poems, of levels of reality as represented in the fiction. What I mean to point out, as a complication to "inconclusiveness", is the self-consciousness of Chaucer's fiction. That is, Chaucer repeatedly calls our attention to the fact that we are, when reading his poems, somewhere in a humanly created fiction. This is more than a simple matter of unrealism. For example, we can be absorbed into a highly fanciful world in Medieval literature and never be troubled by its unreality because of its consistency within its own fancy. Thus, in *Sir Orfeo*, when a flesh and blood Herodis is carried off by the faery king and even when Orfeo penetrates the faery world we are undisturbed because there is a consistency, albeit outlandish, within the fiction's own established terms. Such is common in Medieval literature; realism, much less naturalism, is not a common commodity. Even bizarrely contrived endings, as in any number of romances, are easily accepted within the terms of reality and satisfaction that the poem enforces.

The situation with Chaucer's unrealism is more problematic because of the insistent way in which he reminds us that we are in a fiction. Although such reminders of fictionality appear in Boccaccio, Gower, and other writers, the reminders in Chaucer are much more frequent and diverse.[3] There is the address of the narrator as Geffrey by the eagle in *The House of Fame*; the description of the pilgrims as they would be at home or on the road rather than at the Tabard in the "General Prologue"; the reference to the historical Chaucer in the "Introduction to the Man of Law's Tale"; the surprising verse form of the "Man of Law's Tale"; the Merchant's reference to the author of *The Romance of the Rose*; the allusion to the Wife of Bath by Placebo *within* the "Merchant's Tale"; and the change from third to first person in the description of the Temple of Fame in *The House of Fame* and the Temple of Venus in the "Knight's Tale." And then there are the many more numerous simple impossibilities like the narrator's degree of knowledge and the number of the Knight's battles in the "General Prologue." And there are the ubiquitous direct addresses of narrators to us: as the narrator of the "Knight's Tale" explains how he is shaping his material to the other pilgrims *and to us*, the narrator of *Troilus and Criseyde* asks us to support his deficiencies with our own experience, and many narrators make self-conscious remarks about their abilities and techniques as storytellers.

Now, simple impossibilities and addresses to the audience are common in fourteenth century narrative, but, in Chaucer, their very number, especially when added to the instances where the barrier between us and the fiction or levels within the fiction are transgressed, suggest a habit of mind or angle of vision. The very idea of fiction is forced upon our attention as an object of scrutiny in itself. Of course, there are specific explanations that can be offered for each of these phenomena; for example, Placebo's reference to the Wife of Bath could be a sign of the Merchant's agitation or confusion. But taken all together, the effect is to make fiction itself a perplexing subject. Chaucer is not the only fourteenth century writer capable of ambiguity. For example, in *Sir Gawain and the Green Knight*, it is difficult, if not impossible, to decide whether Gawain's embarrassment or the Round Table's approbation is to be preferred. In fact, both could be embraced simultaneously.[4] The situation, however, is qualitatively different from the bafflement that recurs in Chaucer where neither alternative seems acceptable on its own and the two together are incomprehensible. These are the sorts of circumstances which I intend to address in succeeding chapters.

For the situations that Chaucer describes and the techniques used in his representations defy accommodation even to the familiar confusions of ambiguity, irony, or paradox. Ambiguity allows for alternatives which can be laid out, assessed, selected from, and, at the extreme, lived with. This is the kind of array that John Martti Hill offers as an opportunity to "know feelingly" and to choose with the guidance of benevolent belief.[5] Irony is not quite the thing either. Irony identifies what we should think by prejudicing our perspective on (or making it quite clear) what we should not think. It depends on a fictional context that provides a backdrop for decideability. As Jesse Gellrich explains, Chaucer simply does not provide the fixed context that makes resolution possible.[6] And even paradox is an insufficient category of thought for the radically multiform fictions of Chaucer. A paradox, strictly speaking, is an apparent contradiction and the pleasure and success of the reader in dealing with paradox assumes that resolution is possible. As Gellrich notices, Chaucer has refused to provide the rationalizing connections that ordinarily issue in meaning; there is no authenticating authority.[7] He does not even allow himself the comfort of a faith that explains all. Faith is there and there is a fideistic element in Chaucerian thought, but it is not permitted to intervene as a *deus ex machina* that informs and elucidates the otherwise impenetrable or to preclude both sober and playful intellectual speculation. Thus, although what Delaney says about *The House of Fame* seems apt, that "the tradition . . . is a critical and skeptical tradition, rooted in the awareness of coexistent contradictory truths and the suspension of final rational judgment," the vision of Chaucer seems to me even more fundamentally undecideable, and that I think is Chaucer's pervasive insight.[8]

Nor is the undecideability rooted in abstract formulations of the competing claims of faith and reason. The problem is rooted in the human incapacity to sort through all claims towards an intelligible human reality. It is not that the "truths" of faith are rejected or inadequate; it is just that, despite their indubitability, they are not an answer to the dilemmas of understanding that human beings continually confront in a fallen world: they do not annihilate our passion to understand. This is more than a problem of coping with an hermeneutical circle.[9] It is hermeneutics itself as a topic and it is explored in the ambience of Medieval philosophical speculation not Heideggerian phenomenology. This is not to say that Chaucer was a philosopher, but, as Russell Peck makes clear, he was a philosophical poet.[10] One way of addressing the intransigence of interpretation is offered by Sklute: "I read each work as Chaucer's attempt to represent the complex and conflicting relationship between antinomies such as experience and authority, belief and proof, freedom and necessity, truth and opinion. . . . I see the shape of Chaucer's literary career as a search for an appropriate form able to accommodate the inconclusiveness that these antinomies create."[11] What Sklute says, however, is, in a way, the beginning of my indecisiveness. The antinomies he cites are there and struggled with, though they are not the only indecipherables in Chaucer's vision of the human condition. I would suggest that Chaucer's preoccupation with interpretation goes deeper than this list which I take to be a list of many of the important manifestations of the primary ineluctable vision. We do not see Chaucer coming closer to a resolution of these antinomies through his career no matter how we date the works. And the answer, if there is one, does not seem to be in an achieved or hoped for form that will give shape to the otherwise intractable. That is not Chaucer's vision. Indeed, his forms, or narrative techniques more broadly, are not ameliorative. Rather they themselves are inextricably intertwined with the ideational perplexities. After all, the narrative techniques, themselves the mechanisms of the fictions, are condign with and generative of the intellectual ambivalences. Sklute's contention that inconclusiveness is an attribute of form analogous to skepticism in thought or ambivalence in feeling, however, paves the way for seeing the thoroughgoing way in which form, thought, feeling, and narrative technique are of a piece in the creation of the essential Chaucerian insight that there is, indeed, no form adequate to the vision and no human vision adequate to the reality.[12]

Burlin contends that Chaucer's fiction contains "within its writing structure bipartite elements that seem to be in opposition but interpenetrate imaginatively."[13] Again, I think, close, but no cigar. First, the elements seem not simply bipartite, but sometimes tripartite, quadripartite, or even more partite; second, it is not a matter of "seeming" but of "being"; and third, imaginative interpenetration may or may not result (in Chaucer I think they do not) in a hodgepodge. As with Sklute, there seems to be a root problem that remains to be assessed. It is not sufficient to conclude with Burlin that Chaucer saw that the making of fictions was finally inadequate. Chaucer is fiction; he did not, after all, turn away from it and, as I have suggested and will return to, the elements of fiction are an inextricable and essential component of the perplexity because our perplexity as interpreters of fiction mirrors our perplexity as interpreters of the world.

Despite the sweet reason of the Donaldsonian tradition that wrestles with particular issues and wrings sense out of them, the corpus does not seem to admit of a correlative global analysis. Perhaps that is why Donaldson's most impressive work was in essays. Despite the sour reason of the Robertsonian tradition, that can find an allegory of charity in a cast-iron lawn dog, the corpus does not seem to allow for an interpretive engine that can turn out consistent and uniform units of Chaucerian meaning. The more recent critical tendency to emphasize inconclusiveness and indeterminacy, mediated by irony, paradox, or faith, seems closer to the mark and yet stops short of tackling the collaboration of idea and technique in creating an Everlasting "I don't know."

The "school of inconclusiveness" does, however, recognize that Chaucer's fiction is resistant to solution. Taking into account both the intrinsic ambiguity (or contrariety) of the ideas and the sinuous collaboration of narrative techniques, Chaucer's fiction is not a problem to be solved but a game to be played. This is not meant to trivialize the enterprise. The game is in earnest. Before turning to the techniques that intertwine with ideas to produce Chaucer's instructive indeterminacy, I should make clear that there is a method in the confusion and a sanity in the madness, an ultimate sanity that will not let us complacently think that we know what we do not know, or that we think what we ought to think and feel what we ought to feel, or that thinking and feeling are always reconcilable. It will be essential, then, to examine the context of Chaucer's thought, the connection between that context and the fictional techniques that represent Chaucer's place in the context, and the questions, issues, problems, and dilemmas to which Chaucer repeatedly turns his attention. Briefly, my contention is that Chaucer held a view of the world that saw its inconsistencies as intrinsic but intriguing, various but beautiful, and problematic but satisfying, satisfying in the only way that a person can be satisfied who struggles with the impossible, revels in multiplicities, and rejoices in the splendors of diversity without finding it either necessary or possible to evade all by snuggling in the bosom of faith, even a faith that is deeply and joyfully preserved. Chaucer will not let God solve his confusions partly because the confusions that Chaucer cherishes must disappear if fideism prevails wholly and destroys the multifarious contradictions and confusions that make life worth living and thoughts worth thinking. Before faith resolves what it must resolve, it is only human to explore human capacities for understanding in the manner of the philosophers who scented the air of the High Middle Ages. Although Chaucer does not despair of meaning, he does apply his courage to worrying this world's meanings through all of its contradictions and surprises. His method, however, is not that of the systematic philosopher or theologian nor are the truths that he grapples with arrayed in the same way as those which are the objects of propositional argumentation. If Chaucer's view of the world is inexorably trapped, it is trapped in an especially fascinating and human way, a way that engages the thoughts and feelings of those who are just trying to make sense of a life that is hard to grasp as, moment by moment, we wander through it.

It is not, as some commentators have suggested, that Chaucer is thwarted in the adventure of interpretation by accepting Augustinian versions of Platonic realism. Chaucer's poetry is not a fictional gloss on the Franciscan Augustinianism that culminated in St. Bonaventure. He is insistently unwilling to funnel all knowledge of the world through faith and ignore complications of terrestrial experience. His fictions resist submission to the notion that the world is knowable only by faith in a schema that provides access to ideas that control human life and action. Having indicated reservations about premature fideism, or a fideism that is the only access to understanding the human condition, let me also suggest some skepticism about wholesale allegorization as a key to unlocking elusive, supposedly Augustinian ideas. My hesitation is not just about the monolithic allegorization by Robertson and Huppé, which leads always and everywhere to allegories of charity.[14] Nor do I mean to undervalue charity; indeed, later I hope to show that charity, in the more concrete form of "commune profit," is an essential ingredient for Chaucer both for knowing and unknowing or, conversely, transcendence and limitation. Here I mean only to doubt hasty allegorization that conduces to Augustinian resolutions and solves problems that are more interestingly left as unassimilable irritants.

For Platonists, allegory is both a fictional technique and a way of knowing, but it does not have a privileged authority in Chaucer's narratives. It has no more authority than the finding of correspondences between Chaucer's fictions and contemporary events. To the latter interpretations one may say "well and good, if so," but they do not further our insight into Chaucer's life-long literary project. What I would call allegory proper, or Platonic allegory, does not solve the problem either, for the fact is that Chaucer does make allegories, say in the "Nun's Priest's Tale", but their meanings are rarely, if ever, four-fold and never unqualified by non-allegorical contexts which obliquely call their didactic authority into question. The Nun's Priest teaches both a homely and heavenly message, but the world in which he lives does not leave his conclusions unassailable nor give us confidence that he has embodied transcendent ideas which order and validate our experience ultimately. Less yet does the confusion in the Clerk's allegory issue in a stasis of transcendent ideas; the Clerk's allegory still requires backing and filling to seem pertinent to the messy realities that have come and are to come in the *Tales*.

Now, allegory is not the private reserve of Platonists and Augustinians, but it is especially congenial to those whose metaphysics locates realities in Ideas or Forms and thus to Robertson's reductionist correspondences. The other major tradition of Medieval philosophy, nominalism, rooted in and rebellious from the tradition of Aristotle and Aquinas, avails itself of the particularities of the world, but by way of categorical abstraction.[15] This tradition, firmly present in Boethius, sees reality in the individual and universals in the mind. Of course, Chaucer, despite his close familiarity with *The Consolation of Philosophy*, probably did not know his commentaries on Aristotle's logic. Nevertheless, nominalism, and perhaps the extreme nominalism of William of Ockham, seems better to fit the primacy Chaucer accords to individuals and to experience, by which we arrange individuals in provisional categories.[16] Traugott Lawler, though he does not develop the philosophical connections, tantalizingly entitled his study of the general and the particular in Chaucer *The One and the Many*, a phrase that recalls historical concern with the question of universals. He notes that "diversity is eventually resolved into, or contrasted with, some unity—though that unity is itself usually precarious, threatened, or incomplete".[17]

Ockham is more radical than his nominalist predecessors because he placed certainty entirely in the sphere of the experience of individuals. He separates abstract speculation from the intuitions of individuals and goes so far as to argue that our speculations about abstractions may be logically valid but incorrect because of the radical separation between individuals and abstractions.[18] He does not solve the Chaucerian dilemma of experience as opposed to authority because he allows for the acceptance of reliable authorities concerning matters of intuitive understanding of experience. Nevertheless, here is a world-view that radically unsettles the Thomistic accommodation of faith and reason. Ironically, faith becomes even more potent because the sphere of reason is honored (and to be explored on its own terms for its own sake) but limited and must give way on theological questions to faith. (For Ockham, God's foreknowledge and even the idea of the Trinity were beyond reason, only knowable by faith.[19])

The point is that Ockham's nominalism problematizes allegory (and a lot of other things) by his disjunction between individuals, which are directly intuited by the senses, and abstractions, which can be consistent but unrelated, or unprovably related, to the real world of experience. Whether or not Chaucer knew much, or anything, of Ockham, he breathed the air of the speculations of fourteenth century "clerks." The Nun's Priest and the Clerk are good examples of Chaucerian allegory because charity, properly complicated as "commune profit," does seem implied by both, but neither is the key to all mythologies. All of which suggests that allegory as a literary instrument is more important to Chaucer, with its own hermeneutical pitfalls and promises, than allegory as a constant guide to abstract truths which are otherwise unapproachable. I do not mean to make too much of this foray into the proper uses and abuses of allegory, but I want to insist that it is not a way out of the cognitive prison of Platonic realism, though it can provide a way of turning problems and issues over in our minds that fits better with Chaucer's persistent application to the impossible but productive scramble towards truth. To see meaning in the Book of Nature as well as the Book of Revelation is a commonplace, but neither Book provides a comprehensive exegesis of human life. The meanings of the Book of Nature, allegory at its simplest, are relevant and various and ubiquitous, but they are assays not certainties. Unfortunately, the Book of Scripture, and our approach to it, seems to offer little more cognitive confidence in a confusing, various, highly particularized world.

Although Platonic realism may occasion an endeavor which is intrinsically fruitful, I am persuaded that it is the nominalism of the Thomistic tradition, perhaps even of Ockham, that is closer to the heart of Chaucerian knowing and unknowing. Once again, I emphasize that Chaucer is a fiction-maker not a maker of propositions. Russell Peck's brilliant application of nominalism to Chaucer provides a sounder method of relating Chaucer's confrontations with meaning without compacting Chaucer's variety into an hermeneutical machine. Peck states the nominalist view succinctly: "From intuitional information, the intellect, motivated by the will, abstracts words, images, and concepts, which it holds in the mind for further abstraction and confirmation. Through repetition these processes lead to principles and habits of mind which constitute each individual's sense of reality."[20] Several important words deserve commentary. The beginning of the whole process is intuitive, yet it is essential to remember that intuition has its basis in sense perception; it is not a free-floating cognitive faculty. The nominalist is bound by the dictum that "nihil est in intellectu quod non prius fuit in sensu." As Peck puts it, "For Chaucer, like Ockham, experience is pre-eminently an authority."[21] Second, the notion that the intellect is motivated in this process by the will makes clear that, in nominalist formulations, there is an innate will to know, to make something of the data of both experience and authority, whatever we take each of those terms to mean.[22] Finally, these perceptions are "held in mind" for "further abstraction and confirmation." Knowledge is not certain and immediate, but a process of suspension, testing, probing, and finally wilfully choosing and the result is both "principle" and "habits of mind." Chaucer deals both in principles that may be indefinitely kept in suspension and, more importantly, habits of mind that may be signposts to truth if not truth itself. Peck speculates that as a result "Chaucer's personas often find themselves in the strange position of knowing and not knowing simultaneously."[23]

But several caveats, as important as distrust of allegory as a definitive meaning-maker, are necessary. First, as Gellrich clearly argues, in searching for truth it is not enough to "test our authority against experience."[24] That would assume an illogical priority for experience and, indeed, everything becomes authority once it is written down. And here is an interesting problem: how do we relate the fluidity of experience with the apparent stability of authority as experience continually turns into authority but an authority which cannot automatically be taken to be authoritative?[25] Gellrich finds such stability as is possible in the "text": " . . . voices emanate from language that the narrator does not fully control."[26] This is a version of the liberation of mind and will from the nominalist dilemma.

Second, it cannot be emphasized too strongly that Chaucer's "nominalism" is not an Ockhamite treatise. To emphasize Peck again, "He is not a logician, nor is he a systematic philosopher. He is a philosophical poet, however, and is profoundly interested in the moral implications of nominalist questions."[27] Nor, I would interject, is Chaucer an epistemologist. "Chaucer is not interested in the questions as problems in logic, but, rather, as phenomena of experience."[28] Thus, "what the intellect intuits is the individual not the universal."[29] Consequently, apprehension and judgment remain crucial and both can go wrong. Our refuge is in the explanatory power of the text, yet even that is not definitive and we are left in a world where truth is evanescent but real, elusive but important. For Chaucer, at least, faith is real, but it is not an adequate recourse in the web he is exploring. Divine truth is stable; human knowledge is provisional; and fiction is the means by which nominalist dispositions provide the testing ground for our comprehension of the world we actually live our lives in.

Peck's final challenge is provocative: "Nominalist thought makes one aware of the limitations of human perception and the likelihood of one's being prisoner to his own ideas."[30] One does not have to be a nominalist philosopher to find oneself in this position. One need only be in a world where nominalist speculation has descended from the heights of abstract speculation to the ordinary perplexities of human beings living their lives to be challenged by the nominalist predicament of "two truths"[31]: unchallengeable faith (because faith is not opinion) and suspended opinion, because opinion shapes and re-shapes itself in a world where nominalism suffuses intellectual endeavor. The result is not only twisting and evolving opinions but emergent habits of mind which guide the confrontation of man's intellect with reality.

My speculations about how Chaucer played out this drama of mind, will, and feeling depends upon confidence in the optimistic note that Peck finally strikes: " . . . although Chaucer delights in depicting man trapped by his mental limitations, he also delights in exploring ways in which men break out of their abstractive prisons."[32] *Hic labor est*. Once again, Chaucer's poetry not a problem to be solved but a game to be played. It is, however, a game of the most profound and serious importance because it is the essential human game: how do we pick our way through apparent realities when reason and feeling are both guides but conclusions are intrinsically provisional?

The answers, such as they may be, lie in the nature of Chaucer's fictions and the power he ascribes to them. "Everything that is written is written for our doctrine," say Chaucer and Gower and St. Paul.[33] The problem, then, is the interpretation of the written word, especially when it is a fiction. How do we get at meaning in what is written? And if we understand the writing, what authority do we grant the written text? The problem should be separated both from oral texts and propositional texts. Oral texts, until they are written down, have a wholly different dynamic. If, for example, we look at the vast landscape of popular romance, the confidential relationship between the narrator and his hearers provides, in itself, a kind of authority for the text. The oral romance means to mean something, usually moral, and the combination of structure and means of presentation join teller and hearers in a collaborative community of understanding. One may disagree with an oral text but the context of presentation makes clear what we are to understand. This is so even if the matter is ambiguous, because ambiguity is actually a form of bounded possibilities which can be intellectually encompassed. The ambiguity is, in a way, shaped and framed for us in a determinate whole. Oral literature may not have to be this way, but the circumstances of presentation (I leave aside the level of sophistication of the audience) tend to assure that the narrator is clear in sharing "truths" already accepted by the audience. Community ensures certainty.

The situation with the propositional written word is different. There the writer attempts to validate his own opinions by the use of logic and/or authorities which the reader is expected to accept. Logic may be attempted skillfully or ineptly, but it does imply a set of formal, categorical standards which the reader can apply to a critical reading of the text. Even on the most public of issues, the essential relationship is between writer (philosopher, theologian) and reader and both are constrained by formal rules which are agreed upon *a priori* and can be applied to the text/argument. Appeals to authority within propositional writing add a degree of complexity. If the authority is easily acceptable within the culture, say the Trinity or the divinity of Christ, there is no impediment to the argument. If the authority is doubtful or if its application is problematic, the reader of the propositional text still has the prior tenets of logic as a guide, a meta-authority. The foregoing, of course, did not remove dubiety from propositional discourse in the Middle Ages; one need only notice the *Sic et Non* formulation whether within one writer like Abelard or across texts of, say, idealists and nominalists. So, my argument is not that logic resolves the turmoil of philosophical disputation, but that it does provide an agreed standard for assessment.

The matter is quite different with written, fictional texts, but the common suppositions surrounding Medieval fictions usually submerge the intrinsic dubeity of their arguments, assumptions, or visions. We put ourselves in the fiction and accept its terms in a way similar to but not identical with the conventions of oral fiction. That is to say, we accept, for the moment, the other world, perhaps different from, but certainly comparable to, the world of the reality of our own experience, which, if we are nominalists, is a congeries of intuitions and habits of mind. We may disagree, in whole or part, as we test the fiction against our provisional sense of reality, but, for the duration of the fiction we live in another world devised by another mind. We allow the fiction-writer his otherness and find doctrine in our acceptance or rejection of his construction. Our reaction is something like satisfaction or stability in the provisional acceptance of the authority of the fictional world.

Unlike oral fiction, there is not the rhetoric of present community to envelope us; unlike propositional texts, there is not the formal authority of logic to shore up our confidence as we agree, or disagree, or weigh the propositions against our sense of our own experience. Nevertheless, the tradition of written fictions in the Middle Ages is characteristically one of "little worlds cunningly made" with their validity implied by their own internal consistency. Such is true even of problematical fictions, like Malory, which are on the borderlines of the kind of self-contained worlds I have been describing.

I have made these distinctions (about oral texts, propositional texts, and written fiction) because I believe that the situation with Chaucer is radically different. My contention is that Chaucer's entire career was devoted, probably not in accord with an antecedent plan, to the relentless destruction of the canons of authority which other writers availed themselves of. Without the oral assumption of community, the propositional authority of formal logic, or the willing suspension of disbelief of other Medieval "writers," Chaucer inexorably challenges the conventions, assumptions, and rhetorics which provided others a bastion of authority inherently incorporated into their texts. This is a leap into a world of unresolved and unbounded ambiguities radically different from the tame ambiguities and ironies of even his least confidently didactic contemporaries; the creation of this rudderless world is so familiar to post-modern readers that it takes a leap of imagination to see its uniqueness in the second half of the fourteenth century. Chaucer refuses to make fictions that tell us the truth, because his project is itself the very process of authorityless examination of the world we find ourselves in. It is not a rejection of faith or the authority of the Church, but rather a human-centered, non-self-indulgent exploration of what we as human beings make of the world we find ourselves in. Faith and the Church have answers, but they are not answers to the questions that Chaucer proposes about who we are, where we are, and what we make of it. Renaissance perhaps. Post-modern perhaps. But certainly Medieval in the way that our confusions and contradictions are essential to the human condition. Put another way, Chaucer persistently addresses the problem of interpretation itself. As his fictions present to our senses the raw material for nominalist abstraction, Chaucer never lets us rest with our intuitions or remain comfortable with our habits of mind. Chaucer is about wondering.

Consequently, Chaucer's narrative techniques are a combination of means to represent the fungiplasty of reality as seen from the human perspective *sub specie temporalis* rather than *aeternitatis*. The techniques are familiar to readers of Chaucer. There is the variety of narrators: limited narrators, disappearing narrators, contradictory narrators, incredible narrators, dubious narrators, conscious and unselfconscious narrators. All of these deny us one or more familiar forms for establishing internal authority. There is the development of structures, literal and allegorical, which undercut their own fragilely developed authority. There is the creation of logics (in dream visions, on pilgrimage, and at Troy) which defy the abstract sets of rules which ordinarily give us at least a tentative confidence in fiction. There is the skepticism about ways of knowing that are frequently taken for granted. There are the distinctions between knowing and ways of knowing, often obscured in fiction, but brought to the fore by Chaucer as in his ambivalence about rhetoric. There is *amplificatio* which confounds and *abbreviatio* which mystifies. There is the multiplicity and interpenetration of apparent intents between and among the author and his narrators. There is the insistent preoccupation with contemporary dichotomies of thought, like experience and reality, left unresolved or resolved in ways that do not fully persuade. All of these are familiar techniques, which have been amply explored by generations of Chaucer critics in concrete contexts. Most of all, there is the refusal to allow us to settle on the level of reality in which the fiction resides. This is the technique which I earlier identified as Chaucer's self-conscious fiction and it is the most troublesome, yet characteristic, technique of all. In its simplest form it appears in the ambiguously layered realities of the dream visions. It is developed in the *Canterbury Tales* and *Troilus and Criseyde* into an even more fluid, ever-changing equivocation of what level of reality we as readers stand on. This is not a matter of unrealism; it might perhaps better be called multi-realism. It is more than what has been called Chaucer's bi-focal vision. It is a quicksand of realities that disorients and disturbs the reader who not only lacks an authoritative guide but is deprived also of a consistent terrain. Concretely, it is pilgrims who exist in their own worlds and the world of the pilgrimage. It is a circumscribing world that interpenetrates contingent worlds and is tweaked by them. It is a world that cannot speak the truth because the surrounding worlds dissolve and transmogrify. But it is a fictional world that can represent a multivalent reality that defies assertion, encapsulation, or prescription.

The narrative techniques are necessary for and congruent with Chaucer's vision of the world and our place in it. The interaction is so persuasive that fiction becomes not a means of interpretation, leading to conclusions or even nominalist-like provisional opinions. Community between poet/narrator and audience is undermined, propositions are undermined, and we are left with fictions that are a metaphor for a reality which cannot be fully comprehended. It is like the situation of a person who, in order to make sense of a problem, must keep a large number of variables in mind, while recognizing that the whole is partially falsified if any of the variables is ignored or submerged. In Chaucer, the variables are too numerous for human integration. Faith can supply "answers" but these are transcendent answers to questions other than those being asked. Granted the intellectual incommensurability of the variables, they cannot be sorted, ranked, integrated, or resolved, and we are left in a perpetual state of inconclusive interpretation.

By using fictional techniques that deconstruct his own narratives, Chaucer places a peculiar emphasis on the process of interpretation itself. It is not simply that an individual narrative is inconclusive; a narrator's failure to reach a conclusion is subject to the same kind of delimitation and critical exegesis as ambiguity or irony and we, as readers, are constantly absorbed in the *process* of interpretation itself. Thus, it is not simply that Chaucer's fiction is a metaphor for reality; that is the case, at least in a general sense, with all fiction. Chaucer has taken the process a step further. Because of the effects of techniques he uses on our capacity to understand his fictions, the interpretation of fiction becomes a metaphor for the interpretation of reality. The self-consciousness of Chaucer's fiction, *i.e.*, his repeated reminders that we are *in a fiction*, and the fluid movement between levels of reality, to which he insistently calls our attention, makes the interpretation of the fictions analogous to our ordinary human attempts to interpret reality. We are reminded that there is a higher reality which resolves doubt and confusion, but that is a recognition of the two truths of nominalist thought. Like nominalists in philosophy, Chaucer in fiction is concerned with the meanings of the truths of the other, human reality which is not solved by faith even when the truths of that faith are readily acknowledged. Just as God has created human reality (and therefore has the only total comprehension of it possible), Chaucer has created fictions, not as a god, but with the limitations inherent in being human. What he has done, however, is to insist that we try to understand those fictions and the process that we as readers of text engage in is analogous to our attempt to understand the reality of the human world we live in. Put another way, reality is God's fiction just as Chaucer's canon is man's fiction. The hermeneutical endeavor of the reader with regard to the text, then, is a metaphor for the hermeneutical endeavor of the human being with regard to God's text–reality.

The foregoing is not blasphemous because it recognizes the presence of the pre-existing transcendent realities which are the stuff of God's fiction, and there are even parts of God's fiction which are foolish or dangerous to inquire into: "Goddes privitee," for example. Likewise, Chaucer's fictional texts are the equivalent of a corresponding human creation, but one that we are called upon, again and again, to inquire into, to try to figure out, to try to arbitrate, even though we know that intellectual closure is impossible. There may be an ultimate consolation in faith, but that is not what Chaucer is about. We are left with a never-ending adventure of interpretation. As we inquire into Chaucer's fictions, his techniques have made a text-world that metaphorically stands for the real world God created, which it is the human condition to try to understand. It is not just that Chaucer's tests "stand for" elements in God's created reality, though they often do that, so much as that the interpretation of fiction is the very model for the interpretation of reality. The Truth, in the human world, is not to be had, but it is a necessary and compelling human function to wrestle with the evidence and finally to wonder and even enjoy in fiction the variety and mystery that is the irresistible attraction of God's fiction and our understanding of our place in it.

All of this should not be taken as a dismal assertion that we are abandoned in a world that is disordered and incomprehensible and isolated. We know by faith that the world is indeed ordered by God just as we know that texts are ordered by an author. We know that incomprehensibility is not identical with chaos; our interpretive limitations do not prove that there is nothing out there to understand; rather the relation between the two entice us to the hunt. There is an analogy in Shakespeare's *Troilus and Cressida*. In it, Shakespeare represents a world in chaos and confusion, falling apart metaphysically, politically, and psychologically. Yet Shakespeare's representation of that world is not itself chaotic. It textualizes chaos. Similarly, Chaucer plays with the process of interpretation itself, finding excitement not despair, exhilaration not chagrin, as he ranges over the metaphorical congruence between God's universe and man's textuality. The metaphor illuminates the parallels in process. That Chaucer's texts cannot be solved should be no more catastrophic than that God's fiction cannot be solved; both must be wondered at, both must engage us. And it is precisely in this way that Chaucer does not leave us hopelessly high and dry in texts that are as impenetrable as the reality they figure. In the metaphoric interpenetration there emerges not only the excitement of endless wonder, but also a repeatedly confirmed conviction that we are all in this together and the only way that we can come to despair is by separating ourselves from the process. We are somehow bound together in celebrating what we cannot fully understand, but that is a bond that is the foundation of the "commune profit" that Chaucer urges us, implicitly and explicitly, is the basis for coherence in human experience and our nearest way to "make a virtue of necessity" and bring joy out of wonder at man's texts and God's creation.

Throughout this introduction I have been using terms like "reality," "the world," "the human condition," and "God's creation" somewhat loosely and interchangeably. If we are to understand how the interpretation of texts (man's fiction) is a metaphor (not a solution) for the interpretation of these entities (God's fiction), it remains to play with them more directly. If my thesis is that Chaucer's literary achievement is relational (that text is to reader as these entities are to man, and that the relation is interpretation), I should explain what I mean these terms to comprise, because I have in mind not objects or artefacts but circumstances, situations, relations, and our provisional means for and results of trying to understand.

My terms are meant to comprehend several areas of human experience. They are not things so much as conventional constructs and habits of mind for the ordering and shaping of the constructs. I list them here not in a comprehensive or exhaustive way, but as a suggestive list of items that will be the objects of scrutiny in the chapters to come. Since these items interpenetrate (or permeate) each other, they are not chapter headings, but entities of human experience that existed in

Chaucer's human experience and that he made part of our textual experience.

First, perhaps most important, are the broad paradigms for human experience that were prominent in the fourteenth century. The two most important and most recurrent in Chaucer are courtly love and chivalry. It is immediately obvious that they are not things but matrices for the interpretation of experience. As Chaucer turns over, in his and our minds, these paradigms, they become the opportunity for the examination of the array of human actions and ideals that are associated with each. They are interesting in themselves as ways of knowing, or attempting to know, the world, to make sense of human experience. In each case, Chaucer goes beyond the paradigm itself to explore the limitations and alternatives to the paradigms. All heuristic devices are man-made and limited.

For example, in the case of courtly love, in, say, *The Book of the Duchess*, "The Knight's Tale", and *Troilus and Criseyde*, Chaucer identifies defining characteristics of the paradigms, elements of the paradigms, and alternatives to the paradigms. Although satire is sometimes a useful instrument in this anatomization, it is not the main point. Chaucer's focus is rather on the cohesiveness and explanatory capacity, ingredients, and alternatives which perhaps distort less our understanding and behavioral imperatives. Thus, courtly love becomes not a paean to Andreas Capellanus or Chretien de Troyes, but an opportunity to survey the varieties of love (sexual, domestic, and divine) which the paradigm incorporates, ignores, or falsifies. Courtly love is not a model or a taboo; it is an opportunity to explore its constituent parts in relation to each other and to the rest of our experience.

Similarly with chivalry, Chaucer is interested in both the adequacy of the paradigm and the elements incorporated and ignored by the paradigm. Thus, Chaucer concentrates not on a systematic analysis of, say, the five virtues of the pentangle or even the truth, honor, freedom, courtesy, and gentillesse attributed to the Knight in the "General Prologue". He is curious about the explanatory power of the construct as a whole *and* he is interested in the operations of the constituent elements. Chivalry is tested as a device for shaping and understanding human morality, and its parts are scrutinized as to their effectiveness or futility. Consequently, the paradigms of love and chivalry become testing grounds for how we should live our lives. Even if faith is the ultimate determinant, and I think Chaucer never really calls this into doubt in what is finally an orthodox vision of the world, there remain these niggling questions of how life should be lived and conceived from a tentative and imperfect and necessarily incomplete human perspective, rather than *sub specie aeternitatis* which removes the perplexities which we inevitably feel in ordinary life regardless of the power of our faith.

These two major paradigms involve Chaucer in their subject matters but also in their explanatory power as hermeneutical devices, thus providing the overarching categories for thorough exploration. It has often been said that Chaucer was interested in all of the major controversies of his day that involved ways of knowing and doing. Love and chivalry are the paradigmatic *topoi* in which these items are weighed and assessed. Thus, recurring themes like experience versus authority, rhetoric, anti-feminism, and others are not separate objects of inquiry, but parts of the overarching categories of love and chivalry as ways of knowing and doing. This is not to imply that such questions are of limited importance but that they are put in the forefront as surrogates for the larger enterprise. Take experience/authority for example. It was a hot topic. But it is a question of ways of knowing rather than a paradigm for knowing and doing. The opposition between the two is either false or more complex than it is usually taken to be. From one perspective, authority necessarily incorporates experience, at least in narrative. As Gellrich pointed out, once written down experience becomes an authority.[34] On the other hand, authority may be seen as simply an account of intellectual (or fideistic) experience. Chaucer wants to test both, and he does that in the context of the ideas and ideals of the two pervasive paradigms.

Rhetoric is a way of knowing as well as a means for communicating knowledge. Only in its application can it become clarifying or obfuscatory, a virtue or a vice, and it is the proper and improper applications that Chaucer praises, ridicules, and wonders about. It should be noted that rhetoric, the rhetoric of fiction itself, pervades Chaucer's canon as text. Thus, while specific examples may come under the microscope, Chaucer is aware that his whole endeavor as a creator of texts is a rhetorical one and therefore self-reflexive. That is, it is an instrument inseparable from the making of fiction. So, in a larger sense, rhetoric is the medium of Chaucer's exploration as well as an object of scrutiny as a means of working through the constituent parts of the two paradigms. Rhetoric for Chaucer is both a contingent subject and an encompassing hermeneutic, and must be called into question itself. There are Chinese boxes here that Chaucer refuses to fully unpack, Gordian knots that he will not untie but only ask us to inspect unceasingly.

Genre may be seen as an aspect of rhetoric or at least the rhetoric of fiction. As such, it receives peculiar manipulation by Chaucer and requires constant attention by us. Chaucer tried out most of the literary genres available to his French, Italian, Classical, and native traditions. Indeed, Fragment VII has been seen as an anthology of genres. It is important to keep in mind, however, what many have said: for Chaucer, genre is not a formal package for narrative, but is itself subject to variation, complication, and manipulation. Whether the narratives are dream-visions, romances, legends, fabliaux, or whatever, they themselves become something new as Chaucer plays with his traditions by subjecting formal fictional categories of organization to inspection and complicating and opening them up as new opportunities for inquiry and wonder. Thus, Chaucer complicates genre itself in order to continually re-focus our attention on the potentials and perils of the imperative to interpret. However, Chaucer's brilliant use of genre is finally in and of our quest to deconstruct the two paradigms and anatomize their elements.

Perhaps the foregoing is to say nothing more than that Chaucer was interested in the world as a complex of ethical imperatives too intricate to be confidently understood, too important to be put aside. In the inevitable, in Chaucer's view, attempt to try to establish and tease out these imperatives, Chaucer employs a rhetoric of fiction that makes his texts profoundly self-reflexive. That is, to address the substance of ideas implies, even necessitates, simultaneous attention to the means of representation. And that is why Chaucer's fiction is so focussed on the necessity and limitations of interpretation. That is why the interpretation of Chaucer's texts is inextricably intertwined with the interpretation of substance in a way that makes interpretation, and wonder, the subject itself.

To return, then, to the underlying idea that guides my opinions, my contention is that the interpretation of Chaucer's texts is a metaphor for the interpretation of the very world that gives rise to the necessity of textual interpretation. Now to an examination of how this is all done. It is tempting to organize the following substantiation of my contention by arranging chapters according to paradigms, like love and chivalry, or ways of knowing, like rhetoric and genre, or "subject matters," like truth and experience and sexuality and gentilesse, or fictional techniques, like self-conscious fictionality. I have decided that to use any of these principles of organization would "falsen my matere" by imposing a kind of hardening of the categories. I have chosen instead to use the texts themselves as my structural format so that it will be possible to keep attention on them and the problems of interpreting them while allowing free play to introduce those features which complicate and indeterminate the texts. Only thus can I represent in my procedure the ways that the agonies of the interpretation of texts are the same agonies that plague an honest, if "unclosed," interpretation of the human condition, while suggesting the efficacy of the ideal of "commune profit" as the only consolation of an unresolved and unresolvable human philosophy.

Chapter II: The Interpretation of Dreams

1. *The House of Fame*

Because of the high level of interest in the significance of dreams in the Middle Ages, it is not surprising that poets wrote a large number of dream-visions, which imply a relationship between the dreaming and waking states and provide a useful laboratory for the study of interpretation itself: nowhere more than in *The House of Fame*. John Fyler's comment on this vision might stand as an epigraph for all interpretations of the poem: "*The Hous of Fame*, above all, is Chaucer's fullest exploration of the poet's position and responsibilities, the sources of his knowledge, and the limits of his vision."[1] Despite the frequent identification of *The House of Fame* as a poem about love, and Chaucer's own categorization of it in the "Prologue to the Legend of Good Women", references to love are intermittent and, with the exception of the Dido episode from the *Aeneid* (actually more from Ovid's *Heroides*) brief. The narrative concentrates on interpretation, an attempt to understand both how we live and how we understand.[2]

Although dream visions by their nature call upon us to interpret the dream, to find significance in it, *The House of Fame* is particularly insistent on this imperative and equally resistant to univocal analysis. For example, the "vision" falls into several parts: the flight with the eagle, the House of Fame itself, and the House of Rumor. Each has its own peculiar opacity and it remains difficult to discover systematic correspondences among these parts. And then, of course, we come to the ending which is not an ending. Nevertheless, we are recurrently exhorted to interpret.

The "I" who introduces the poem has no particular call on being identified with the poet Chaucer himself. The dreamer is himself a character within the circumscribing, if confusing, world that Geoffrey Chaucer draws us into. Thus, from the first line we are in a fiction, not in an overtly pedagogical relationship with the speaker. Within that fiction, the speaker, platitudinous, confused, but curious, launches directly into a discussion of dreams, whether they have meaning and, if they do, what kind of meaning. However, the narrator is hopelessly confused about the categories of dreams. His terminology overlaps but does not coincide with the authoritative division of Macrobeus (or anyone else); it is even hard to tell, for example, what the difference in his mind is between "sweven" and "drem."[3] He decides to leave such philosophical speculations to clerks. What is clear is that he wants to tell us his dream. He does not say why, but his speculations make us suspect that on a level beyond him we are being called to attend to some matter of significance regardless of the dreamer's level of understanding. Indeed, this is a special dream, unlike any that anyone has had before:

> For never sith that I was born
> Ne no man elles me beforn
> Mette, I trowe stedfastly,
> So wonderful a drem as I . . . (59-62)

Moreover, the dreamer's invocation of the drowsy god of sleep to help him "My sweven for to telle aright" and his chatty and homely (or ironic) movement to a wish that everyone should get what they dream for does not give us confidence that he is likely to speak with interpretive authority as he recounts his dream. He can tell us what he saw in his dream, but it seems unlikely that he can as reliably tell us what it means. The confusion about how dreams work does not even assure us that the dreamer is the maker of his dream and therefore intellectually responsible for its interpretive content. But he does want to tell us his story, and the responsibility for the meaning of the dream is thereby left with the Chaucerian

"I" who exists beyond the world of the dreamer even when he is awake. At any rate, we are primed to pay attention and suspect the dream will have significance whether the dreamer understands it or not. This ambiguity is retained because we never return to the world of the dreamer proper; we are left in the end in the world of the dreamer as narrator of his dream.

With apparent factuality the dreamer places his dream on the tenth of December. There are speculations about external historical significances of the date, but in the narrative we can only be sure that it takes place at the opposite end of the year from traditional love visions. Appropriately, then, the dreamer, upon beginning his dream-narrative, finds himself in the Temple of Venus. He doesn't know where he is. His surroundings are unfamiliar, but in some unexplained way he knows that he is in the Temple of Venus. We are now in the dream though it is never made explicit how this world relates to the world of the dreamer waking or the poet making. The layers are at this point inseparable. There is, however, one important distinction: the dreamer is in an opulent world of images and the art has meaning, or at least our impulse is to try to make it mean, though we are ignorant of the authority that the signifiers in this world may have and for whom–for the consciousness within the dream, for the dreamer, for Chaucer and us, or for all simultaneously.

The primary experience within the Temple of Venus is the dreamer's observation and description of the *Aeneid* (supplemented with Ovid) that is depicted in the images in the Temple. Surely there will be a lesson of love; but what will it be, how will it be taught, and where will it fit into the layers of consciousness that have produced it or been instrumental in representing it? The artist of the images is left, unmentioned, beyond our inspection. What is curious is that the dreamer, in the dream, turns these images into story. Whether the artistic maker of this building is the poet or the dreamer, the first interpreter is the dreamer and our job, the job he has charged us with, is to interpret what he represents. This is not to avoid that Chaucer is the ultimate maker of the fiction; but to what extent does the dreamer make it his own when he turns images into story and to what extent do we in turn make it all our own when we read the dreamer's story?

The main sculpted event is the Troy story, but it is a Troy story fashioned out of a combination of Vergil and Ovid. The emphasis on the Dido episode, compared to the whole rest of the *Aeneid*, certainly suits the Temple of Venus. The piety and prowess of Aeneas are acknowledged in the moving tableau, but it is the love and suffering of the Ovidian Dido that takes center stage. The narrator does not tell us that there is writing associated with the pictures, but he quotes, lengthily and sympathetically, Dido's lament. He simply ascribes the words to his dream:

> In suche wordes gan to pleyne
>
> Dydo of hir grete peyne–
>
> As me mette redely.
>
> Non other auctour allegge I. (311-314)

He reminds us that he is looking at engravings but he gives both "speeches" and his own commentary. He digresses briefly on the dangers of mistaking appearance for reality and the perfidy of wicked men and the consequences of bad Fame that have attached to Dido.

Along the way, the narrator hides several times. He shies away from recounting the details of the consummation of the love of Dido and Aeneas. It is too long, he says, but it is also not to his purpose:

> And eke to telle the manere
>
> How they aqueynteden in fere,
>
> Hyt were a long proces to telle,
>
> And over-long for yow to dwelle. (249-252)

He also shies away from the story by referring us to Vergil and Ovid for the details: "Rede Virgile in Eneydos/Or the Epistle of Ovyde . . ." (378-9). He says it would take too long, but he proceeds to a description of wronged women, presumably not treated in the images at all: this is the commentary of the dreamer himself. By the time he returns to the narrative of the founding of Rome, the narrator's stance is clear and it is much more Ovidian than Vergilian. Thus, we have not just an account of the visual representation viewed by the dreamer but a critical commentary on the substance. Dido has been betrayed, and this has become clear as the dreamer has turned visual art into narrative. The dreamer concludes this section by asserting that he does not know who made the engravings, but what is of primary importance is that he has turned the images into a story and thereby imposed his view. Whether this view is Chaucer's or not is undisclosed. What we can tell is that the unadorned visual stimuli have become the raw material out of which the dreamer has made a moral narrative.

Where do our perceptions come from? Who knows? But they are there for us to complete with the significance that we choose to impose. Just as the art at Troy becomes a moving (in both senses) account of the Fall of Troy for Aeneas at Carthage in the *Aeneid*, the stimuli which are merely inexplicably present in the dream become the occasion for the mind of the dreamer to find meaning. No matter what is in the images the narrator has gone beyond them. Thus, the experience in the Temple of Venus is a creative process for the dreamer, and we are asked to see not just images but significance as created by the dreamer. We have observed the dreamer as poet, taking data and explaining it to us. As we come to the end of this segment, granted that we have been involved in the dreamer's story of Dido, we have some expectations of the substantive vision that might ensue from his creative act. But that is precisely what does not happen. (The line between wicked Fame in this section and fickle Fame later on is a very thin one.) What does happen is that the turn of events, by means of a properly dream-like transition, makes the dreamer subject of narrative (the dream narrative again) rather than interpreter of dream data within his own dream. This confusion may bear some relation both to the creative/interpretive process and our situation in the world. The dreamer's opinions may be justified, suppositious, sentimental, revelatory, or whatever; the point is that he is an interpreter who takes on an active role, then returns in the next section to someone in our position who needs phenomena explicated just as he does.

The transition, which many have seen as characteristic of dream logic, seems to me that and more in that the change in the dreamer's circumstances is so radical. Suddenly he is outside of the highly wrought world of art/artists or nature/God and in a blank and barren desert removed from what gave him substance to deal with. The blankness of the world he steps out into is significant and, appropriately, he is lost and fearful. The scene is frightening. He is alone in a barren landscape, man entirely on his own, without the guidance of authority or even stimuli for his imagination to work on to create meaning. And then he sees the eagle. His situation will be changed now as he finds an authority. Will, as we might expect, the eagle/authority confirm or confound the foregoing imaginative activity of the dreamer? The result turns out to be not that simple.

The "Proem" of Book II begins with another insistent combination of an invocation asking for inspiration and exhortation to interpret:

>Now herkeneth every maner man
>
>That Englissh understonde kan,
>
>And listeth of my drem to lere. (509-511)

This is an important dream, of more significance than Isaiah's, Scipio's, Nebuchadnezzar's, Pharaoh's, Turnus's, or Eleanor's. Curiously, the narrator invokes Venus, from whose temple he has just emerged and who might therefore be seen as providing the substance from Book I's meditation on Dido, and Thought, an abstraction that is called upon to help him tell his dream "aright." He must get things right so that we can get things right.

On cue, the golden eagle, glimpsed at the end of Book I, swoops down, picks him up, and carries him off into the air. The eagle's dramatic entrance, his quick movement into the air from where, presumably, it will be possible to gain perspective, and his confident straight-talk establish him as an authority of some sort. Yet, he is different from the literary authorities that helped the dreamer shape his own understanding of Dido in Book I. The eagle, clear-sighted, confident, and in control, takes it upon himself to instruct the dreamer. Understandably, the dreamer swoons, but the eagle's command to wake up not only emphasizes the relationship between the two but highlights that there is much for the dreamer to learn. The dreamer awakes to what he feels is a new state of awareness:

> My mynde cam to me ageyn,
>
> For hyt was goodly seyd to me,
>
> So nas hyt never wont to be. (564-6)

The eagle explicitly tells the dreamer that it is for his enlightenment:

> ☐ And this caas that betyd the is,
>
> Is for thy lore and for thy prow.
>
> Let see! Darst thou yet loke now?
>
> Be ful assured boldely,
>
> I am thy frend. ☐ (578-82)

and the dreamer wonders what his experience might mean.

Amusingly, the narrator (dreamer/storyteller) first thinks that he might have been stellified, turned into a heavenly body like heroes and poets, but the candid eagle quickly disabuses him of this fancy and bluntly tells him that he is to be instructed because he is a writer of love poems who is in fact bookish and introverted with no knowledge of the real world of love. The lesson is the dreamer's reward for his devotion to love, but it is also, according to the eagle, correction and instruction. In short, there has been something admirable about the dreamer's endeavors (the flight is a reward), but now he is being given an opportunity for a more direct understanding that is more accurate and profound than what has been accessible to him heretofore. In one sense, of course, the eagle might be seen simply as an authoritative teacher, but the shape of the fiction accords him a different kind of authority; he is not the mentor of the literary study, but a symbolic, mysterious, powerful symbol of access to a world of reality outside. And the eagle specifically promises, from this privileged position of authority, knowledge of love by experience. So this experience is about revealing to the dreamer how the world works and how love is.

The eagle, completely in charge now, tells the dreamer, whom he has addressed in l. 729 as Geffrey, to look down. That naming necessarily raises for us the question of where we are in the concentric realities of the vision and reminds us of the fictional structure of the whole. Just as much as the Temple of Venus, this is a made thing, which simultaneously interprets and must be interpreted like the artefacts in the Temple of Venus and the poet whose consciousness is the artificer of the whole. When Geffrey, as I shall now call him to keep the ontological ambiguity in mind, looks down, he sees the physical geography of the world. Nothing to be learned or interpreted here, but the eagle streaks higher, higher than Alexander or Scipio or Daedalus and Icarus, and he urges the nervous Geffrey to look up at the universe; they have flown free of the quotidian constraints of the terrestrial world. The eagle's explanations in ll. 935-958 are somewhat pedestrian; he has not really explained anything of much import yet, but Geffrey is getting into the spirit of the journey and what it might, because of the authority of his guide, have to offer:

> He gan alway upper to sore,
> And gladded me ay more and more,
> So feythfully to me spak he. (961-963)

So far, all the eagle really has had to offer by way of interpretation has been his explanation of the motions of sound, a legitimate scientific explanation for the terrestrial world, but nonsense for this stratospheric world. The exposition on sound waves makes sense on earth, but the eagle's extrapolation to the stratosphere, indeed to an upper realm beyond the ordinary experience of anyone heretofore, is a fancy upon which his interpretive value depends. He explains that all sounds come to the House of Fame, but the significance of that movement is held in abeyance until Book III. What is important here is that Geffrey has moved from "reality" into a Boethian, indeed Platonic, world of ideas where real meaning is to be found. But the important distinction is that Geffrey now has the opportunity to view this exalted world not as the product of bookish speculation but as a direct experience open to nominalist analysis and generalization. The eagle asserts that poets do not know this world, but are trapped in a world that imagines but does not know directly. As it turns out, learning will not be that simple. As they approach the House of Fame through the air, Geffrey is struck not only by the opportunity not granted to other poets but even more powerfully by "the grete soun." The eagle explains what it is:

> "The grete soun,"
>
> Quod he, "that rumbleth up and doun
>
> In Fames Hous, full of tydynges,
>
> Both of feir speche and chidynges,
>
> And of fals and soth compouned." (1025-31)

The task of understanding because of the compounding of truth and falsehood, will not be easy, but the eagle has transported Geffrey to where he can see for himself and exhorts him, quite explicitly, to examine and interpret:

> "And here I wol abyden the;
>
> And God of heven sende the grace
>
> Some good to lernen in this place." (1086-8)

More confident now, though his unease will return, Geffrey parts from the eagle to get a first-hand look.

What has been accomplished so far? The eagle has promised knowledge, specifically of love as a kind of run-on from Book I and from Geffrey's performance as a bookish poet. But we have certainly drifted far beyond love or any human construct of love to the question of understanding itself. Perhaps it is not possible to understand love without understanding how to understand. Thus, Chaucer, the dreamer, Geffrey (the dreamer within the dream and the poet beyond the dreamer), and the eagle have transformed a love-vision into a philosophical fiction that provides a basis for understanding. We are all getting more than we bargained for.

The "Invocation" to Book III moves us further in this direction. The invocation is to Apollo as god of "science and of lyght." The dreamer again stresses the primacy of engaging our powers to interpret. He dismisses poetry in the narrow sense of verse by telling us to ignore technical weaknesses, say of prosody, and to keep our eye on the central enterprise–interpretation of a vision of an inaccessible world that has imaginatively been given a reality available for direct experience. We can be informed nominalists in this Platonic world. However, we must not ignore the reflexive reference to the technical medium of verse that the speaker introduces. We are still in a dream in a poem, and the heart of the poem is its interpretive potency.

What Geffrey sees in the House of Fame further expands the purview of the poem, for this is not just the House of Fame of Love but it is a House of Fame of all human experience. But Geffrey is, like us, now on his own. The eagle is not now present to tell him how to interpret or what to think. His earlier misgivings return as he approaches the castle itself. We are now back in a world reminiscent of the House of Venus with its icons of love, but here the icons and their medium are of broader significance and, paradoxically, chancier existence. The foundation of the castle is ice not iron, brilliant but unstable. Geffrey is suitably skeptical:

> Thoughte I, "By Seynt Thomas of Kent,
> This were a feble fundament
> To bilden on a place hye.
> He ought him lytel glorifye
> That hereon bilt, God so me save!" (1131-5)

This instability accords with the sound emanating from the palace "of truth and fals compounded." Getting at truth, even here, is going to be hard. The first thing Geffrey notices is the names of "famous folk" carved into the foundation. Some are clear, some are indistinct, some are obscured, all because of the chance of where they happened to be carved, in sun where they will melt or in shade where they will abide. *Sic transit gloria mundi*.

Again we are in a world of art, the interpretation of art being somehow analogous to the interpretation of reality, though both in need of being made into story for us to comprehend. Geffrey proceeds upward towards the House itself and is astonished by its opulence and elegance, though we are now prepared to be cautious in our praise of its excellence. Niches abound with the figures of great artists and magicians, the earthly preservers of fame, but the combination of them once again gives us pause about the epistemological reliability of these icons of communication. There is great diversity, but as Geffrey approaches the gate itself, his observation enforces the uneasiness which has already been hinted about this place of revelation that we and Geffrey are privileged to visit:

> The castel-yate on my right hond,
> Which that so wel corven was
> That never such another nas;
> And yit it was be aventure
> Iwrought, as often as be cure. (1294-8)

Unease is compounded by the confusion we find when we enter.

Quickly our attention is drawn to the central figure, which ought to be the most significant, the most meaning-laden, Fame herself. She glitters with opulence and the Muses are singing her praises: she is the darling of the artists. But she is a shape-changer, growing larger and smaller, and equipped with a superfluity of ears and tongues. All of which is to say that she is glorious but unreliable. On a first level, we might see her simply as a symbol of the capriciousness of fame as reputation. But her meaning, as elaborated by the continuation of the vision, suggests that her significance extends as well to fame as renown and report. When one later discovers that she is Fortune's sister, we cannot simply comfort ourselves with the platitude that reputation is precarious. Much more is at stake: our capacity to understand past or present events at all. The frightening suspicion arises that she may be the central symbol of the intrinsic inability to preserve the past or make sense of the present.

The figures arrayed from her shoulders downward develop this perception. They are "authorities" who have preserved for us the cultures of the past. But the tableau remains confusing in several ways. First, these authorities, recreated here from the "sounds" they made on earth, must be vulnerable simply because of where they are. Second, the array is too much to understand:

> The halle was al ful, ywys,
> Of hem that writen olde gestes
> As been on trees rokes nestes;

>   But hit a ful confus matere
>   Were alle the gestes for to here
>   That they of write. . . (1514-9)

The problem here is our problem, expressed through the narrator, as interpreters. Thus, their presence and aspect represent the central epistemological problem with respect to our ability to learn from authorities: they are too many and too confusing. The general confusion is intensified by the groups of indistinct petitioners who chaotically approach Fame to request a reputation that they may or may not deserve. The permutations presented are almost a complete survey: the undeserving who get good fame, the deserving who get bad fame, the undeserving who get bad fame, those who ask for obscurity–and get it–, *etc.*. The ambient confusion in the scene and the obvious randomness of the assignments leave the narrator perplexed.

At this point, he is moved along in a dream-like transition by a nameless interlocutor. The narrator is unsatisfied. He tells the stranger that he has not really learned anything new, anything he did not know before, and thus is left in the same curious confusion which his primary guide, the eagle, had promised to solve. The narrator makes clear (1873-7) that he has not come here seeking fame for himself, nor has his desire to understand "tidings" been satisfied. What does he want to know?

>   Quod y, "That wyl y tellen the,
>   The cause why y stonde here:
>   Somme newe tydynges for to lere,
>   Somme newe thinges, y not what,
>   Tydynges, other this or that,
>   Of love or suche thynges glade." (1884-9)

Something of love or "glad things," but the fundamental impulse is "to know." The guide, apparently understanding, promises knowledge of "the way things are" and leads him out of the castle. We cannot but expect that some revelation is at hand, but, as we soon find out, the revelation of the "tidings" the narrator desires is again thwarted despite the interlocutor's promise:

> "But now no fors, for wel y se
> What thou desirest for to here.
> Com forth and stond no lenger here,
> And y wil thee, withouten drede,
> In such another place lede
> Ther thou shalt here many oon." (1910-5)

As they emerge, near the castle, in a valley, the narrator sees the central vision: an enormous house, "the house of Daedalus" and therefore a labyrinth. Now labyrinths are puzzles, but they do have answers. Still, this is a daunting vision. He sees an enormous wicker house, sixty miles long, whirling and whirling in the air, exuding a multitude of competing and incomprehensible sounds. The large but unstable house is full of holes. Still trying to understand, Geffrey asks the eagle to let him see the wonders of this place and the eagle-guide assures him that such is his purpose, to instruct and comfort him. By now, we must be aware of the ironic role of the eagle as guide. The House of Fame itself has not been illuminating and this wicker basket of confusion is not promising. Inside there is total chaos. It is the very image of "sothe and fals compouned" so that it is impossible to make sensible distinctions. There is a limited understanding granted: once inside, the narrator is able to see and assess more clearly. From the outside, the house is a whirling and mysterious enigma. From the inside, there is relative stability (akin to the way we get used to travelling at 500 mph in a jet.) But the vision within is itself chaotic, so that as we seem to move closer to the stability of truth we in fact are confronted with an essential inability to understand because of the total confusion that prevails. The eagle's revelation merely confirms Geffrey's perduring confusion.

The chaotic information flies out the window, in unintelligible, bits to the House of Fame for distribution by Aeolus. This, by the way, is Geffrey's direct observation, not an explanation by the eagle. The assertion of the unreliability of information available to human beings is complete. And once more Geffrey is confounded in what has been presented as a journey of interpretation by means of a dream, which we are predisposed to expect to be explanatory, and with a guide who turns out only to be able to point Geffrey towards the essential chaos of information, the inevitable frustration of human attempts at understanding.

There is one last hope. We may not be able to understand everything, but perhaps, we are encouraged to believe, there is some hope: there is a stirring in the "love section" of the House of Tidings. If all else fails, there may be some comfort in our ability to understand love. This would indeed be worthwhile because it would at least provide a refuge of solace from the otherwise impenetrable chaos, and the poem has in fact implied (from the first invocation to the story of Dido, to the eagle's references to Geffrey as a bookish lover) that knowledge of love is central. There appears a man, whom Geffrey is unable to name, who "semed for to be/ A man of gret auctorite...." (2157-8).

And at this point the poem breaks off. Now, it is certainly plausible to assume that Chaucer just stopped, left the poem unfinished, and many critics have seen the ending this way. Others, however, have at least suggested that the poem is unfinished, but complete.[4] But whether the poem was left intentionally or unintentionally without a formal literary conclusion, the meaning is already clear. I would argue that, if that is the case, then an intentional lack of a conclusion is more probable than, say, Chaucer losing interest in the poem or giving up on the possibility of making an adequate conclusion. What, indeed, could the mysterious man of great authority add? The abrupt ending fits with all of the preceding frustrations of our expectations of discovery. The authorities in the precarious House of Fame are too numerous to comprehend, the petitioners are themselves flighty and dealt with as capriciously as one would expect by the sister of Fortune, the raw information that is mixed into an ambiguous soup in the House of Tidings is distributed in unintelligible combinations by Fame's servant Aeolus. In each case, Geffrey finds confusion and caprice obstructing his desire to know. The ending before any explanation of love by the man of great authority is a final representation of the bleak epistemology that the poem demonstrates at every turn.

The "conclusion" does suggest that, regardless of the impenetrability of the rest of human life, there might be a salutary comfort in understanding love, but we are denied even that. Perhaps it is better that the man does not speak. If he did, it would not be a direct vision of love anyway even though we are in a dream vision. He would still be an authority and our knowledge would entail acceptance of authority as the only way to understand even love. The dilemma does not seem to have an answer. As such it is the final statement of the practical epistemology figured in the poem. Each hope for revelation is dashed. Is the human condition thus unremittingly bleak? Certainly the data presented to Geffrey do not admit of interpretation in the sense of resolution. And that is exactly what human beings face. But to understand that is not to be plunged into despair. The very quest that Geffrey has participated in (humorous, playful, unremittingly hopeful) is a representation of where we really are. The problem of interpretation is not a doom but a metaphor for the paradox of the human condition. That the boundaries between the vision of the dream and the experience of waking life have been blurred by the character of Geffrey (dreamer, dream reporter/interpreter, and Chaucer/poet) implies that fiction and reality are complementary. Our inability to comprehend the fiction, to see a determinative lesson in it, is analogous to our human quandary about our experience. Chaucer deconstructs his own fiction as we inevitably deconstruct "God's fiction," the reality that we daily confront. The poem's indeterminacy does not leave us with simple frustration at lack of closure. Geffrey never gives up and there is an awareness of the joy that is in the process, a human joy that Geffrey does not blunt with an appeal to *The Ultimate Interpreter*. Here we stand curious, confounded, and engaged; we can do none other. Geffrey never comes out of the dream.

2. *The Book of the Duchess*

To proceed to *The Book of the Duchess* from *The House of Fame* may be anachronistic insofar as we understand the chronology of Chaucer's works, but the issues raised in the *Book* may clarify the nature of the practical epistemology represented in the *House*. In the *Book*, we have an insomniac dreamer. How he falls asleep, how he behaves in his sleep, and what, if anything, he learns in his dream raise epistemological questions similar to those in the *House*, but structured in a different baffling way by a differently troubled narrator. Like the *House*, the *Book* deals with love, but equally obliquely so that we become aware not only of the power of love but also of the inherent problematics of understanding love, ourselves, and the world in which we and love are entwined. The poem is interesting here not as an historical document, nor as an elegy or allegory, but as a problem in human understanding.[5]

The structure of the *Book* is significant in that the layering of parts becomes our key to understanding the narrator's predicament. The dreamer is the circumscribing reality of the poem: it is in his consciousness that it begins and ends and we become curious about what he learns in part because of his confusion and desire to understand his own predicament and its meaning. He tells us his situation. Then he recounts the story of Seis and Alcione, which is in a book of romances he is reading because he cannot sleep; at this point he is not in a dream, he is in fiction. Subsequently he has a dream for which we are asked to find significance. Then we return to the narrator and the representation of his state of consciousness (and understanding) at the end of the dream. Throughout he is wondering, trying to understand; his perplexities become ours as we accompany him on his interior journeys.

In approaching the dreamer, we should be careful not to overspecify what we know of him, his concerns, and his confusions from the opening section. He tells us, enigmatically, that there is only one physician who can heal him, and he turns away from speculation on his own condition to his "first matere," which must, therefore, have to do with his reading and his dream. All we are sure of is that his present situation is "agaynes kinde," against nature. Presumably, this will relate to his waking state which, in the introduction, is in the present time. The romances are from the past "While men loved the lawe of kinde." (56)

The story of Seis and Alcione is an odd one to provide comfort regardless of what the narrator's affliction is:

> Such sorowe this lady to her tok
>
> That trewly I, that made this book,
>
> Had such pittee and such rowthe
>
> To rede hir sorwe that, by my trowthe,
>
> I ferde the worse al the morwe
>
> Aftir to thenken on his sorwe. (95-100)

We know immediately that Seis has drowned; our attention is on Alcione's grief and the narrator's pained reaction. Alcione wants to know what has happened to Seis, she appeals to Juno, and Juno sends Morpheus with a meaningful dream. The playfulness of the description of the embassy to Morpheus is at odds with the tone of the dreamer's situation and Alcione's. Indeed, Alcione dies within three days when the truth is revealed to her in her dream. The narrator's reaction is sympathetic, but uninformative: he is sorry for Alcione but he avoids dwelling on her grief: "But what she sayede more in that swow/ I may not telle yow as now" (215-6). Returning to his "first matere" again, he marvels at the existence of Morpheus. The comic blandishments to the god of sleep (a perfect bed and bedroom, just what would appeal to Morpheus) are, condignly in the fiction but surprisingly anywhere else, rewarded with sleep and a very special dream.

At this point we cannot help but wonder: what is the narrator's plight (besides sleeplessness) and what does the story of Alcione have to do with it? The circumstances are calling for interpretation about the nature of grief, the nature of love, and the nature of nature. No answers yet, but the dream that does come to the narrator promises to be interpretive, though hard to understand. It is so "wonderful" that not even Joseph, who interpreted the dream of Pharaoh, or Macrobeus, who interpreted the dream of Scipio, might interpret it properly. We are primed to interpret the dream ourselves. Central to the dream is the paranomasia of "hert-hunting." That is what the dreamer has highlighted in his own experience, Alcione's experience, and throughout the dream. Many commentators have noted the centrality of this pun; I am interested in the way it relates to both the subjects of the poem and the narrative's epistemology.[6]

In his dream, the narrator paradoxically awakens to a world, at least initially, far different from the gloom of his own and Alcione's. It is a beautiful world, but it is also complex right from the start. The physical beauty and the birdsong evoke the charmed world of romance. Not only the weather; the walls of his room are painted with stories of love and pain: Troy, Jason and Medea, the *Romance of the Rose*. Although there is not enough detail given for precise interpretation of the significance of the scenes, paintings are usually meaningful in Chaucer and they do portray love, lost or gained, but always glittering and glorious. The narrator's idyllic room and his romance context at least evoke the splendors of love and, from the pictures and setting, probably courtly love. Now, courtly love is one of the central Medieval paradigms for love and grief, so it is tantalizing to see the dreamer emerge into and from this context which is, at least in fiction, explanatory of fundamental mysteries of nature. He is brought to action by Octavian's "hert-hunt" in this context, but the preternatural hunt is unsuccessful. Love thwarted? Understanding thwarted? Regardless, the narrator/dreamer is led by a charming little dog on to the next vision within the dream, a beautiful garden, perhaps still a garden of courtly love, where winter is forgotten (but mentioned): "All was forgeten, and that was sene,/ For al the woode was waxen grene" (413-4). The dog, itself a playful, innocuous bit of nature, leads him to a thick forest, dark, dense, but full of animal life, where he sees the man in black, separated from the sensory paradise. We have entered an area of significance. The setting provides the obscure and dark side of the celebratory courtliness of the bedroom, garden, and hunt. We are ready for even a more particular and poignant expression of sentence for the dreamer.

The project of the dreamer, from this point on, is to understand the situation of the black knight. The knight in black is in great sorrow, similar to that of the waking narrator, except even more intense and affecting:

> Hit was gret wonder that Nature
> Myght suffre any creature

> To have such sorwe and be not ded. (467-9)

As the dreamer approaches, we already have in our heads the insomnia of the dreamer and the suicidal grief of Alcione.

The source of the black knight's grief is clear; he explains directly and profoundly:

> "I have of sorwe so gret won
>
> That joye gete I never non,
>
> Now that I see my lady bryght,
>
> Which I have loved with al my myght,
>
> Is fro me ded and ys agoon.
>
> "Allas, deth, what ayleth the,
>
> That thou noldest have taken me,
>
> Whan thou toke my lady swete,
>
> That was so fair, so fresh, so fre,
>
> So good that men may wel se
>
> Of al goodnesse she had no mete!" (475-86)

His lady is dead and the dreamer must overhear, but the dreamer behaves, until the very end of the poem, as if he does not understand the nature of the knight's grief. Is the dreamer a dolt or a therapist trying to get the knight to "talk out" his agony? Both alternatives have been vigorously argued. The dreamer's ignorance might even be a refusal to understand and an opportunity to act out in the situation of a grieving courtly lover an explanation for his own malady. Consciously or unconsciously, the narrator, inquisitive and sympathetic, seems to try to work towards an understanding of the knight's grief. His continuing failure to understand the knight's veiled revelations betrays the dreamer's incomprehension but also his genuine sympathy.

The knight, unfailingly polite and courtly, patiently and pathetically interprets for the dreamer. The elegance and delicacy of the knight's revelations reveal his dignity in extremity. The narrator wants to understand the knight's grief; is it perhaps the unsuccessful hunt? The narrator wants to help, but the knight's grief is beyond the consolation the naïve dreamer struggles to offer. The extremity of his grief is so great that he sees death, who will not relieve him by taking him, as an enemy. He is sorrow itself: "For y am sorwe, and sorwe ys y" (597). His joy has, in every respect, been turned into a corresponding sorrow. The totality of his grief is beyond straightforward explanation so he turns to the allegory of the chess game with Fortune. The elegance of the knight's revelation of his grief throughout is in sharp contrast to the sympathetic but pedestrian efforts of the dreamer at consolation. The chess game with Fortune is an explanation but not a consolation for the knight. For the dreamer, astute through the fog of his naïvete it is not even an explanation. He, consciously or not, rejects the allegory; he does not take its "sens," but does compare it to the losses of other lovers. In a sense, the dreamer both understands and does not understand the situation of the knight. But the knight courteously offers to explain if the dreamer will really listen:

> "I telle the upon a condicioun
>
> That thou shalt hooly, with al thy wyt,
>
> Doo thyn entent to herkene hit." (750-2)

Here comes the kernel; the dreamer and we are ready to try to understand, to interpret.

The black knight's explanation is a rhapsody of courtly and more-than-courtly love, a complex conjunction which occupies most of the rest of the poem and is the crux of the grief and its consequences. The knight has always honored Love; he has performed all of the conventional courtly behaviors which appropriately stellify him, his beloved, and their relationship in the constellation of courtly love. The description of his courtly beloved is one of the most beautiful tributes in Medieval literature. Yet, it has an even more powerful impact on us for two specific reasons. First, it is courtly love and more, or perhaps courtly love transformed into real life and love. Second, all is told in retrospect in the context of the knight's overpowering grief. Yes, he describes the physical appearance and the virtue of his beloved with the proper exaggeration and with an elegance that few courtly lovers could hope to attain. She is both physical and moral perfection itself, one of a kind!

> "The soleyn fenix of Arabye,
>
> For ther livyth never but oon,
>
> Ne swich as she ne knowe I noon." (982-4)

Of course, she is the phoenix who will not rise again and therein lies the pathos of the panegyric. She has given great joy and moral improvement, like a courtly lady, but beyond because she rejected the artificial stratagems of the courtly love tradition. As a courtly symbol of human perfection, she rises above the courtly to an ideal sublimity. She was the very best, the paragon, and not a paramour but a wife (1036-41).

When the knight concludes this panegyric to the courtly love paradigm and the human love reality in elegiac terms, the dreamer interjects an enigmatic comment:

> "Now, by my trouthe, sir," quod I,
>
> "Me thynketh ye have such a chaunce
>
> As shryfte wythoute repentaunce." (1112-4)

The knight has just been speaking of how his lady ennobled him. The narrator, learning the history in wholly conventional terms offers a conventional consolation: your experience is as magical as a sinner who receives forgiveness without the pain of or need for repentance. She has beatified the knight. The knight's response is equally curious. He says that repentance is not in it at all, leading to the dreamer's question about what the knight has lost. Although it is hard to tell, it seems that the dreamer suspects that the knight is a forsaken courtly lover, suitably improved, but the knight quickly explains that his situation is much more than that: " 'Yee!' seyde he, 'thou nost what thou menest;/ I have lost more than thou wenest.' " (1137-8). The narrator has grasped the courtly, as he grasped the literal in the chess game, but he has not grasped the extremity of the loss. So, the knight returns to his panegyric as if this will somehow explain all to the slow dreamer. He idyllically recounts their courtship and concludes with the duration of their married love, always perfect, always new: " 'And thus we lyved ful many a yere/ So wel I kan not telle how' " (1296-7).

The narrator, apparently aware as we have been for a long, expectant time that the knight's narrative has been entirely in the past tense, asks the obvious question: " 'Sir," quod I, "where is she now?' " (1298). The knight tries to answer by repeating what he has said before, but the dreamer requires an explicit answer, which the knight bluntly gives: " 'She ys ded!' " (1309) and the narrator is simply and powerfully sympathetic: " 'Is that youre los? Be God, hyt ys routhe' " (1310). When the narrator says that the "hert-hunting" is now done, the pun is even clearer than it was earlier. There is no more from the knight who repairs to his castle at the stroke of twelve. Our exploration of the human heart is over for now, but the narrator must bring us back to the circumscribing reality of his own world. Curiously, when he awakes, he is holding the story of "Seys and Alcione" but there is no reference whatever to the psychological state of the waking narrator, no analysis, no glimpse into his own heart.

The swift departure from the narratives (the fiction of Seis and Alcione and the dream of the narrator) is not analyzed or applied to the speaker who, we remember, was suffering so severely in the introduction to the poem. What are we to make of the experiences within this quizzical frame? One thing is clear: the poem is an unrelenting search for meaning. Although this may not be superficially as clear as the cognitive quest in *The House of Fame*, we are continually asked to examine successive episodes as if there is something to be understood. It is important to remember that the dream, dominated by the soliloquies of the knight, is the narrator's "first matere," but it is necessary to view that matter in the context of the circumscribing circumstances. After all, what are we and Chaucer, the narrator, trying to understand?

There is no clue in the opening section as to what the source of the narrator's perturbation is; Chaucer does not tell us. Certainly he is suffering and consequently insomniac. He seeks relief, desperately and unsuccessfully, in sleep. He is in a world where he cannot think, so overwhelmed is he. It is tempting, because of the experiences of Alcione and the black knight, to infer that he is grieving a death, but we are never told that: neither at beginning nor end is there an application directly to himself. What he wishes for is the oblivion of sleep. He gives no evidence that he himself is the source of revelation for us. We only know that eventually he sleeps and finds his dream "queynte."

Although the story of Alcione is not his "first matere" and he draws no clear conclusions from it, it is a fiction, which invites interpretation from us and somehow makes sleep possible for the narrator. We know that Seis is dead before Alcione does. Our attention is on her process of discovery and reaction. She is distraught and fears that Seis is dead; she will not rest until she knows and she can only find out the truth in a dream, a vision within the fiction. When that vision comes, a vision that she unquestioningly takes to be the truth, she commits suicide. She cannot bear the uncertainty and even less the reality of the death of Seis. The fiction is about grief: the truth is in the dream, but that is a literal truth; the human agony is in the response, suicide. She presents, therefore, the human perplexity about how to deal with the ultimate grief: loss of love, death. For her experience is not that of a betrayed lover, but the universal experience of bereavement. That is our focus, but she does not provide us with a satisfactory answer, rather with a retreat into oblivion. This is not an answer; the fiction does not solve the problem; it sets rather than explains the human suffering from the pain of loss. She excites the sympathy of the narrator but does not resolve his agony: she is instrumental but she is not "first matere."

Nevertheless, the placement of her experience between the narrator's insomniac struggle and the dreamer's vision invites speculation about her instrumentality, for her story does, in some way, make it possible for the narrator to sleep. It seems improbable that there is comfort for the dreamer here: she commits suicide. Neither does the narrator's discovery of Morpheus, in itself, seem an adequate explanation as we move through the phases of narrator *in propria persona*, fiction, and dream. The narrator's only hope, only learning, from Alcione's story is of the existence of Morpheus. Before he had known only one god and, although his reaction to the vision does not seem to be a theological crisis, he becomes, even within his suffering, whimsically aware of the power of sleep as personified in Morpheus. The treatment is playful, but it does provide an entry, no matter how unrealistic or fanciful, into a vision, and perhaps in that vision we will find meaning in the grief that deprives the narrator of sleep and Alcione of life. Simultaneously, fiction does not provide a resolution for her or the narrator but it does provide a whimsical direction. Fiction, or rather the examples of fiction, do not provide an answer, but they do provide in their conceits an entry into a land of vision where the meaning of the central agony of grief can be anatomized. Thus, fiction does not explain in itself, but may be a gateway to insight if we, like the narrator, are willing to pursue our "first matere."

The suspended state of the narrator and the destroyed state of Alcione may find interpretive understanding, if not consolation, in the vision which is the central focus of the poem. Here is another instance of Chaucer's playing with layers of reality as a representation of our existential perplexity. In *The House of Fame*, if the man of great authority had spoken, he would have blurred the distinction of experience and authority, so Chaucer pulls back from explicitness. Similarly, the story of Alcione is a stimulus and instrumentality towards a vision which may provide insight, but it seems will not in the end provide answers. So we proceed to the substance of the vision. The medium of the vision is that great paradigm of love and loss–the courtly love tradition. The garden to which the dreamer awakes and the terms of the black knight's soliloquies comprehensively place us in that tradition, as do the love portraiture and the hunt metaphor. Courtly love, as artificial as it necessarily is, is explanatory, interpretive. Here, I would suggest it is a vehicle for an exploration and explanation that transcend the tradition itself. Throughout his career, Chaucer never seems to see courtly love as an answer, but as an instrumental phantasm that allows inquiries that go beyond its artificial constructs. Here it is a vehicle for profounder inquiry into the labyrinth of the human heart.

The vision begins in glory, the beauty and consolation of the physical environment and the excitement literally of the hunt and metaphorically of courtship. But the hunt does not lead to success: there is frustration in human experience. Still, this is superficial; there are depths to be plumbed. The playful puppy, innocent and unconsciously helpful, leads us into the dark wood of underlying human experience to the black knight and his complex narrative. When the dreamer comes upon him, he is saying, in prose not in the beguiling sounds of music, the lay of his grief. The dreamer is now in a dark wood of interpretation, but why does he not simply understand what the knight says so explicitly: that the woman he loves is dead? Is the dreamer stupid? Insensitive? Probably no more than we are. In the narrator we observe a suffering that disables insight; in Alcione we have seen limited insight that leads to death rather than regeneration. Thus, in the dreamer's apparent insensitivity (he is, after all, Chaucer's mechanism and the narrator's exegete,) we recognize our inability to confront grief immediately and directly; it needs the mediation of vision-fiction to transform our paralysis into capacity, if not transcendence.

The black knight can express himself, but it is not so easy for the dreamer really to hear what he says: this is a central paradox of the nexus between human suffering and understanding. The experience that the black knight describes is framed in the language and conventions of courtly love. It is courtly in his praise of his beloved, his description of her excellences, his own feelings towards her, and the ennoblement that he claims as the consequence of his love. Now, the perennial danger of courtly love and the constant fear of the courtly lover are of the essence of the whole process. Bereavement by desertion or discovery is the constant terror of the courtly lover and these are made relevant to the revelations of the knight. The very exaggeration that he is sorrow itself and sorrow is he recalls the extremities of joy and grief that characterize the tradition. This experience, whether ultimately salvific or tragic, is at the heart of the precarious apotheosis that is courtly love.

This language and matrix thread through the reflections of the bereaved knight and in its extremity are the source of the confused sympathy of the dreamer. We find eventually that the knight's experience has been of all the blisses of courtly love; this is not a rejection of the tradition. But here it is only a medium not a subject, and it is a medium made applicable to human love and grief beyond the tradition while using the tradition to inquire into an intrinsic human grief more profound than the conventions of the paradigm. For all his good will, the dreamer tries to understand the knight's grief by the paradigm: this is the main source of his difficulty in understanding. He is not stupid, but he must work through the metaphors of human bliss and grief that the knight relates. For example, Fortune is prominent in courtly love, but its enigmatic operations are also present in the substratum of human experience that courtly love images.

The knight's language is the language of the tradition, but his experience is something more, something merely imaged in the conventions; the bridging of that gap is the unconscious focus of the dreamer's sympathetic engagement in understanding the totality and extremity of the knight's grief. His anguish is not simply the loss of the beloved; it is the much starker reality of the death of the beloved. The knight has prepared us for this leap of imagination: his beloved did not force him through the hoops of meaningless quests, her reserve was not "daunger" but honorable caution, and they lived many years in married bliss. How can the dreamer penetrate to this profound level beyond the conventions by which we express our joy and grief? The knight's story, which the dreamer is trying to interpret, represents the bliss and despair of genuine human love, heightened by the paraphernalia of the conventions. But the final goal is to pierce through the fictions, which the knight gives the dreamer the information to do, but the dreamer cannot. Finally the knight, to communicate with another human being (to make manifest the territory of his heart,) must make the stark and painful direct statement. His grief is not resolved, but the emotional journey of the dreamer is ended. There is no further to go, so the knight retires and the dreamer awakes.

What, after all, has been the substance of the whole book? What have the dreamer and we been trying to interpret? It is not the cognitive problem of *The House of Fame* but the affective reality of a grief as profound and perplexing as any concept human beings have to struggle with. Grief is a fact of our experience no matter how we try to act it out. The successive presentations of grief in the dreamer, Alcione, and the knight do not give answers. This is not a poem of consolation in any ordinary sense. It goes beyond that to assay the nature of the experience itself. Alcione dies; the knight is not relieved; the dreamer is not cured. Even when the narrator awakes, we are not given a remedy that he can apply to his own unnamed suffering. Grief is every bit as much a part of the human experience as ideas. And in his elegiac anatomy of grief Chaucer does not provide answers. The struggle to understand the interlocking segments of the poem is analogous to our hopeless but inevitable attempt to understand and cope with grief. We are not allowed the comfort of heavenly consolation or platitudinous dismissal. Grief is there and to be endured. The only alternative is the sad capitulation of Alcione, but this is not satisfactory. In human life, if life there is to be, grief can be given utterance but not remission. Of course there is joy in life but the remembrance of joy is not a palliative when grief descends. What cannot be avoided must be endured, as Chaucer will say in other contexts. But this is not a matter of fate, but a fact of human experience. It can only be named as the inscrutable and undecipherable operations of Fortune seen not as a force so much as a way of talking about the pain that comes to us all, nowhere so devastatingly as in the unchangeable reality of death. The dreamer has slept and inquired, but at the end of the poem he has not been saved. He may sleep, but he and we cannot be relieved. We can try to understand and perhaps extend our feelings to others, but there is no escape. The unresolvable inquiry of *The Book of the Duchess* stands as a metaphor for an inquiry which we are all sentenced to experience. We do not transcend grief but, with powers as limited as the dreamer's, and problems as severe as the narrator's and the knight's who surround him, we inquire and suffer.

3. *The Parliament of Fowls*

The problems of human understanding are as various as the cognitive and affective dilemmas represented in the assaying structures of *The House of Fame* and *The Book of the Duchess*.[7] The third of the major dream visions, *The Parliament of Fowls*, the most polished poetically in its rime royal stanzas, also asks us to inquire with the narrator about "the way things are." The nominal topic in the introductory material before the dream is Love and the narrator's relationship to it, but even here there arises a reflection on how we know, which is soon related to the question of dreams. The narrator identifies himself as a bookish lover who is inquiring into "a certayn thing." Although that "certayn thing" is not specified, the narrator insists upon the importance of gaining new knowledge from old sources. The epistemological question here is how the reading of texts, all written for our doctrine in one way or another, can yield understanding, especially the kind of understanding that might transform the narrator's knowledge into something beyond the "bookish." A connection between reading and vision is implied as in *The Book of the Duchess*. However, the relationship here is more direct if not more obvious.

The narrator, trying to garner new knowledge from old sources, is reading the *Dream of Scipio*. At l. 29, the narrator, a seeker after some kind of knowledge, begins to summarize for us what he has read. In the process of summary, however, some kind of interpretation is inevitable. To recount the writings of another is to provide "a reading" of the other's text; that is what the narrator does, for this is clearly not a comprehensive recitation of everything that is in the much longer *Dream of Scipio*. The narrator promises (35) that he will give us the "sentence," the significance, of the Ciceronian work known through Macrobeus. He will give us the kernel of meaning and that, of course, is in the form of a dream. African's description in the dream is of a universe of order, culminating in heaven. Man is immortal and our human life "nis but a dethe" after which we awake to heavenly bliss. The changeable universe will eventually resolve or restore itself to its original perfection and we have the opportunity to become part of that blissful order. Interestingly, there is a purgatory for those who have transgressed during this temporary life (though there is no mention of a hell), implying that oneness with the perfection of the universe depends upon our behavior in this transitory life. Barring the absence of hell, which may just be a delicacy in this joyful poem (and, happily, accurate to what is in Macrobeus,) this could all be taken as a metaphoric version of the Christian cosmos.

What are the means beyond the avoidance of sin (78-84) that lead us to salvation as part of an ordered creation? African is explicit twice on this moral imperative, once in ll. 46-49 and again in direct answer to Scipio's question about how to achieve "salvation": work towards "commune profit" (73-77). This injunction is African's main moral guideline, that will raise Scipio (us) to everlasting participation in the order of the universe figured as musically harmonious celestial spheres. So far this is a pagan vision of orthodox Christianity if, indeed, commune profit can somehow be seen as consonant with Christian moral injunctions.

The summary is what the narrator makes of the dream, but it is not a resolution for him; it is not curative of whatever is troubling him. The narrator is troubled, although his unease is not directly attributed to what he has just read. The narrator's state of mind is perplexing as well as perplexed and there is no unambiguous answer in the text. What does he have that he does not want and what does he want that he does not have? There is no clear connection between this and his summary of his reading, although one wonders whether the quest for understanding of Love in books may be at its source. The narrator is a persistent seeker; his readings, even of the *Dream of Scipio*, have not solved his perplexities. What is it that he would know? The *Dream* seems a comforting text but the definition of commune profit is not made clear and he goes to bed with a "heaviness" that is attributed to a divided self that echoes St. Paul's dilemma.[8] Structurally, the poem seems to ask us to seek illumination in the narrator's own dream that follows. The narrator's observation that people often dream of what has been absorbing their waking attention points to a relationship between whatever has been troubling him and the *Dream of Scipio* on the one hand, and the vision that is to follow on the other. As we have been in other poems, we are invited to see the dream as interpretive, particularly of the context that the frame has created. Our suspicions are strengthened first when the narrator invokes Venus to aid him in recording his dream accurately and African appears as his guide within the dream.

The dreamer immediately confronts a gate that is reminiscent of Dante's revelatory entrance into the Inferno. But this is a double gate with two inscriptions which describe the two aspects of love: a salvific gate of idyllic, immutable love and a forbidding gate of the pains of love.[9] The dreamer is hesitant but is thrust through by African, who chides the dreamer that since he knows of love only second-hand, by books, the inscriptions cannot cause a direct threat to him. This is comic, but it is also perplexing. A vision suggests direct experience of what can otherwise only be known by report (authority.) But the dreamer is hurried on his way with only the comfort that he will somehow remain immune because he is and will remain, in some sense, an outsider. The epistemological quandary is here acute. A vision awaits, but the dreamer's safeguard is his personal distance from the vision. Then African disappears, and the dreamer is left to make what he can or will of the sights he is about to see.

The dreamer finds himself in a garden of beauty and permanence which has all of the harmony of the celestial world described by African in the *Dream*. The garden is perfect: all of nature is in accord, the climate is temperate, there is no sickness or age or even night, but a perpetual glorious day. There are, however, multiple serpents in this paradise, and they all take the form of personifications or artistic representations of the realities of human love, in fact courtly love. In the garden of innocence and harmony are discordant figures: Cupid and Will, his daughter; Plesaunce, but in company with Aray, Lust, and Curteysee and Craft; Delight under a solid oak with Gentilesse; naked Beauty and Youth; Foolhardiness, Flattery, Desire, Love Messages, and Meede (bribery); and "the other three" (the Fates, the Furies, or who?). The temple of Venus, which the dreamer then comes upon, is ruled by Priapus, and contains images of a catalogue of lovers good and bad.

This breathless array of inhabitants, personified and artistically enshrined in the Temple, is an abundant confusion. They are the reification of courtly love. The possible sources are many; all are in the tradition. The specific relational interpretations have been many within the tradition of critical commentary.[10] What is apparent, however, is that this is the melancholy panoply of human love as represented in the courtly tradition, and it seems to be the love of the inscription on the first gate. The dreamer, a bookish lover, is safe, an observer, but what he sees is disquieting, not to him but to us. He is not interpreting at this point; he is representing the "reality" of his dream. He has gloried in the first idyllic garden, but does not comment on the discordances within the garden represented by the *dramatis personae* of courtly love. He simply does not explain; he does not even reveal how he feels, so we are left with our own sense of discordance to ponder.

On leaving the Temple of Venus, we return to a garden, more like the idyll we first saw, with the goddess Nature presiding over the convocation of birds on St. Valentine's Day. Although much can be, should be, and has been said about the convocation, it is its intrinsic character and placement within the whole of the visionary garden that is of importance to us here.[11] This is the representation of the love of the inscription on the other gate. Here is Nature presiding over the whole creation of birds, complete and in order. As there was no negative criticism of the disordered vision heretofore by the dreamer, there is no special encomium to Nature or the order that she presides over here. This is pure reporting. Incidentally, it is not interpretation in the sense that the narrator's recounting the *Dream of Scipio* is interpretation, at least from the narrator's point of view. But even if mysterious, with any interpreter either distant or affecting distance, it is interpretation from the point of view of the poet who has chosen the elements for inclusion in this internally uninterpreted vision. The narrator simply seems relieved to be back out in the comforting garden.

Forgotten are the personifications that preceded the Temple of Venus. Our attention is on Nature and her perfectly ordered hierarchy of birds. This is the other gate of love, where birds are the symbols and come to choose mates, thus participating in the communal perpetuation of society. They are presided over by Nature who is the symbol of God's providential order projected into the sublunary world and the polar opposite of Fortune, the personification of disorder or apparent disorder, as projected into the world by a God who understands to us who do not understand her caprices (as they seem to humans.) In any case, Nature is God's vice-regent for order and it is appropriate that she should preside over this assembly. We are treated to a catalogue of birds that suggests the fullness of God's created world. It is what happens in this exercise of commune profit that creates the benign, and sometimes amusing, atmosphere of this scene even when discord enters.

Nature's purpose is to proceed from highest to lowest (the birds are in amusing categories, apparently of Chaucer's own devising), so it is the favored tercel eagle who is, according to plan, to choose first as he sits on the hand of Nature, the "vicar of the almighty," the principle of order in the created world, the antithesis of Fortune. The tercel makes his highly conventional, polite, courtly speech confirming his fidelity and the depth of his love. But there emerges, ever so politely, discord, as a second tercel, "of lower kynde," claims he has loved the formel eagle longer, will never be jealous, and will preserve her honor. And a third tercel, arguing the virtue of the intensity of his love rather than its duration, simply asserts his unparalleled fidelity. There is nothing to choose among these elegant representations. And there is a popular mini-rebellion among the lower orders of birds, who, in one way or another, assert the undecideability of the contention on the grounds upon which it has been argued. Nature has put the decision up to a council of the various species, each of which is to choose a spokesperson. The various representatives propose appropriately foolish solutions. Combat is rejected; indeed the notion that the one who loves the formel eagle most should have her is rejected on the grounds that such a decision is impossible to make. Their debate about the value of steadfastness is as ineffective as and more comic than the stately formalities pronounced by the contending eagles.

Courtly debate has not solved the problem; democratic choice has degenerated into an amusing but futile bird-bicker, made all the crabbier by the fact that evening is coming on and the rest of the birds, of a more practical turn of mind, are eager to have the question of mates throughout the aviary hierarchy decided. Nature is clear that neither courtly argument nor popular debate will bring a resolution, so she intervenes. Two aspects of her formulation are prominent: first, she will leave the choice up to the formel eagle because arguments about who loves her best are inconclusive:

> "For sith it may not here discussed be
> Who loveth hire best, as seyde the tercelet,
> Thanne wol I don hire this favour, that she
> Shal han right hym on whom hire herte is set,
> And he hire that his herte hath on hire knet . . ." (624-8)

Second, Nature does counsel the formel eagle on what she ought to do:

> "But as for counseyl for to chese a make,
> If I were Resoun, thanne wolde I
> Counseyl yow the royal tercel take,
> As seyde the tercelet ful skylfully,
> As for the gentilleste and most worthi,
> Which I have wrought so wel to my plesaunce
> That to yow hit oughte to been a suffisaunce." (631-7)

Nature says that the rational thing to do ("If I were Resoun") would be to choose the first tercel as the most royal, "gentil," and worthy. Nature lets us know whom she judges such; as God's agent, she has formed him. Her abstractions, gentilesse and worthiness, are, of course, difficult to define precisely. (Chaucer will deal extensively with the definition of gentilesse in the *Canterbury Tales*.) But these are the terms of her ordering advice. Nevertheless, she acquiesces to the tercel's request to delay the decision for the year and, being Nature, her word prevails.

The decision is put off and, in this sense, the whole movement of the poem is inconclusive. But in other respects it is not. Nature has not enforced her own decision and has allowed the female choice. Abstractions are made subsidiary to the dictates of the avian human heart. Their suspension with regard to the highest order of birds, allegorically the humans of bird creation, does not impede the orderly, and joyfully received, directives of Nature for the lower orders. Nature provides order over the other orders of creation and establishes a harmony that suits the idyllic introductory garden and culminates in the paean of praise "Now welcome, somer. . ." (680-92). Thus Nature, as the primary principle of God's order, does arrange the world of the poem, does have an idea of who, according to abstractions, ought to be selected, but leaves the final choice to the human heart of the formel eagle. Neither the rhetoric of courtly love, nor the disputations of the rabble, nor the abstractions which she understands overpower the right to choose in Love. Nature can tidy up the lower orders, but the indeterminacy of human beings must be respected.

Thus we come to the ambiguities of the final stanza and its relationship to the narrator's entry into the dream. When the dreamer awakes, Scipio is no longer around, because he has awakened both from the dream and the vision, and he is left where he was at the beginning of the poem. The narrator asserts that he must go on to other books to continue his search for peace. Now, what is it that the narrator wants? The ambiguity in "mete" is important: he hopes in his reading to "come upon" some solace which he does not feel or "to dream," have a vision, that will better answer his unrelieved unease. Has the narrator missed the important teaching of the dream? I think not, though his situation is left appropriately unspecified. He has seen what we have seen in the dream and yet it is not a resolution for his distress. What is there to do but to hope for something more satisfying in other books, perhaps also in another dream vision. That, like the suspended state that the formel eagles must live in, is the human condition.

There remains, however, for us, as critics trying to make sense of the whole of *The Parliament of Fowls*, to struggle with the interrelationship of the parts, because the poem is not merely coextensive with the dream. That African was the guide in the beginning of the dream suggests that there is some connection between his presence as "mover" and the doctrine in the *Somnium* that the narrator summarizes before the beginning of the dream. That doctrine, clearly implied to have been the stimulus for the dream (we dream about what we are thinking about when we are awake) must have, we feel, some connection with the vision, so let us return in the end to that doctrine. The world is orderly; yes, Nature has established order in the dream. That order is not so clear or ubiquitous as Scipio taught, but it is there. The most perplexing connection has to do with the notion of "commune profit" which is the moral imperative that the narrator gleans from the *Somnium* while he is awake and simply reporting Scipio's dream. Have we seen, in the narrator's dream, an acting out of the implications of commune profit?

Commune profit is a political as well as a human imperative. It is what earns salvation. Thus, it is an ordering principle that goes beyond politics in any narrow sense. It is the politics of human relations and thereby the politics of order in human reason and emotion. However, it remains an abstract ideal. Within the dream, Nature as God's instrument works things out in human (bird) affairs as well as it is possible to do. But there is a point beyond which commune profit, for human beings, is not to be imposed, because there remains the territory of the heart. This is a different kind of "heart hunting" than in *The Book of the Duchess*, but "heart hunting" it is. The narrator is troubled at the beginning of the poem by Love and, although his reading of the *Somnium* provides a rational explanation of the loftiest imperatives of love, those that extend to our relationships with all other human beings, the dream vision stimulated is not enough. True, we see that there is a providential Nature that acts on God's behalf to give order and meaning to the world, and in this we should rejoice. But that is not all there is to the human condition. Although the dream can celebrate an ultimate order, it is not able to resolve the ambiguities of love and the confusion about abstractions. The narrator will go on to seek explanations in books (or perhaps a revelation that the books inspire), but he and we have not come to a stasis, a resolution. The divine answer is ultimately in "commune profit." The human answer remains locked in the inscrutable labyrinth of the human heart, and we must continue to search. We are thereby locked into the narrator's search for meaning (or rather the meaning of the meaning that has been proposed to him.) We are drawn into the continuing attempt to interpret the most fundamental and important issues that confront us as the characters in fictions. Our attempts to interpret the fictions are counterparts to the interpretive endeavors represented in the fictions themselves.

In *The House of Fame*, we faced the cognitive impediments to the whole enterprise. In the *Book of the Duchess*, recognizing the contingent nature of our cognitive capacities, we explored the human meanings of grief. That grief was associated with love, or the loss of love, but the focus was on the essence of grief and the necessity to bear it and to transcend the barriers to its communicability, which communicability could bring solace to a human community in suffering. In *The Parliament of Fowls* we are drawn into the incomprehensibility of love and our inadequacy to fully comprehend. We are comforted about the existence of a God-given circumscribing order for which we ought to strive, but we, like the formel eagles and the narrator, are left to wait, to continue our quest to understand the nature of love, the foundation of human feelings, and the ultimate instrumental bestower of understanding. We are like Chaucer's narrators. As we struggle with their fictions, they struggle with the realities of their worlds, and the two processes become aspects of the same thing. The consequence is not despair, but a necessity and determination, despite our limitations, to persevere in our quests. As we puzzle over the varieties of the fictions, so do they puzzle over the structure of reality.

Chapter III: The Approximation of Truth

I should acknowledge what will become clear, that I am making some assumptions about the order of the *Canterbury Tales*, the "plan" of the *Tales*, and perhaps even about Chaucer's intention.[1] All of these assumptions are dicey, especially the latest, but in each case I am adopting one side of a long-standing controversy which has not been resolved. Thus, though my assumptions are not certainties, they all fit within the range of contested possibilities. This situation is similar to many critical cruxes in Chaucer where mutually exclusive alternatives must, at least provisionally, be accepted while keeping our uncertainty alive and well in the back of our minds.

My first assumption, that Fragment I is a single unit and that it is intended to come first, is safe. It is structurally logical and is attested to by the order in the manuscripts. My second assumption is that Fragment I was intentionally, though perhaps temporarily, abandoned in the midst of the "Cook's Tale" because the sequence, which makes good sense from the "General Prologue" through the "Miller's Tale", began to deteriorate as Chaucer proceeded to the "Reeve's Tale" and the "Cook's Fragment". This implies my third assumption, also attested by some commentators, that Chaucer, during his lifetime, was continually revising and re-shaping the *Tales*, most notably in the fundamental change from the four-tale plan in the "General Prologue" to a one-tale plan implied in Fragment X, a change which implies a profound change in the metaphor of the journey from a survey of fourteenth century life (perhaps particularly through "estates satire")[2] to a journey from this life (London) to the next (the New Jerusalem of Canterbury.) Finally, I am assuming that the "Man of Law's Tale" is what would follow whatever Chaucer might have revised Fragment I to be, and would have formed a conclusion to a single segment of the *Tales*. I do not go as far as Kolve to see the "Man of Law's Tale" as a conclusion to the tales of the first day, though that too is possible.[3] I merely assume that the "Man of Law's Tale" makes an appropriate connection to what Fragment I probably would have come to be.

My comfort with my assumptions, although not complete, is made less outrageous by the fact that plausible contradictory arguments can be made and accepted provisionally as long as one does not insist upon an absolute validity. This tentative state of mind, a playing with both the mutually exclusive and the mutually compatible, seems to be of the essence of the project of the *Tales*. The *Tales* are both inconclusive and incomplete, but by playing with provisional arrangements, assumptions, and interpretations, it is possible to get at the embedded indeterminateness that no completion could resolve.[4] The *Tales* are Chaucer's most ambitious, or at least most comprehensive, assay of the human condition and it is necessary that we play with the possibilities, but in such a way as to bring their complexity into accord with, rather than thwart, Chaucer's exegetical enterprise.

The essentially paradoxical nature of the *Tales* is clear in the metaphor of the opening eighteen lines. It is presumptuous in the extreme to try to say anything new about the metaphor, but it is necessary to establish the guiding paradox that informs the "whole" of the *Tales*, so as not to be simplistic in understanding the function of the "General Prologue". Many have noted that the *Tales* differ from other collections of tales by the very nature of the "General Prologue": the characters are laid out for us in portraits so that we have the panoply of fourteenth century society as context, and so that we have a foundation for the teller-tale relationships that are developed in most individual prologues and almost all the tales. I would caution that we not overestimate the explanatory quality of the "General Prologue" or assign it a definitiveness that may go beyond its fictional capacity.[5]

To return to the opening metaphor. It begins with the images of new life implied by Spring. The complication comes in line I,12, which for a twentieth century reader is an astounding non-sequitur: "Thanne longen folk to goon on pilgrimages." When the new life of physical nature bursts forth in the tantalizingly sexual terms of the first eleven lines, it is startling to see the direct connection between that rebirth and the impulse towards pilgrimage. My observation, of course, is familiar to all students of Chaucer: the experience of pilgrimage is also a manifestation of new life on the spiritual level. Religious pilgrimage is as much a spiritual new beginning as Spring is a physical one. This connection, though familiar, is the paradox upon which the whole ensuing narrative is based. Not only must the connection of the physical and spiritual be kept in mind simultaneously and persistently, but the implications of this paradox must be embraced as the portraits and the journey unfold. We must be able to keep two apparently contradictory views in mind: pilgrimages, especially the main ones like those to Canterbury, or the Holy Land, or St. James Compostela, were genuine religious experiences with the expectation of a plenary indulgence for participation, a radical opportunity for new spiritual beginning. But pilgrimages were, in actuality, also human celebrations of camaraderie and community. If pilgrimages were spiritual quests, they were also travelling picnics, which the human participants enjoyed as extended outings. The simultaneity and compatibility of spiritual quest and secular picnic is the guiding paradox if we are not "to falsen our matere." This paradox, a true paradox because it is not logically resolvable, is the double vision that is the essence of the *Tales*. Its consequence is an inexplicable acceptance of the simultaneity of the human and the divine in human experience.

Accepting the paradox is consistent with an understanding of the paradoxical role of the narrator both in the "General Prologue" and as he peeks through the tales. Ever since Talbot Donaldson's brilliant essay on "the two Chaucers," pilgrim and poet, rearranged our thinking about the role of the narrator, we have largely given up the view of the narrator as a *naif*.[6] Yet, it may not be necessary to see the narrator simply as a compound of writer and limited narrator. It is possible to do so and it establishes one important possibility of doubleness, but it is equally important to see that the poet and narrator need not be taken as two structural entities in paradoxical conflict. It is also possible to see the narrator as one Chaucer, speaking sometimes unequivocally and sometimes ironically. These two ways of viewing the "Chaucer" of the *Tales* may in themselves generate another paradox by equivocating the relationship between the poet and his narrative in a very complex way. Chaucer is both in the narrative and outside of it at the same time. As a character/pilgrim he is a more or less reliable interpreter. As a poet, he is the manipulator of that character, of other characters, and of the narrated fictions. If we prefer, as is equally plausible, to see a single ironic Chaucer, an overarching narrator who is responsible for the tangled ambiguities of the whole, then Chaucer, the guiding consciousness, is never really *in* the narrative, but always its ambiguous architect. That both of these possibilities exist reinforces the foundational confusion of where we are in the narrative as a whole. In either case, or better yet if we can hold both cases simultaneously in mind like the paradox of the opening metaphor, there is a blurring of levels of reality, perhaps best understood as a kind of "self-conscious fiction."

Thus, there is a "Chaucer" who is both inside the narrative and outside of it. This bilocation of the narrative voice establishes a peculiar relationship between narrator and audience. It is both a matter of where the narrator stands and what authority he commands, and a matter of where Chaucer has situated us, as audience, in relation to the fiction. We, like Chaucer, are both inside and outside. As a result, authority, both Chaucer's as creator/interpreter and ours as reader/interpreter, is always undermined. Put another way, the "two Chaucer" theory creates a tension between an ironic, urbane creator of the whole and a bookish, limited character within the fictional world. The "single ironic voice" theory blurs the distinction. If we put the two theories together (do not decide between them), then the reader is situated in a clarity of confusion about which world he is in. This is the essence of the problematics of interpretation of the "General Prologue" and, by extension, of the *Tales* as a whole. Chaucer, as creator, has made a fiction which requires interpretation. As we are reminded of the fictionality of the fiction by the equivocal nature of the narrator, we are led to an understanding of the complexity of the interpretive project. We are inside and outside the fiction and, as he insists on the fictionality of his constructed fiction, we are aware of the fictionality of the world in which the poet himself lives. That is, even as fourteenth century poet *in propria persona*, "Chaucer" is imbedded in a fiction as much constructed by the process of interpretation as the conventionally fictional world he creates is. We are put in a position where we must both interpret the fictions presented and accept the circumscribing "real world" as a fiction which itself must be interpreted.

Yet, and here is the essence of the paradox, there is one Chaucer we listen to throughout, but he is a "Chaucer" of these many inevitable manifestations. The result is that the interpretation of the "fictional world" of the pilgrims becomes a simultaneous interpretation of the finally ineluctable "fictional real world" of Chaucer the guiding, interpretive consciousness. We will return to this self-reflexive interpretive scheme, but first a few comments about the nature of the presentation by the one voice that we have immediate access to.

The problem of "reality" in the *General Prologue* is intrinsically insoluble because the created circumstances of the fiction are unrealistic, thereby reflecting on the corresponding "unreality" of the world that the controlling consciousness lives in. The portraits are not fixed, determined entities. That is to say, as many others have, that the portraits are not those of persons/characters as they could conceivably be understood by the "participant Chaucer." Sometimes they are, but the narrator's assertion is problematic:

> Me thynketh it acordaunt to resoun
> To telle yow al the condicioun
> Of ech of hem, so as it semed me,
> And whiche they weren, and of what degree,

And eek in what array that they were inne . . . (I, 37-41)

"Condicioun" is a vague word, but "degree" and "array" are narrowly observational and the subjectivity is clear in "so as it semed me." But to whom?

This is the first essential problem of "interpretation" in the "General Prologue". Is the pilgrim Chaucer an ironic narrator in charge or is the poet Chaucer an omniscient narrator in charge? Whether by irony or persona, Geoffrey Chaucer shapes and arranges the portraits in a way that will mean, not in the simple way that types mean but in a more complex set of orders (the order of the portraits is not the same as the order of the tales), and an even more complex pattern of expectation and frustration or gratification of expectation. For example, the narrator, in an orderliness that would be beyond any but the luckiest of *naïfs*, begins with the party of the knight, a slice of chivalric life, from the fully achieved knight, to the promising but amusing squire, to that simple backbone of English virtue, the yeoman. The use of order becomes even more complex. The Prioress seems to ignore, or be oblivious of, her vows; the Monk contradicts his vows; the Friar perverts his vows; and the Merchant, unencumbered by vows, is a logical conclusion of the sequence. The Parson and Plowman, brothers, represent the ideal complement of spiritual and secular. The Summoner and Pardoner harmonize their iniquities. These groupings are significant; they bear meaning.

In addition, expectation and frustration/gratification bear meaning. The knight, although hyperbolically, fulfills our expectations of his degree. The Monk, the Friar, the Pardoner, the Summoner, the Merchant, and the Doctor of Physic come from orders of society from which we do not expect much, according to contemporary reputations. The Parson and the Plowman fulfill our expectations more happily. The Clerk, however, is an honest scholar, not the charlatan we might expect, whose type appears in many of the tales. And then there are the ambiguities in the Franklin and Wife from whom we hardly know what to expect. Geoffrey Chaucer has engaged us not just in a social anatomy, but in one that teases and plays with our expectations. We are in a familiar world which bids fair to turn out not to be as familiar as we might comfortably expect. By frustration, gratification, and ambiguity, conventional wisdom is called into question or at least kept off balance. Can we understand the world by formulated generalizations? Sometimes. Can we understand the world by close examination of detail? Sometimes. But if our generalizations are chancey, what confidence can we have in the filtered authority of the narrator who, as persona or ironist, gives us our details? Not complete confidence, I suggest, because of the medium through which the details ("facts") we receive are filtered. These are the problems of knowing/interpreting interior human behavior and ideals that the "General Prologue" proposes.

The fact that the portraits are not stock figures is cognitively unsettling. Even more unsettling is the narrator's professed methodology. It is "accordaunt to resoun" to tell their degree and array, but what does that tell us? Well, the narrator, in his curious position both inside and outside the fiction, does not tell us just that. It should be unsettling that his whole process of description is intrinsically unrealistic, for he goes beyond degree and array to tell us both of experiences and interior dispositions that would not be literally accessible to him. The Knight's exploits, the Wife's behavior in her parish, and the Franklin's public service are possible but violate the canons of probability concerning what even the most convivial narrator might garner in the evening. The motives of the Friar and Summoner should not be knowable in the circumstances; nor should the ambiguities in the honor of the Merchant, Doctor, or Man of Law. The narrator's knowledge is, therefore, equivocal. We endow him with a reliability that springs not from his location on the pilgrimage but from his elusive existence both inside and outside of the *Tales*. Thus, his opinions are revealing, but not necessarily determinative or authoritative. We need to think only of the almost universal approbation he accords almost all of the pilgrims, both deserving and undeserving. Likewise, the knowledge of the controlling consciousness is revealed only partially because of the capacity of his narrative intermediary. The consequence is that we both know, and do not know, and yet the portraits are revealing. They are most revealing, however, in the way they represent the problematics of the interpretation of the peopled world around us. Geoffrey Chaucer does not give us divine insight or interpretive authority but asks us to come to grips with the various ways that truth and falsehood, honesty and infamy, present themselves to us. Geoffrey Chaucer invites us into the interpretive process rather than providing conclusions to be conned, and we thereby become active participants in the quandaries of knowing.

The effect corresponds to what Chaucer has done for and to us with his dreamers in the visions. What is real and what is not? What is appearance and what is reality? What is doctrine and what is illusion? Where are the canons of authority in the world as presented? Regardless, we are put in a position where we are called upon, though perhaps not as explicitly as in the dream-visions, to be interpreters. It may be that we will also be called upon to be moral arbiters, but our first job is to understand. The unrealism of the portraits, even more so the unrealism of the professed realistic context in which they are presented, calls upon us to fathom the fiction in ways that are analogous to Geoffrey Chaucer's, and ultimately our goal is to interpret the world. Sometimes the challenge exists because of what we are told, reliably or unreliably, as the data of our experience of the fiction. Sometimes it is the very absence of direction that is most intriguing and invites most forcefully our interpretive speculation.

Before leaving the portraits themselves, one in particular is worth noting, one that it is easy to pass over in our fascination with the racier and more ponderous figures: the Cook. Here we do not have ambient expectation. We have the narrator's reported catalogue of the Cook's professional excellence (I,379-84). Let us leave aside how the narrator might know this with any reliability and instead look at what the narrator can see directly: "But greet harm was it, as it thoughte me,/ That on his shyne a mormal hadde he" (I,385-6) It is tempting to see this portrait as an emblem for a cautionary view of the world. We should at least be aware of the possibility that idealities, no matter how discovered, may very well also have palpable running sores. Small as the portrait is, it is a view of Geoffrey Chaucer's view, uncritically reported by the narrator, and left for us to find significant, or not. We seem to be looking at the world, but we are looking at Geoffrey Chaucer's opaque fiction. Now that may seem simply to be what we do with any fiction. The difference is that Chaucer is insistently and self-consciously inviting us into the process of interpretation itself. That interpretive enterprise is as much a focus of the fiction, as Chaucer presents it, as the fiction is a reflection of reality. Thus, life is an interpretive process and our confrontation with Chaucer's fictions is a metaphor for the larger problem of interpretation of "the real world." The figuration will only amplify as we examine the elaboration of these narrators and the tales they tell, tales which inevitably are one layer more deeply embedded in the world of fiction.

The narrator is satisfied with the service he has done us (I, 715-9), but he goes on to be garrulously reflective on the rest of his mission by commenting on the responsibilities of a narrator. He asks pardon of our sensibilities in case he offends, on the grounds of a narrator's responsibility to fidelity in recording and transmitting the narratives of others, as if such recall and presentation were possible or necessary. But he does claim it as necessary on the grounds of a narrator's responsibility to accuracy:

> Whoso shal telle a tale after a man,
>
> He moot reherce as ny as evere he kan
>
> Everich a word, if it be in his charge,
>
> Al speke he never so rudeliche and large,
>
> Or ellis he moot telle his tale untrewe,
>
> Or feyne thyng, or fynde wordes newe. (I, 731-6)

Narration of fiction, reality from the narrator's point of view, must be accurate in every detail. It may be that Chaucer through the narrator is excusing himself from responsibility for the lewdness that will ensue, if only ironically. However, the commentary on narration seems the much more important point. The narrator asserts, and cites the authority of Plato, that a storyteller's first, sacred responsibility is to literal recording, to avoiding the falsification of the hypothetical reality that he is recreating. This puts the narrator in a curious position: his goal is to be pure conduit for events that have transpired. His attempt is a noble devotion to precise, reportorial accuracy: no manipulation or interpretation here. What people have said, they have said. Because of the equivocation in the narrator, a figure either as persona or ironist both inside and outside this created world, we are reminded of the contingent reality of the whole. There are no keys to all mythologies here. Chaucer is a narrator and we must take data and interpret although we are perfectly well aware that, as in the dream visions and the preceding portraits, data never exist in a simple, uninterpreted state. We are inevitably involved, regardless of the narrator's protestations, in an interpretation of an interpretation; and this is the problematic state that draws us into a process analogous to the struggle of the controlling consciousness to understand God's created universe.

The narrator then does a bit of housekeeping about the plan of the journey and the tale-telling competition that the Host will judge. The latter implies some standards by which a winner will be chosen, but we have no confidence in the Host's qualifications. Indeed, we do not even know the standards that he will apply. How, after all, does one judge narrative? Entertainment value? Insight? Highmindedness? We are not given to know, but we are directed to the process itself as exercised by the Host/stage-manager and ultimately as entered into by the pilgrims in regard to each other's tales as they proceed. The Host takes charge and has the pilgrims draw lots so that the selection of the first narrator will be wholly a matter of chance. The narrator, in reporting that the knight gains the honor "by aventure, or sort, or cas," chance, luck, or destiny, professes a lack of design, in his story and in the "reality" it depicts. But who can be surprised or disappointed that the process should produce the Knight as first narrator. His social primacy is clear; his virtue is uncontested. This is an auspicious beginning, but its very self-consciousness calls attention to its structural, fictive artificiality.

The Knight accepts gracefully and embarks on a lengthy chivalric romance. What could be more appropriate for "the ideal knight" described in the "General Prologue". Like the use of interpreting narrators in the dream visions, the selection of genre for the Knight invites interpretation of the narrative, with a hope for insight, because the Knight will take on the two great interpretive paradigms of the fourteenth century, chivalry and courtly love, the forms that traditionally give shape, order, and meaning to our moral and emotional experiences. Of course, our confidence depends on the slender evidence of the portrait of the Knight in the "General Prologue". Great chivalric hero, both spiritual and secular, but we have no reason other than slender conventional expectation to be confident that the Knight will be a reliable explicator of how the chivalric and courtly ideals inform human life.[7]

Even without antecedent dubeity, it becomes clear early in the tale that the Knight does not have complete control of the story as narrative, and that in itself may be a caution against simple acceptance of his formulaically asserted authority. The Knight repeatedly refers to sources for his tale in old books. At first, this might encourage us to expect at least traditional wisdom. Quickly, however, it becomes clear that the Knight is shaping his narrative primarily by the use of *abbreviatio*. Early on he asserts: "But shortly for to speken of this thyng . . ." (I, 985). And these indications recur throughout the tale. I am not suggesting that the Knight is manipulating his sources to suit his own ends; this is not a source study. Within the narrative itself, however, it is clear that the narrator is making choices about what to tell and what to leave out and thereby he assumes responsibility for the structure of the whole.

Our confidence in the narrator is further attenuated by the way he effects transitions from episode to episode. Although there is a storial necessity to move from scene to scene, the way the narrator effects the transitions is often intrusive:

> This passeth yeer by yeer and day by day . . . (I, 1033)
> Now wol I stynte of Palomon a lite . . . (I, 1334)
> And in this blisse lete I now Arcite,
> And speke I wol of Palomon a lite. (I, 1449-50)
> Now wol I turne to Arcite ageyn . . (I, 1488)
> And in this wise I lete hem fightyng dwelle,

> And forth I wol of Theseus yow telle. (I, 1661-2)

The examples could be multiplied, but even so it might be possible to attribute these technical awkwardnesses to the Knight's unworldliness, his lack of literary skill. This may be, but it nevertheless has an effect on the way we apprehend the sequence of events and their significance. The consequences become all the more prominent when the transitions occur at peculiarly inopportune places: when he leaves Palamon and Arcite disputing over Emily like two dogs fighting over a bone, or fighting ankle-deep in blood. The effect is almost comical. He explicitly refers to his use of sources and lack of skill:

> Who koude ryme in Englyssh proprely
>
> His martirdom? For sothe it am nat I;
>
> Therefore I passe as lightly as I may. (I, 1459-61)

The Knight is doing his best, by his lights, although early on we suspect, from recurrent homely imagery, that he may not be up to the ambitious task that his placement in the structure of the *Tales* led us to expect: "I have, God woot, a large feeld to ere,/ And wayke been the oxen in my plough" (I, 886-7). It is not that the Knight is discredited, nor is the nobility of his aspirations in question in the large and nobly purposed tale he has undertaken to tell. It is rather that we lose confidence in the authority of his voice as teacher by fiction: the Knight does not seem to be in control of the foundational story he is doing his best to tell. Thus, we are left without an interpretive voice that we can rely on as the fiction unfolds. As narrators in dream visions cry out for us to interpret with them, the Knight undermines our confidence that he will be able to provide answers to the basic human issues for which chivalry and courtly love are the normative heuristic paradigms.

Our uncertainty about the reliability of the Knight as narrator/interpreter is condign with the uncertainties, contingencies, and vagaries which his story represents. The awkwardness of his narrative techniques fits well with the slipperiness of the matter he has chosen. After all, this is a story of Fortune, its consequences, and our reactions to those consequences. There is throughout an attempt by the Knight to make sense of these frustrations and calamities that human beings face: they are presented in the story as the inevitable workings of Fortune which human beings have to deal with. It is just that the Knight as formulator and presenter does not seem in control of his fictional world any more than we are in control of our real worlds. The great paradigms are honored in the telling but not entirely confirmed by the Knight's narratorial limitations and not confirmed by the sequence of events in the tale. This is not satire of the probity or intelligence of the Knight nor is it an indictment of the paradigms of chivalry and courtly love, nor a refutation of the Boethian consolation of philosophy that the Knight offers. Rather it is an erosion of our confidence in the full explanatory power of conventional wisdom and idealism as I hope an examination of the structure of events will show.

Although the core of the story is the origin, progress, and outcome of the love triangle of Palamon, Arcite, and Emily, it is the fallout of their experiences that most engages the Knight's and our attention. Yet, the context of the triangle is as important as the Knight's intentions and authorial capacity, because the story begins not with the triangle but with Theseus and the Amazons. The ambient presence of Theseus makes his actions, decisions, and interpretations crucial to an understanding of the world and, if the Knight sees Theseus as a model philosopher-king, we must attend to his role in the story, what the Knight makes of it, and what we make of this connection.

Theseus, we are told uncritically, even admiringly, has conquered the Amazons and taken Hippolyta (to wife) and Emily, and is returning home. We are asked to assume with the Knight that this conquest is just, that it establishes some kind of order, and that his marriage to Hippolyta is a confirmation of that order. When he meets the grieving Theban ladies, Theseus is overcome by pity; their suffering is, according to the women, the result of Fortune, and Theseus takes on the role of rectifying the effects of Fortune. This is praiseworthy, but the plunder that follows his restoration of order in Thebes, though mentioned only briefly, can hardly be ignored or received with total equanimity. For the Knight it is right and just; for us it is a mildly troublesome semi-preterition. In any case, Theseus quells but does not put an end to chance as ubiquitous in human affairs. It is by chance that he finds Palamon and Arcite still alive in a pile of bodies. It is to enforce justice that he summarily imprisons both of them for life. His plundering and his sentencing makes us uncertain that "pite runneth sore in gentil herte," and, in any case, this resolution is just prologue to a concatenation of chances, philosophized and dignified as Fortune, that ensues.

We shift, almost mechanically, to the plight of Palamon and Arcite in prison: justice from the point of view of Theseus, ill Fortune from the perspective of the lamentations of the two imprisoned young heroes. While Theseus is engaged in living as happily ever after as this world allows, Palamon and Arcite languish in prison until Emily appears. We are jerked into a courtly description of her doing her May observances in a garden, and Love enters the poem in beauty and artificial splendor. The plight of Palamon and Arcite is plunked into the middle of this courtly idyll: " . . . the knyghtes weren in prisoun/ Of which I tolde yow and tellen shal . . ." (I, 1058-9).

But Palamon, by chance (Fortune?) sees her and is totally smitten with the unfulfilled extremities of courtly love. Sympathetic Arcite tries to comfort Palamon with the balm of resignation; he attributes Palamon's grief to Fortune, thereby elevating the chance sighting, and offers philosophical consolation: " 'So stood the hevene whan that we were born./ We moste endure it; this is the short and playn' (I, 1090-1). This is a kind of resolution or stasis, but thereupon Arcite sees Emily himself, philosophy flies out the window with his heart, and the cousins become heated contenders for a love that seems impossible to consummate for either of them. Their courtly longing is compound; not only is Emily inaccessible in a traditional courtly way, but there is also their imprisonment. They engage in a courtly *disputatio* over who has priority in love for Emily, using familiar courtly arguments such as who saw her first (Palamon) and who saw her first "as a human being" (Arcite). Their disputation is rancorous, disrupting their pledged camaraderie, but it is at least a veneer of order in its association with the familiar conventionalities of the courtly tradition. But the intellectual conflict is clear as the formal disputation degenerates into two dogs fighting over a bone, and it makes Arcite's return to philosophy all the odder in I, 1185-6.

Chance strikes again in the unexpected and flimsily motivated liberation of Arcite and their reactions are complicated, perhaps even trivialized. Arcite, the recipient of apparent good fortune, laments that he will be free but separated from Emily under pain of death by exile. He paradoxically envies Palamon who will be near Emily, able to see her but unable to do anything about it, and attributes his fate to cruel Fortune. Palamon sees the matter otherwise; he is the victim of Saturn/disorder. The Knight concludes Part I with a conventional love question about who is worse off. Though the Knight resolves this segment with a courtly convention, the behavior of Palamon and Arcite has already left courtly traditions in a confused shambles. So much for the superimposition of a tenuous convention on the disordered perspectives of the two young knights. Book I has not set up the operations of Fortune conveniently for a solution.

We then bounce back and forth between Palamon and Arcite and between chance and purpose. Arcite suffers love-longing in exile but contrives to return to Athens, put himself in service to Theseus, and thereby be near Emily. His disguise, neatly the simple result of the physical suffering of love-longing, allows secret return and gives his natural nobility an opportunity to flourish. Just at this point Palamon escapes, according to the Knight "by aventure or destynee" (I, 1465). But only the timing could be either; the escape, like Arcite's preferment, is purposive. That they should meet in a grove (Arcite in courtly enjoyment of May, Palamon in flight) is clearly chance. They descend quickly from disputation to bickering and, after Arcite is a good enough sport to get armor for Palamon, they fall to fighting like a lion and a tiger (I, 1656-7) rather than courtly rivals. When Theseus, by chance, comes upon them they are fighting "breme as it were bores two" (I, 1699). The Knight's sententious explanation of destiny as the working out of God's foreknowledge seems overblown in context. Although Theseus' first inclination is to execute them both, the intercession of women and the overwhelming power of love allow "pity to runneth sore" in his heart in an astonishing 83 lines (I, 1742-1825). Theseus avoids bloodshed and establishes order, but the pace of resolution is disquietingly rapid.

Nevertheless, in this world that is confusing chance and purpose, elevating chance to Fortune, equivocating Fortune and destiny, and equating destiny with God's foreknowledge, Theseus attempts to impose order: the two will fight a formal and proper battle at a tournament one year hence. Book III, in its description of the design of the lists, is an emblem of order and balance; it is as if Theseus believes that he can give shape and meaning to the chaos of human life by means of his human will to order and symmetry. The emblem is important to the Knight. In a story which he has been parenthetically hurrying along, he insists that every care be given to the description of the lists, the champions Lycurgus and Emetrius, and the temples of the prevailing deities Venus, Mars, and Diana.

The order, however, is all on the surface. The association of Palamon with Venus and Arcite with Mars is arbitrary; the association of Emily with Diana is paradoxical, the courtly lady who would be a virgin. Even the devotions of each at the temples is superficial and arbitrary. In the iconography of Book III Arcite will get what he asks for; Palamon will get what he asks for; Emily will get what she can get: barring chastity, whoever loves her more. The mischief lurking beneath the surface of Theseus' elaborate attempt to impose order on human experience is apparent at several points. After lingering over the initial descriptions, the Knight decides he must speed his story along, so he does not describe the big celebration. Then he becomes leisurely again as he recounts the balanced visits to the temples. Emily in the temple of Diana is particularly poignant. The inescapable bawdry in the response to Emily's prayer to Diana

cannot but be seen as humorous, an intrusion into the high seriousness of the Knight/Theseus' order-making:

> The fires brenne upon the auter cleere,
>
> Whil Emelye was thus in hir preyere.
>
> But sodeynly she saugh a sighte queynte,

> For right anon oon of the fyres queynte
> And quyked again, and after that anon
> That oother fyr was queynt and al agon;
> And as it queynte it made a whistelynge,
> As doon thiise wete brondes in hir brennynge,
> And at the brondes ende out ran anon
> As it were blody dropes many oon . . . (I, 2331-40)

The four puns on "queynte" and the conclusion with a symbolic deflowering suggest an unconsciousness on the Knight's part of the underlying realities.[8] Similarly, Theseus has established a proper and conventional content for ordering human affairs, but his gentle heart seems unaware that the result, even when he eventually forbids the spilling of life, inevitably causes far more spilling of blood than any single combat between Palamon and Arcite could. Thus works the imposition of human order on the chaos of human experience. The Knight, wrapped up in the high-minded dignity of his narration, fails to notice his unintentional punning. Theseus, wrapped up in his quest for dignity and propriety, brings on a blood-letting out of proportion to the dictates of chance, Fortune, destiny, or whatever. Indeed, the incompatibility is reinforced by the quarreling of the gods in heaven over how the conflicting promises will be resolved. The result is that the power of resolution falls to Saturn; thus despite all of the efforts of Theseus, Saturn, the ancient god of disorder, will prevail. Theseus will be thwarted and the Knight seems as unaware of this irony as he is of the puns in Diana's temple. Theseus is implacable in trying to bring order, or at least sense, out of chaos; where the Knight as narrator stands with regard to all of this is ambiguous and is further explored as the tournament proceeds. At the beginning of Book IV he is eager to get on with it.

The resolution does not come about in single combat, if at all. The battle is bloody and Arcite's triumph is not single-handed. It is attributed to Fortune, even Satan, but what is most clear is that Theseus' artificial order of the lists is unravelling. Theseus proclaims an unaccountable three-day feast; celebrating what, except superficialities, is hard to tell, while we are treated to a coldly clinical description of Arcite's death agonies and final reconciliation, full of "allases," with Palamon. The death of Arcite is almost as long as Mimi's in *La Boheme* and as full of sentimental protestations which have no force but pathos: a pageant of the meaninglessness of it all. All mourn, but especially Theseus, for whom there is no comfort except in the wisdom of the speech of his father Egeus:

> "Right as ther dyed nevere man," quod he,
> "That he ne lyvede in erthe in some degree,
> Right so ther lyvede never man," he seyde,
> "In al this world, that som tyme he ne deyde.
> This world nys but a thurghfare ful of wo,
> And we been pilgrymes, passyinge to and fro.
> Deeth is an ende of every worldy soore." (I, 2843-9)

The problem is that this most fatuous of platitudes answers nothing, solves nothing. It leaves Theseus with only one more drama to manage: the funeral of Arcite incongruously protracted through a long preterition (I, 2743-2815).

Our only consolation, apparently, is to be the long explanatory philosophical speech by Theseus, long-winded, conventional, and not even a very imaginative presentation of traditional doctrine. Asserting that an immutable God is the source of all created beings, he draws the familiar Boethian conclusion that as God's creation moves down from His changelessness it descends into unstable spheres where change is the only rule and degeneration is the universal character of the change. Such is true of man as well as of physical nature. After all of his striving to control, Theseus relaxes into an attenuated Boethian consolation:

> "Thanne is it wysdom, as it thynketh me,
> To maken vertu of necessitee,
> And take it weel that we may nat eschue,
> And namely that to us alle is due.
> And whoso gruccheth ought, he dooth folye,
> And rebel is to hym that al may gye." (I, 3041-6)

All works out for the best and it is futile, even wrong, to rebel against the divine plan: "The contrarie of al this is wilfulnesse." (I, 3057). Theseus is left with a superficial version of Boethian consolation.

It is Boethius without the substance of philosophical explanation. Theseus is, after all, shallow. He gets the idea that it is necessary to "make a virtue of necessity," and this is a "home truth" which, of course, is not entirely trivial: life must go on; we must make of it what we can; Palamon should marry Emily (disregarding her preferences entirely) so as to make the best of a hard world. But the heart of Boethius, the part that gives Boethius consolatory power, is missing. The exploration of the relation between chance and fortune, the transformation of Fortune to destiny, the confusion of destiny with God's foreknowledge, and the explanation of Divine Providence as the benevolent working out of human life in ways that man cannot and should not understand: all of this is left out of Theseus' final speech and without it Theseus is reduced to a pompous presentation of pop-Boethius. He more than anyone may have learned to accept destiny and to have the resilience to try to turn "wo" into "wele." There is a pathetic insight here as Theseus does all that he can in promising Emily to Palamon. But there is no metaphysical foundation. Theseus is not a fool, but neither is he a philosopher. He may try to ward off suffering or pick up the pieces in the end, but he never demonstrates the equanimity of understanding, the transcendence of vision.

Theseus is to be admired because he tries, not because he sees. And in the sympathetic relationship that the Knight establishes between himself and Theseus we see that the Knight too is representative of what is good and noble about human attempts to live in a mutable world. The Knight is an idealist; for this he is to be admired. He believes in the nobility of man and his capacity to fashion a better world out of adversity through moral idealism. Idealism is a way to live in the world, but it is not necessarily a way to understand the world. Chaucer, having established the interpretive ambiguities of the world in the "General Prologue", contrives to give idealism as his first, best answer to the dilemmas of the human condition represented in the *Tales* as a whole. The Knight, in associating himself with the idealism of Theseus and transcending it, shapes a world as he sees it. For him, idealism is a satisfactory philosophy. He sees neither its limitations nor its dangers. Although we are not finally sure whether the Knight understands what he has done, he has affirmed the idealisms of love and chivalry as moral imperatives in a mutable world. He deserves reverence, but also should inspire caution, because his is the idealism that can fall in the ditch while gazing at the stars. The virtues asserted of him in the "General Prologue" are borne out as he associates himself with Theseus, but he is a flawed narrator who does not always seem to understand what he is doing in shaping the tale or associating himself with Theseus. Still, he is man at his aspiring, and most vulnerable, best.

The reaction to the Knight's tale is general approbation, especially among the "gentils." Who, after all, could object to the nobility of the Knight's aspirations? Internally to the *Tales*, this is a good start as the Host affirms, and he attempts to sustain the level of high seriousness by soliciting a tale from the Monk. The ironies here are clearer to us than the pilgrims: there are the chinks in the idealism of the "Knight's Tale" and we already suspect the moral reliability of the Monk from his portrait in the "General Prologue". But Chaucer abandons a schematic didactic structure in favor of a different form of development. He allows the drunken Miller to interrupt and the *Tales*, and the pilgrimage seems to take on a life of their own. The progression seems to escape from the authorial constraint of both Chaucer and the Host. Of course that, from the point of view of Chaucer, is illusion, but the narrative calls upon us to see this world at this point as independent of authorial manipulation. By force of rudeness the Miller seems spontaneously to take control and to thwart the Host, insult the Reeve (who is a carpenter and the Miller intends to feature a stupid carpenter), and insert by force a "realism" which the idealism of the Knight has avoided. The Miller is the guy in the bar who is really going to tell us "what's what."

The Miller explicitly promises a tale that will "quite" the Knight's: pay back, retaliate against, equal? All of these are possible, but what emerges most clearly, whether the Miller realizes it or not, is a vision of human life and love that is antithetical to that proposed by the Knight. The genre of his tale, a fabliau, is an antithesis to the chivalric romance of the Knight. As a piece of narrative it is not rude; it is the Miller and his vision of the world that are rude. The tale itself is a highly sophisticated conjoining of two familiar fabliaux (the duped husband and the misplaced kiss) which come together in a comically splendid denouement at John's cry "Water!"

In every respect, the Miller's Tale is an antithesis to the Knight's. There is a love triangle: two men vie for the favors of a beautiful woman. But Alison is married, Nicholas is clever, even cynical, and Absalon is foolish. It is a degraded love triangle, and if there is any correlative to Theseus it is the hapless husband John. The goal is not the winning of a fair virgin, but the seduction of a sexy young wife. Such is the matter of fabliau and fabliau is at the core of the Miller's vision of human relations. Our expectations from this genre are as important in viewing this tale as were our expectations of chivalric romance in the "Knight's Tale". The "Miller's Tale" is efficiently, compactly narrated. There is nothing in it superfluous to the Miller's vision. When we see a stupid old man married to a frisky young wife, especially one stupid enough to have a clerk as a boarder, we know what will happen: cuckolding is an inevitability. Even the complication provided by Absalon's misguided, foppish aspirations have predictably unsuccessful, and comic, results.

The tale is very funny. But we should remember the context in which it is told. The Miller's comments in the preamble to the tale betray a dark, cynical view of marriage and human nature. It is bad enough that the Miller asserts that "who has no wyf he is no cokewold;" that is merely a black and absurdly exaggerated expression of conventional anti-feminism and a fabliau donné. It is the Miller's connection of female infidelity with the divine that is more ominous: "An housbonde shal nat been inquisityf/ Of Goddes pryvetee, nor of his wyf" (I, 3163-4). Even here we have a perverted echo of the "Knight's Tale". "Goddes privitee" is that area of knowledge which human beings ought not inquire into. In the "Knight's Tale" it is the source of the Christianized Fortune that must be accepted and endured. In the Miller's mind it is linked with the intrinsic baseness of infidelity and becomes almost blasphemous by being drawn into unworthy company. With this blackened preparatory atmosphere it is revealing but not surprising that the narrator or Chaucer (whatever avatar of narrative authority we choose) sees fit to offer a disclaimer. His reporting of the ribaldry and immorality that is to come is, from his perspective and according to his role, simply a matter of fidelity in recording: he must not "falsen his matere." He must, if he is to recount the world of the pilgrimage truthfully, transmit his "text" accurately. His puckish suggestion that those who might be offended choose a more congenial tale serves only to ironically imply that if we do not face up to the "Miller's Tale", we will miss something important. This ambiguous stance apparently distances the narrator from the vulgarity while preserving the sense that he is transmitting a text of the way the world is, like it or not, and it reflects the way the *Tales* have ostensibly taken on a life of their own by virtue of the Miller's intrusion.

Chaucer, characteristically, has it both ways. He is a faithful reporter of a world that he does not necessarily approve of but cannot control, and which he must present if he is to represent the actualities of this apparently independent world. Interpretation, he implies, is our problem. We must wrestle with the disturbing, though hilarious, ways in which narration, characters, and events correlate and contrast with the "Knight's Tale". First, there is the economy of narration noted above; there is none of the clumsiness in transitions and *abbreviatio* that characterize the Knight's more morally admirable narrative. The "Miller's Tale" is 700 lines of compact action stopping only for portraits which are directly relevant and to be savored.

Nicholas and Absalon cannot be specifically correlated with Palamon and Arcite, but in portrait and action, they are contraposed characters to the high-minded protagonists of the "Knight's Tale". Nicholas is a clerk, so we expect him to be clever rather than wise (interesting in view of the unexpectedly virtuous Clerk in the "General Prologue"). His main characteristic is in the supple adjective "hende": skillful, courteous, gracious, and near at hand. The application is both literal and ironic. He is a devotee of "hidden knowledge," perhaps even forbidden knowledge, but certainly factitious and fraudulent knowledge. Truth and honor do not enter into knowing for Nicholas. Knowledge is for practical application towards goals that are material and sensual. His forbidden knowledge is not explored; it is used in a ruse to achieve practical goals quickly and effectively. His operative knowledge is pragmatic and he is the manager of the action up until this cynical manipulation receives a practical, painful, comical come-uppance.

As Nicholas is a degradation of wisdom, Absalon is a degradation of the courtly. His foolish aspiration to consummation with Alison is put in courtly terms, but Absalon is absurd as a courtly lover. His courtly attributes are a parody of the noble paradigm and his goal is more forthrightly fornication rather than love. Like Nicholas, he is clever, but he is not clever about himself. He is self-deluding and foppish rather than self-abnegating and dignified. Yet he is as clever as Nicholas in prosaic human terms when it comes right down to it.

Nor is Alison Emily. The introductory description of her associates her with animals and a kind of earthly vitality (I, 3233-70). The tone of this portrait is delicious; it establishes her sensuality and inclination towards sexual adventure without arousing our moral disapproval. She is more a warm form of nature rather than an evil woman, but she is no ideal, courtly or otherwise. When she and Nicholas have the opportunity to satisfy their sexual inclinations, little time is lost. Presumably it is at least nine years from the time Palamon first sees Emily and adores her as a goddess until the consummation of their pure love in holy matrimony. Thanks to Nicholas' cleverness and Alison's compliance, they are in bed as soon as opportunity allows. Indeed, Nicholas's approach to her lacks the rhetorical and real delicacy of the courting of Emily by Palamon and Arcite: "prively he caughte hire by the queynte" (I, 3276) and "heeld hire herde by the haunchebones" (I, 3279). They get right to the point and the point has no redeeming social or moral value. This is the very antithesis of the elegant self-control and self-denial that ennobles and dignifies in the "Knight's Tale". The plan is practical, comical, unchivalric, anti-courtly, and successful. Retribution, if that is what it is, comes when they try to be too clever even for Nicholas: "to amenden al the jape." They will add relish to adultery by humiliating Absalon. Now, we are pleased when the artificial Nicholas kisses Nicholas's real ass. But we are equally pleased when the vindictive Absalon takes revenge on the overweening Nicholas. And Alison just seems to be enjoying it all. Crass efficiency, vulgar language, and ignominious aspirations in the Miller's tale contrast at every point with the idealism of the world that the Knight portrays at such great length.

We are not, however, revolted by the world of the "Miller's Tale". Even the obviously harsh treatment of John does not generate moral opprobrium. He is an unperceptive gull, and this is not a world that stops to pity the doltish. Wit, ingenuity, the human at its least common denominator define the "moral" ethos of this world that allows for sympathy no more than for idealism. This is no place for pity "to run sore in gentil herte." Such is just not in the cards where sensuality and cleverness are the energizing ideals. Despite ourselves, or perhaps because of a part of ourselves that the "Knight's Tale" does not acknowledge, we laugh with and at the characters and revel in base human comedy.

Part of our pleasure comes from the juxtaposition of this tale with the long-winded morality and sententiousness of the "Knight's Tale" and, in this way, the Miller really does "quite" the Knight. But is the implied moral vision one that we would want to accept as an alternative to the Knight's? No. The tale is funny and appealing, a fair enough representation of one aspect of our humanity. But it is not satisfying as a characterization of the entire human condition. Its cynicism, which cleverness allows us to enjoy while the tale lasts, cannot ultimately prevail. One of its consequences is that it generates the "Reeve's Tale", a still darker quiting of the "Miller's Tale" which has as its purpose only a mean-spirited, though funny, character assassination of millers. Its point is personal and mean and it reduces the larger comedy of the *Tales* to personal retribution rather than human comedy. Thus, if the "Reeve's Tale" is crabbed, the "Miller's Tale" is inadequate despite its comic appeal. And in this way its own intrinsic failings disqualify it as a comprehensive "quiting" of the "Knight's Tale".

What we do have in the juxtaposition of the "Knight's Tale" and the "Miller's Tale", especially in their apparent "life of their own" within the *Tales*, is an approximation of truth. It is not, however, that we just take the two tales and find a satisfactory elucidation of the human condition by finding the mid-point between their contrasting visions. The relationship between the "Knight's Tale" and the "Miller's Tale" is subtly reciprocal. That is, each of the tales answers the other and undercuts itself. Not that the "Knight's Tale" does not represent much of what is admirable in human behavior and laudable in its attempt to find order, humanly and philosophically, in a world that seems defiant of human potentialities and comprehension. Nor that the "Miller's Tale" is a cynical representation of a human baseness that we can easily distance ourselves from. Both are true; both are flawed or inadequate as free-standing interpretations of the human condition. It is rather that the relationship between the two tales is bi-polar. That is, the "Knight's Tale" betrays the insufficiencies of the radical idealism embodied in the paradigms of chivalry and courtly love. The "Miller's Tale" betrays the vacuousness of a radically alternative realism. Thus, each tale is a caution about itself and each comments on the excesses of the other. This bi-polarity sets the tales in a relationship to each other such that a mid-point is impossible to determine; we and our condition as human beings float indeterminately somewhere between idealism and cynicism, between our sense of the inadequacies of idealism and realism. If we view the world as the Knight does, we may fall into the pit; if we view the world like the Miller, we may live in the pit.

What happens in the rest of Fragment I is hard to determine.[9] It may be that Chaucer abandoned the sequence or intended to return to it. The space left after the 'Cook's Tale" in the manuscripts suggests the latter, though it may only suggest that early fifteenth century scribes thought so. In any case, the "Reeve's Tale" degenerates into a quiting that has fewer heuristic possibilities than the counterbalance between the "Knight's Tale" and the "Miller's Tale". And the "Cook's Tale" seems only to be cognizant that dirty stories are the order of the day. Such is a conceivable consequence of the apparent "life of its own" that

Chaucer has given Fragment I, as he withdraws as far as possible from restrictive commentary and apparent control. Maybe he thought he had reached an irretrievable dead end in his structure; maybe he would have come back to resolve the feathery descent of the significance of this free-floating world. In any case, the complex counterpoise of the "Knight's Tale" and the "Miller's Tale" is an excellent emblem of the quest for interpretation that Chaucer invites us to join him in in the *Tales*.

Although definitive evidence cannot be adduced, it seems fair enough to see the "Man of Law's Tale" in conjunction with Fragment I. It appears next in almost all of the manuscripts and makes a curious, if inconclusive, commentary on the world and issues which have emerged in Fragment I. First, and prominently, we are jerked out of the apparent "world of its own" back to a more directive sequencing of the *Tales* as the Host calls upon the Man of Law who acquiesces, if reluctantly. The "Introduction to the Man of Law's Tale" not only takes us out of the independence of Fragment I, but also emphasizes the fictionality, the made-upness, of the *Tales* as a whole fictional artefact. Partly it does this by foregrounding the nature of fiction and the relationship of fiction to a circumscribing "real" world. The "Introduction" is a self-conscious fiction in that it calls attention to fiction itself and unsettles us, as we try to interpret what world we, as readers, are in. In the "Introduction" the Host regains control over the sequence of narration. His reference to time suggests that time must be used wisely and that we are coming to the end of the day, perhaps the first day of the pilgrimage. One need not accept the latter to notice that the Host's observations imply a point of closure. The sequence is once again under management. Thus we have emerged from "the world on its own" to the fictional structure.[10]

The Man of Law assents gracefully to the Host's request, but his preamble to his tale raises further issues. Here as later he peppers his comments with legal terminology and that may imply a thread of fragile human order that his legal mind tried to impose on the matter of his tale. But his continuing comments complicate the narrative structure. In explaining his difficulty in coming up with a tale, he refers directly to the historical Chaucer. This complication has no easy resolution. He cannot be the "pilgrim Chaucer" because he says that Chaucer has told all the good stories (II, 45-56). He is somewhat critical of Chaucer's versification, but he emphasizes the breadth of Chaucer's work and Chaucer's restraint in not telling tales of incest. His references are to real works reliably attributed to the historical Chaucer. Thus this creates an ontological problem even if we wish to see the overall narrator as Chaucer the poet speaking with an ironic voice. The problem, essentially, is that levels of reality lose their boundaries: a fictional character, ultimately created by Chaucer the poet, or intermediately by Chaucer the pilgrim or Chaucer the ironist, is commenting on a reality beyond him. It is at least ironic that a fictional character should comment on his maker; at most it is an obliteration of the distinction between the levels of reality of the fictional and real. It may even be an analogy to the situation that man finds himself in with relation to God, the ultimate maker of the fiction which is human reality. This has an effect on the context in which we attend to the story, the only one he knows, fortunately told to him some years ago by a merchant. Its fictionality is both emphasized and self-consciously called attention to.

And one other feature calls especial attention to his tale: he says that it will be in prose, but then the tale, and even its brief prologue, is in elegant rime royal. The verse form, especially in the mouth of the Man of Law, gives the tale a disembodied quality that reinforces our sense of the peculiar situation of this tale within the whole of the narrative structure. The tale itself is not very complicated, at least from a narrative point of view. Constance is subjected to a series of misfortunes, eventually to be restored to safety, security, and wealth. The unrealism of her castings adrift need not trouble us; this is an easy "given" to allow in the development of a fiction placed deep in the past in a world of almost magical interpenetration of pagan and Christian worlds. The tale, however, has attracted an unusual amount of contradictory interpretation, even for Chaucer.[11] For example, Constance has been seen as everything from a flawed ideal of womanliness to a hagiographic ideal. The diversity of interpretations is a confirmation of my sense that the interpretation of fiction is one of the most difficult of human tasks because it is analogous to our multivalent interpretations of "reality." I have no quarrel with these disparate critical perspectives; they are, perhaps, just what Chaucer invites.

Yet, there is also something to be said for the simplicity of the tale, despite the complexities that can be layered upon it or segments of it. It is, after all, a very popular tale and, in its essence, a very simple one. Constance, the constant Christian, is continually made vulnerable to the evils that underservedly surround her in the pagan worlds into which she is thrust. It is an allegory of the precarious position of the Christian in this threatening world we live in, and she is saved by repeated divine interventions occasioned by her unwavering fidelity to Christianity. She is not clever or ingenious, but the recipient of God's favor because of her virtue. It is, at heart, a simple tale (told, ironically, in an elegant verse form, one the very flaws the Man of Law had noted in Chaucer's poetry), efficiently narrated, complicated only by the narrator's occasional. significant use of legal terminology and his predilection for apostrophe.

So what do we make of the simple and conventional narrative that is at the heart of the "Man of Law's Tale"? What, that is to say, are the terms of the simple experience of Constance? Constance is unfailingly good in a world that is penetrated with the evil of the unscrupulous unbeliever. Evil is associated with the pagan, who obstinately refuses to be incorporated into the community of God and therefore works his headstrong, willful way. In the tale it is impossible not to see them, in their ultimate futility, as instruments of divine testing of human fidelity. This can be complicated by making Constance the Church itself, but let's keep it as simple as the Man of Law seems to do. What emerges then is the moral centrality of unwavering faith in the face of extreme, undeserved trials.

Despite the occasional legal terms, we do not get much sense of the narrator and that contributes to our sense of the disembodied quality of the tale. Perhaps this lack of narrative voice, or its faintness, explains why critics so often contradict each other about the ramifications of the narrative. And despite her virtue, Constance is also very flat: she is a simple symbol bobbing around in a hostile sea. Evil is made by the perverted human will, by the invincible ignorance and malevolence of the pagans. Good is brought out of it by a combination of Christian constancy and Divine Providence. Miraculous events and providential fortune keep Constance alive and return her to security and happiness within the Christian bosom of Rome. Everything in this allegory is on the surface though we may torture it to find complexity and ambiguity, and perhaps should; but I am looking here at what the Man of Law is basically doing and sees himself to be doing. Constance is flat; we do not look beyond her surface and therefore concentrate on her circumstances and the simple unfolding of what happens.

The metaphor of the ship, however, is temptingly persistent. She repeatedly finds herself, literally and figuratively, aboard a rudderless ship: the essential predicament of the terrestrial Christian in a world that offers concrete threats. And she is unfailingly rescued by chance, but chance that is here, clearly and simply, the operation of Divine Providence. As Kolve puts it, God is the unseen rudder who eventually brings good out of evil for the devoted Christian.[12] The tale addresses many of the issues of Fragment I: chance, Fortune, Providence, idealism, moral virtue, leading Kolve to see the tale as a "provisional palinode." I believe it is, but in a strange way.[13]

The "Man of Law's Tale" is a flat, non-interpretive exemplification, simplification, assertion of the issues raised in the bi-polar complexity of Fragment I. It does function as a kind of palinode, but a miniature version of the kind of palinode that Chaucer offers, at greater length and with greater complexity, in the "Retraction" to the *Tales* and from the eighth sphere in *Troilus and Criseyde*. A highly conventional statement of undoubtedly true Christian doctrine, it neither contradicts nor solves the complex issues that have been raised and that remain. The Man of Law wraps himself in conventional wisdom; he submerges himself, and can be neither praised nor blamed for the disembodied rime royal that glides above the morass of experience and the struggle to interpret experience that pervades Fragment I. Because of its orthodox doctrine and its narrative flatness, the "Man of Law's Tale" does not lead anywhere. It is conventional, not penetrating: for the Man of Law astrology is as good as Providence, or indistinguishable from it. Providence is undeniably operative, but conventional and unimaginative.

Nevertheless, the simple circumstances and resolutions cannot escape the ontological ambiguities established in the "Introduction" to the tale. The immanence of Chaucer, inside and outside the fiction, mildly betrays the artificiality of the Man of Law's unconscious palinode. As palinode, the tale cannot finally be successful. It is a resolution which is a resolution only on the surface and therefore, in context, in Chaucer's penetrating interpretive world, is no solution at all. It is a conclusion in which nothing is concluded, especially with the presence of Chaucer hovering about it. Of course, Providence prevails, and idealism, truth, honor, fidelity, *etc.*, but, having asserted that, where does it get us in the intricate world where we really constantly strive to figure out who we are, where we are, and what all of this means?

Chapter IV: Gentilesse

Ever since Kittredge it has been common to see the tales in Fragments III to V as "the marriage group."[1] And it is true that each tale, except those of the Friar and Summoner, usually dismissed as an interlude, comments in some way on marriage. As usual with a multi-faceted text like the *Tales*, no generally accepted consensus has emerged. Certainly this sequence of Tales comments recurringly on "gentilesse," originally a catch-all for the virtues associated with members of the aristocracy, but examined and transmuted and extended by Chaucer in this sequence of tales. But there is not critical unanimity.[2] I suspect that the focus of this group of tales should be broadened even further to an examination of human relations, both internal, the relationship with self, and external, the relationship of the self with others. Marriage is an apt metaphor for these complex human relations and gentilesse, as developed and explored in these tales, is the recurring standard of judgment. The consequences are revealing but not determinate. Our understanding of our own or others' principles for personal behavior and human relations can never be complete. Not that these matters are totally unknowable; rather that they are incompletely specifiable. We know ourselves only partially and occasionally, and then from a limited, self-constructed perspective; *a fortiori* others. One cannot be certain in the unstable fragmentariness of the *Tales* that the tales of Fragments III to V were meant as or were coming to be, as the plan of the whole changed, a discrete unit. Yet, unless one accepts the Bradshaw shift, their contiguity in the manuscripts is persuasive, and their echoes of each other's tales (and the Knight's and Miller's) tempt us to investigate related issues in a common context. So, at a Wife then will I first begin.

The sequence, as I presume to call it, begins with the "Prologue" to the "Wife of Bath's Tale." There is no introduction; the Wife simply plunges into an 828 line "Prologue", which dwarfs the 404 line "Tale" that follows. This is entirely appropriate for the Wife, who is less interested in fiction than in the progress of her own life, insofar as the reality of anyone's own life can be presented as anything more than one's own self-reflexive fiction. It is not that the Wife is lying; it is just that we each have our own interpretations of our own lives, and we are put in the position as readers of interpreting the Wife's conscious and/or unconscious rhetorical shaping of her own life. Throughout this sequence, Chaucer plays with literary genres as themselves formal instruments for various presentations of the truth. Chaucer's frequently noted exploration and manipulation of genres is yet one more sign of his curiosity about means of interpretation.

The Wife's "Prologue" is a "confession" in the strict sense, though it may also be a confession, whether she means it as such or not, in a looser sense. Chaucer uses the familiar figure of "La Vielle," the old bawd, as the skeleton of the Wife, but here "La Vielle" is given flesh and scope, her own voice to reflect upon and interpret the complex meaning of her own life.[3] I am pleased to note that critics have found the Wife to reveal herself as everything from a "sociopath" to a "secular saint."[4] Such interpretive discord may be the key to the revelatory opacity of the "Prologue". Mussolini is reported to have said that it is not so much impossible to govern Italy as pointless. And something similar seems to be true of the Wife in her "Prologue". She will be what she is and what she thinks she is; the rewarding part of our interpretive venture is to play with these possibilities as she affirms and contradicts herself.

The absence of an "Introduction" (how would one invite her to tell a tale? how could one keep her from telling a tale and more?) allows her in her first two lines to plunge headlong into two of the major controversies that run throughout the Middle Ages: the competing claims of experience and authority as ways of knowing, and the hoary anti-feminist tradition. Curiously, in these two lines she asserts her subject: the woe that is in marriage. It is intriguing that that is not very much what she ends up talking about at all. She discusses her own five marriages in a way that interweaves woe and joy in a tantalizing tapestry. The structure of her self-exegesis seems to be development by digression, and that itself is part of who she is and who she thinks herself to be.

Having stated her topic and the simple fact of her five marriages, she embarks not on an analysis of the pains of these marriages, but on a reflection on the validity of her marriages. That is, she stops to defend the propriety of her five marriages and, as she proceeds in her argumentative defense, she makes deft use of authority, a technique she has subordinated as a way of knowing in her opening lines. She establishes the issue by reference to the story of the wedding feast at Cana, which ostensibly shows that Christ approved only monogamy. Yet there is a real theological issue here that she is aware of: it was not entirely clear in the fourteenth century church that even serial monogamy was licit. After all, what would the multiply-married do at the time of the resurrection of the body? This focus of attention has several complicating effects. First, it avoids the nagging question of extra-marital sex. She bypasses the ambiguity of "withouten other compaignye in youth"; was she with or without other company before her first marriage? Indeed, the "Prologue" raises uncertainty about whether she was always faithful when ravaging her first three husbands and getting even with her fourth and on her many pilgrimages. These ambiguities recall those unresolved aspects of her portrait in the "General Prologue". Was her hurrying to be the first at the Offertory religious zeal or egoism? Are her pilgrimages devotion or dalliance? We think we know from her "gat-toothedness" and her knowledge of "the olde daunce" but there are not enough words for us to be sure or, even if we are reasonably sure of her sexuality, sure of her culpability. Thus are we left in her own "Prologue".

Her first digression, if digression it can be called, is a vindication of the technical legality of her five marriages; sadness and happiness are pushed aside in the lively movement of her mind. Her arguments, paradoxically, are primarily from the authority of Scripture. She cites the scriptural injunction to increase and multiply and the multiple marriages of Solomon as justification. She goes beyond citations of Scripture and traditional arguments urging monogamy to the fact that Christ never married at all, and that virginity is seen as a higher state than marriage. And she goes further afield from Scripture when she cites not the Bible but the traditional argument of the construction of the universe according to a divine plan. Her untutored genius is in the relentless turning of the authorities to her own purposes. After all, how can we increase and multiply without sex? Most important is not the way she chooses her authorities in order to support what she "chooses" to believe, but the tone of joy in which she accepts the authorities that she likes. For example, the Biblical injunction to increase and multiply is heartily approved: "That gentil text kan I wel understonde" (III, 29). And the argument on the other side, from the marriage feast at Cana, is explained away as inconclusive (III, 9-25). She finds joy in the authority of Scripture in so far as it confirms what she wants. Similarly, the familiar argument from design is neatly turned to her purposes when she cites the "members of generation" as part of God's plan, easily ignoring the potential objections to her argument in favor of a flamboyant acceptance of her interpretation of God's will. The tone again is important as she rejects the possibility that they are simply for excretion. Similarly, there is her contention that virginity is a counsel of perfection. She accepts humbly that she is not a golden vessel nor white bread, and is pleased to recognize that the world needs brass and brown bread as well. Her humility issues in a kind of triumphal joy as she shapes tradition and authority to a form that she can revel in. Is she heretical? Is she disingenuous? There is just not enough text to tell with certainty. Thus we suspect her accuracy, but revel with her in her transcendent joy both in her own experience and her vivacious presentation of it. She has used authority for her own purposes to present a self in a tone that would be mean-spirited to condemn. So we are uncensorious when she concludes this section with a celebratory account of how she will follow God's plan and the apostle's counsel to "render the debt" with exuberance and a tenuous mantle of approbation.

It is curious, in this celebration, that she is interrupted by the Pardoner who says he is about to take a wife and is somewhat daunted by the sexual energy the Wife has just expressed. It is curious because it is the Pardoner, a eunuch from birth, who could not engage in the sexual tournaments she has extolled and who, in fact, would be technically excluded from marriage by his inability to perform sexually. A reminder, but of what? The interruption has some pathos as the Pardoner pitifully tries to place himself within the general run of mankind from which he is, sadly and self-consciously, excluded. His joke is pathetic, but it returns the Wife to her "first matere," "tribulacion in marriage." She is either unaware of his state or unwilling to interrupt her celebration of joyful tribulation with a crass recognition of his sexual deficiency. Joyful tribulation it is because, as she now returns to her subjective autobiography, her "confession," she adds a caution:

> But yet I praye to al this compaignye,
> If that I speke after my fantasye,
> As taketh not agrief of that I seye,
> For myn entente nys but for to pleye. (III, 189-92)

What is serious and factual and what is exuberant fancy? Again, there will not be enough words to tell or there will be words that are aslant in such a way as to defy specification. But on to her matter, which she summarizes thus:

> ... tho housbondes that I hadde,
> As thre of hem were goode, and two were badde,
> The thre were goode men, and riche, and olde. (III, 195-7)

The division of her husbands into two groups, three good and two bad, is at the heart of the complexity and indeterminacy that permeate the rest of her "Prologue". Amidst her celebration, to which she returns over and over again, the three whom she defines as good are those who were sexually inadequate but domitable, while the two who were bad were the most promising and, once she arranged things suitably, the most sexually satisfying. What are her standards of judgment and what do they imply? There is almost a gleeful sadism in her treatment of the three "good" husbands: "As help me God, I laughe whan I thynke/ How pitously a-nyght I made hem swynke!" (III, 201-2). Sexuality has become a tool, which she gleefully recounts, and material gain, venality, has been her successfully accomplished goal:

> They had me yeven hir lond and hir tresoor;
> Me neded nat do lenger diligence
> To wynne hir love, or doon hem reverence.
> They loved me so wel, by God above,
> That I ne tolde no deyntee of hir love! (ll. 204-8)

Her triumph (her sexual vitality) has been transformed into materialism and even beyond materialism to human domination. For all her sexual activity, a cynicism seems to intrude. Their sexual performance was inadequate and irrelevant to her. What has seemed to define her essence is revealed as a weapon in the battle of the sexes for money and power.

The ensuing sample of the sort of tirade she subjected her first three husbands to further develops our skepticism concerning how they could be described as good in any sense other than that they were easily subdued and trivially rewarded with the lavishing of a sexuality that she took no joy in. The sample tirade is an extended exemplification of the very vices of which the antifeminists, particularly St. Jerome, convicted women.[5] In demonstrating the virtuosity by means of which she subdued her first three (old) husbands, the wife exemplifies the duplicity, lechery, greed, materialism, and manipulation that were traditionally taken to be the identifying characteristics of the daughters of Eve. Her harangue is full of intimidation, impossible innuendo (she accuses the poor old fellows of lechery), and overbearance. She is the very model of what St. Jerome warned against. And yet we are not repulsed by her. What saves her from the application of the conventional opprobrium that ordinarily attaches to the behavior she exhibits?

Well, the literary tradition of the old man married to a young wife may provide some exculpation, especially if we know about the more complex relations with her fourth and fifth husbands; the first three are three old fools and, conventional harridan or not, she may just be giving them what they deserve, like Alison before and May later. After all, they bring nothing to the marriages but their material possessions. They are wraiths about whom we know little and our attention is on Alice. The text displays her as venal rather than sensual and yet, somehow, she avoids our censure. Perhaps it is our respect for a virtuoso performance; perhaps it is the high spirits and flourishing vitality in the tone of her tirade that stays our condemnation. We are rather sure that these relationships are materialistic, yet there are not enough words to definitively convict her, and what words there are are delivered with a gusto that would make blame on our part feel mean-spirited. Does she understand what she has done or what she is doing in describing it? Certainly, her conclusion is an explicit statement of the female desire for dominance in marriage: "Oon of us two moste bowen, doutelees" (III, 440) and since man, according to the anti-feminists, is more reasonable, it only makes sense for him to give in and bring accord and consequent sexual rewards.

Her intentions and predilections are further complicated by her narration of her last two marriages. Her fourth husband was unfaithful but she really loved him. She remembers her youth and sexual vitality and this leads to a moment of introspection rare in the "Prologue":

> But—Lord Crist!—whan that it remembreth me
> Upon my yowthe, and on my jolitee,
> It tikleth me aboute myn herte roote.
> Unto this day it dooth myn herte boote
> That I have had my world as in my tyme.
> But age, allas, that al wole envenyme,
> Hath me biraft my beautee and my pith.
> Lat go. Farewel! The devel go therwith!

The flour is goon; ther is namoore to telle;

The bren, as best I kan, now moste I selle . . . (III, 469-78)

She recalls the joys of youth with pleasure, recognizes her age with pathos, and determines not to be defeated. This, in a kernel, is what is attractive and intelligible about the Wife. That she should insert it within the brief description of her fourth marriage is curious. He was unfaithful while she was at her sensual peak, but she wreaks a revenge, by stimulating in him a jealousy that more than pays him back and asserts her control. Money is not made an issue in this marriage, but the rest is there: she will prevail by making herself his purgatory, not by actually being unfaithful, at least according to her account, but by making him jealous. Having manipulated him successfully, she can magnanimously wish him joy in heaven. "Lat hym fare wel; God yeve his soule reste!" (III, 501).

Her fifth marriage is the most complex, and draws together the strains of love, money, and power that have run through the first four. The fifth husband, a clerk and not an old man, is the most severe challenge to her sexuality, venality, and will to power; yet the joyful energy of her narration makes it clear that this marriage was the best of all. She married him for love, not money, and he is "daungerous" in love, inflaming her desire because of course women, especially she, most want what they can't have. Indeed, with her philosophy of "provide, provide" she had had him on her mind for the future at least as far back as the death of her fourth husband, and had sized him up at the funeral through crocodile tears. The fourth marriage, then, was as empty, though in a different way, as the first three. In the fourth marriage, desire had been transformed into a contest which she won. Her narration at this point wanders back and forth, but she returns to Jankyn whose legs she had admired at the funeral.

Jankyn was only twenty; she was forty. One wonders about his motives; hers are overpoweringly sexual. At least that is what she says, and we are inclined to believe it when she signs over her accumulated wealth to him upon their marriage. It is not long until she rues the day, for her husband is an articulate anti-feminist clerk who makes a habit of reminding her at length of women's treachery by reading her anti-feminist tracts. Here is the Wife in her most complicated situation. She truly loves him, sadly enough even when he beats her physically and textually. But she is ultimately no passive victim of battered wife syndrome. Amid her account of his anti-feminist tracts (which he reads aloud to her), she intrudes barbs at the underlying impotence that must motivate such anti-feminist clerks and a very modern analysis of their perspective:

> For trusteth wel, it is an impossible
> That any clerk wol speke good of wyves,
> But if it be of hooly seintes lyves,
> Ne of noon oother womman never the mo.
> Who peyntede the leon, tel me who? (III, 688-692)

Nevertheless, one can see her indignation rising as she finally rips three pages out of his book and casts them into the fire as to deny their validity and end their existence. This is the Wife, loving and desirous, exerting power over her beloved persecutor. The closing events are a paradigm of her powers. He strikes her, but she takes this as an opportunity to seize all that she wants. She plays upon her pathetic situation (indeed, his blow has left her "somdel deef") and his guilty response. The result is that she wins on all fronts:

> He yaf me al the bridel in myn hond,
> To han the governance of hous and lond,
> And of his tonge, and of his hond also;
> And made hym brenne his book anon right tho.
> And whan that I hadde geten unto me,
> By maistrie, al the soveraynetee,
> And that he seyde, "Myn owene trewe wyf,
> Do as thee lust the terme of al thy lyf;
> Keep thyn honour, and keep eek myn estaat"—
> After that day we hadden never debaat. (III, 813-22)

He gives up her money, his anti-feminism, and his sovereignty in marriage. And they lived happily ever after. Or at least that is the Wife's story, and we have no words to disprove it even though we cannot but wonder at the tidy convergence of all the things she holds so dear: money, power, and Jankyn.

By the time that the Wife says: "Now wol I seye my tale, if ye wol heere" (III, 828), we have virtually forgotten that we have not been listening to her tale. The narrative of her life has indeed become a tale, a fiction in the sense that it is her own version of the story of her married life. However, she is so complex, so self-contradictory, so mysterious about what she wants including and besides the sovereignty that pervades all five of her marriages, that we do not feel that we have a definitive hold on who she is. Interpretation is so stymied by the unsorted complexity of her motives and behavior that we admire something about her spirit without confidence in her rectitude, but it can hardly be bad to be so much alive. Still, our desire to understand remains: who is she and what if anything have we learned, by positive or negative example, about how terrestrial life should be lived? So complex is the confession in the Prologue that our tendency to use prologues as guides to the interpretation of tales is reversed. We look to the tale for explanation.

Superficially, the tale is exactly what we might expect if we reduce the Wife of the "Prologue" to the will to power made manifest in sovereignty in marriage. The crime of the knight fits perfectly: rape, the ultimate physical violation of woman by man and a metaphor for the depravity of male domination. His fate, at first certain death, is put in the hands of Guenevere; justice of the Wife's preferred kind will be meted out by a woman. And the quest that Guenevere assigns seems an interrogative precis of the Wife's Prologue: what do women want? The offending knight has no choice. His quest, enlivened by anti-feminist suggestions about what women want, comes perilously close to failure, a failure which is itself a demonstration that the anti-feminist solutions are irrelevant. They are there however, so the Wife, in her "Tale" continues to raise the prejudices which surround women. But resolution is only achieved in the familiar story of the hag who gives the knight the right answer, an answer quickly approved by all the ladies at court. The woman/hag has saved the man/knight.

Fitting for the Wife since it satisfies the ostensible main burden of her discourse in the "Prologue". But the "Prologue" is more complicated than that, and so is the resolution of the "Tale".

The knight has made his unfortunate, compromising promise, which once again puts him under the power of a woman. The irony is made comedy by the knight's reaction to his enforced marriage to the hag. His discomfort at the wedding and his even greater discomfort in bed are enjoyable to us and presumably consummately enjoyable to the Wife. That the hag is magnanimous enough to offer a solution to the knight's revolting dilemma again proves a happy point for the Wife. Within the tale it gives the hag an admonitory lesson on true "gentilesse." She makes a simple, persuasive argument that gentilesse is not the prerogative of the rich, not a privilege of birth. Good doctrine here. Logically, nobility can give birth to treachery and rude parents can produce virtuous children. This is a fact of experience. That true gentilesse is compatible with poverty is proven by Jesus himself; this is a lesson of authority. Indeed, every authority shows that gentilesse is a human virtue that is a gift of God to be nurtured by man. No precise definition of gentilesse is provided in the hag's sermon, but its general dimensions are clear. It is all of the virtues epitomized by the Knight: truth, honor, fidelity, generosity of spirit, not as an artificial accident of birth but as a gift conferred by God and nurtured by man. This is sound Christian and proletarian doctrine, which the Wife certainly likes as much as her preferred Biblical texts at the beginning of her "Prologue". Thus informed and thus chastened, the knight of her "Tale" can receive the ultimate magnanimity of a proffered secular redemption from his predicament by the generous though controlling hag.

What she offers, demonstrating her own gentilesse, is a choice. The choice that she offers differs significantly from that offered in the analogue of this tale told by Gower.[6] The choice in Gower had been to have her beautiful by day and foul at night or vice versa. What the Wife's hag offers is fair and unfaithful or foul and true. There are two important differences here. Chaucer/the Wife has changed the terms from the social and superficial to the moral. And the dilemma is more truly a dilemma. Appropriately, the knight leaves the choice to the hag, thereby submitting to her and granting her sovereignty in marriage, a conclusion, we would think, much to be approved by the Wife. It is a vindication of whatever argument can be extracted from her "Prologue". Is it cynical to imagine that the knight, a much better educated man now in morality and the ways of women, submits to the hag because he knows that that is the only road to his secular salvation? The Wife explicitly draws the first conclusion as she ends her tale; we may wonder but do not have enough words to disagree. The closure is not perfect.

Thus it is with the Wife of Bath. Her confession reveals much and shows much to be admired, but what it reveals and what is to be admired remains shrouded in the mystery of human experience to the end. We may, perhaps should, be skeptical of sovereignty in marriage as we are ambivalent in our reactions to and interpretations of the wife in marriage, the wife as a human being. But two things remain in the intractable indeterminacy of attempts to interpret human nature and the human spirit: the energy of life is our power and gentilesse is our guide. We are deprived of any further context of pilgrim reaction by the eagerness of the Friar to get on with a scurrilous tale about Summoners and we return to marriage, gentilesse, and the human spirit in the "Clerk's Tale", physically but not thematically separated from the conclusion of the Wife's *tour de force*.

From the description of the Clerk in the "General Prologue" we expect that his tale will mean something important. His scholarship and his desire to teach characterize him as a "man of grete auctorite." So imposing is the learning of the Clerk that the Host adds to his request for a tale a plea that the tale be neither too serious nor too highly decorated. The Clerk complies with the latter: his style is restrained, almost plain. Certainly it is not clouded with confusing figures. In a larger sense, however, the literary structure and narrative techniques are obscure, as attested by generations of critics who have interpreted the Clerk's teachings in different ways. The tale itself is a simple and familiar one, told by Boccaccio, Petrarch, Gower and many others and apparently common in oral versions in English, French, and Italian.[7] There is no doubt that the story of the patient

Griselda is a fascinating one. It has almost a soap opera quality as we follow injury upon injury piled on the long-suffering Griselda and a final restoration of her to the joy and prosperity that she has deserved all along. Superficially, this has the unreality and extremity that can be entertaining in a folk tale.

However, put into the mouth of the Clerk the story becomes much more problematic, both because of his reputation for teaching and because he ascribes the tale to the learned authority of Petrarch. We know that "everything that is written is written for our doctrine," and the borrowing from Petrarch increases our expectation of "high sentence." The problem with our understanding of the Tale emerges when we look at it more closely, as we are invited to do by its context, by interspersed comments by the Clerk, and by the Clerk's gloss at the end of the Tale. All of these press us beyond the simplicity of folk-tale and cry out for interpretation of what the Clerk has done with *De obedientia ac fide uxoria mythologia*. Although I have frequently pointed out critical controversies which depend upon the emphasis of one apparently solvable aspect of a narrative coming into conflict with other solutions which depend upon the emphasis of other aspects of the narrative, nowhere in Chaucer is the critical dissonance more radical and nowhere does any one solution seem to come so obstinately into fundamental conflict with others. There is no doubt that the tale comments on familiar Chaucerian themes: marriage, the definition of gentilesse, Fortune, Providence, and commune profit. The problem is: how does the Clerk draw these themes into a compatible whole which teaches us something?

Critics have seen the tale as a paean to wifely patience especially as part of a natural order, as a "remedy" for the extreme and doctrinally unsound views of the Wife of Bath, as preparation of the receptive Christian for salvation, as an allegory of the adversity that must be faced by the faithful Christian or of the inscrutable workings of Divine Providence in the mysterious guise of Fortune. And there are many variations on these general approaches.[8] The problem remains that none of these solutions seems wholly satisfactory as an interpretation of the Clerk's doctrine. But the problem is even more basic than the disagreements of critics: the Clerk's narrative seems to be intrinsically at odds with itself and the Clerk's commentary on his narrative at the end seems only to confound the discovery of any univocal message in his tale. To take a couple of extremes, it is as hard to see Griselda as a model for wives or for Christians more abstractly as it is to see Walter as even the most forbidding, testing God of the Old Testament. And when the Clerk concludes, he explicitly says the tale is not a model for wives:

> This storie is seyd nat for that wyves sholde
>
> Folwen Grisilde as in humylitee,
>
> For it were inportable, though they wolde   (IV, 1142-4)

He does say that it is a model for Christians in adversity, but even if we do not go so far as to equate Walter with God or the mysterious workings of God, the tone of the tale is stridently at odds with the Clerk's simple gloss: "that every wight in his degree,/ Sholde be constant in adversitee . . ." (IV, 1145-6).

Let us look at what is problematic in the Tale to see whether any generalizations about its "sentence" are comprehensible. In a way, we are told too much to be satisfied with any simple resolution. First, there is the presentation of Walter at the beginning of the story. He is preoccupied by the present and gives no thought to the future well-being of the community. It is the people who persuade him that marriage and generation are necessary for "commune profit," for the continuing stability of the community. His reaction, though ultimately compliant, suggests more about him than would be useful if he is to be the inscrutable instrument of Providence. He is shirtily adamant about his right to make his own choice, a selfish willfulness not necessarily congruent with the demands of commune profit as they have been outlined in the preceding lines, and he sees his decision as foregoing his own liberty. In this context, even his desire to follow his own heart seems less romantic than obstinate.

His desire to marry Griselda, whose excellences he has observed among the commoners in the woods, is suspect. She is a paragon of beauty, moderation, chastity, and filial devotion. That seems good for commune profit, but our sense of her appropriateness, despite her low degree (which fits the developing notion of gentilesse as a matter of Divine gift and internal disposition rather than birth), is confounded by the way in which Walter proceeds with the courtship. He follows the forms of propriety by asking her father for her hand and seems generous in lavishing gifts of expensive clothing upon her. The trouble is that the forms are rendered meaningless by the fact that he has prepared everything anyway, in his wilful and autocratic way, for a wedding that in his mind is determined. He insists on complete devotion as a condition of the marriage and she abjectly acquiesces. Maybe this is how wives and husbands ought to relate, but we seem to know too much about Walter to abstract him from his suspect egoism and self-gratification. Allegory is thereby corrupted, and on a literal level tone and event are not on his side.

When Walter brings Griselda home for the wedding feast, the populace is impressed and her subsequent behavior confirms her in their high regard:

> Nat oonly this Grisildis thurgh hir wit
>
> Koude al the feet of wyfly hoomlinesse,
>
> But eek, whan that the cas required it,
>
> The commune profit koude she redresse. (IV 428-31)

Walter is praised by the populace for his judgment and Griselda is honored for her effective commitment to commune profit. She seems to the people "high born" in their ignorance of the nature of true, internal gentilesse. It is surprising that Walter would want to test her, mean for him to remind her of her humble origins, and duplicitous for him to attribute his actions to the will of the people and their fears about succession because her first child was a girl. Even the Clerk distances himself from Walter:

> He hadde assayed hire ynogh bifore,
>
> And foond hire evere good; what neded it
>
> Hire for to tempte, and alwey moore and moore,
>
> Though som men preise it for a subtil wit?
>
> But as for me, I seye that yvele it sit
>
> To assaye a wyf whan that it is no nede,

And putten hire in angwyssh and in drede. (IV, 456-62)

The mild acceptance of the trial by Griselda could, conceivably, be seen as seemly acquiescence within Christian matrimony, but we have been told too much about Walter and his behavior for us to be at ease or to see this as Fortune or a providential plan. That we know he is preserving the daughter in safety with his sister does not absolve Walter from excess.

The second test complicates the doctrinal and the human, event and tone, even further. It begins with the Clerk dissociating himself again from Walter: "O nedelees was she tempted in assay!" (IV, 621). Walter again blames the test on the people; indeed he does not present it simply as a test, which for him it is, but as her duty to him and to the people. There is a brutal doubleness in Walter's dishonesty: "And forth he goth with drery contenance,/ But to his herte it was ful greet plesance" (IV, 671-2). But Griselda's acquiescence this time is even readier and in fact makes our emotional reaction all the more complex, for her submission itself borders on the inhuman (IV, 644-51). She becomes complicit:

> "And certes, if I hadde prescience
> Youre wyl to knowe, er ye youre lust me tolde,
> I wolde it doon withouten necligence." (IV, 659-61)

Even Walter is amazed (IV, 687-93). Oddly, the Clerk approves:

> She shewed wel, for no worldly unreste
> A wyf, as of hirself, nothing ne sholde
> Wille in effect, but as hir housbonde wolde. (IV, 719-21)

So bizarre, however, is Walter's behavior, and the circumstances, that the people begin to suspect him:

> The sclaundre of Walter ofte and wyde spradde,
> That of a crueel herte he wikkedly,
> For he a povre womman wedded hadde,
> Hath mordred bothe his children prively. (IV, 722-25)

The third test compromises everyone. The narrator is more explicit than ever in his judgment on Walter when he pretends to be seeking a divorce so that he can marry a new, more appropriate wife. Even from the narrator's tolerant point of view Walter has gone too far even if wifely submission is in itself virtuous. The papal dispensation is explicitly noted to be fraudulent. It seems inadequate, even twisted, to ascribe this suffering to Fortune: "Disposed was, this humble creature,/ The adversitee of Fortune al t'endure" (IV, 755-6). And Walter's sanctimonious and disingenuous counsel is contemptible:

> "No man may alwey han prosperitee.
> With evene herte I rede yow t'endure
> The strook of Fortune or of aventure." (IV, 810-2)

The foregoing quotations, compacted together, highlight the outlandish character of the narrative and of the relationships we are trying to understand. Small wonder we are perplexed as interpreters. However, Griselda's compliance is total, so total as to be humiliating rather than ennobling. Her acceptance is put in terms of the acceptance of Fortune: she aligns herself with Walter's will in a self-abnegation that is so complete (IV, 813-33) as to go beyond virtue to stupidity or masochism. The whole scene of her acceptance is put in such pathetic and sentimental terms by an active compliance that it seems to go beyond laudable submission; for all that we pity her, she begins to seem a bit monstrous, unnatural, inhuman herself. She is like Job: " 'Naked out of my fadres hous,' quod she,/ I cam, and naked moot I turne agayn' " (IV, 871-2). And the Clerk extends and makes explicit the comparison when he asserts that in humility and patience women even outdo Job (IV, 932-8). But two things stand out despite the references to Fortune and Job. First, Griselda has gone beyond laudable submission, and second, the narrator's praise is at odds with his condemnations of Walter. The human behavior and the tone of the narrative are incompatible with the moral. If human feeling and authorial judgment are so much on one side in the narrative paradox, they become destructive of the high-minded moral.

All of this is intensified rather than removed in Walter's ultimate stage-management of the ostensibly joyful resolution. He begins by rubbing it in. As if Griselda has not suffered enough, he calls her back for the ultimate humiliation of serving his "new wife," and gratuitously emphasizes her lowness compared to his new wife's nobility (IV, 1037-43). The people, except for a loyal few long sympathetic to Griselda, fickly see appropriateness in the new wife, "for it was for the beste" (IV,987). But even the fickleness of the people cannot keep them from recognizing the native nobility, the natural gentilesse, of Griselda.

It is at this point that Walter makes the revelation that ostensibly is to put all things right: he restores her children, receives her back, and explains his machinations. Griselda rejoices, but can we find in this a happy ending? Despite the restorations, Walter's radical new magnanimity, and the protection of commune profit in the successful marrying of the daughter and succession of the son, it is all, from an emotional and tonal point of view, too quick and too simple. So much so that Griselda's joy seems almost simple-minded rather than grateful. In any case, again from the human point of view that is so insistently inserted in a story that only makes sense on a highly abstract level, time has been lost which, as other pilgrims have told us, once lost never can be retrieved.

The Clerk concludes with an explicit drawing of the meaning of the parable and a reference to his learned source:

> ". . . every wight, in his degree,
>
> Sholde be constant in adversitee
>
> As was Grisilde; therfore Petrak writeth
>
> This storie, which with heigh stile he enditeth. (IV, 1145-8)

If his following analogy is correct, that just as this woman was patient in the face of the incomprehensible demands of this mortal man, so we should acquiesce to the trials and the will of God, then there is a dark connection between Walter and God. It seems that patience in the face of suffering is the Clerk's moral message. But can it all be so clear and neat in view of the way the Clerk has told the tale? Within the tale he has taken such pains to be explicit about the evil of Walter, hyperbolic about the resignation of Griselda, and compassionate in his sympathy with her and his condemnation of Walter, that the moral teaching seems thin, asserted rather than developed from the narrative, tacked on rather than congruent with the human feelings that the tale attends to beyond the requirements of the lesson. Fiction and proposition are in conflict.

The Clerk proceeds to a playful assertion that there would be few wives like Griselda to be found in the current world and to a placatory compliment to the Wife of Bath and her "secte." Her followers may be heretics but here the Clerk countenances them. These comments reinforce our sense of the human nonsense in the Tale, yet the Clerk maintains that he has been serious by calling what he has narrated "ernestful matere." He proceeds to his "conclusion," identified in the text as *Lenvoy de Chaucer*, but claimed by the Clerk as his own (IV, 1176). The envoy is high-spirited advice to wives to use their mouths and wiles to enjoy life and confound men: very un-Griselda-like advice. The playfulness is charming and graceful in the context of the *Tales*, perhaps meant to "take the curse off" the role of woman that he has countenanced in his tale in order to draw his moral.[9]

The problem in the "Clerk's Tale" is not so simple as an allegory in which the literal level is at odds with the figurative, although that does seem to be the case. The two levels are in open warfare: the Clerk condemns within the Tale the very agency that he commends at the end as the inscrutable testing power of God. The Clerk does not seem trapped, and we would not expect a learned man like him to be trapped, by inept allegory. We must, I think, accept the judgments within the tale, based on human feeling and common sense, every bit as much as we accept the spiritual application which the Clerk accepts as doctrine but distances himself from as narrative. What is going on here besides simple contradiction?

I would suggest that the Tale goes beyond both its fable and its moral, or perhaps uses their incompatibilities and contradictions, to demonstrate the impossibility of teaching. In our sublunary world it is impossible to demonstrate the higher logic of philosophical and theological truth. We are human beings and our proper human feelings provide an impediment that simultaneously effects and confounds teaching. Regardless of these complexities, as we proceed in the Tale there are subsidiary moral lessons that are taught, compatible or not with the overarching abstraction that the Clerk asserts and the reality he recants. There is the recognition of human adversity, the definition of gentilesse as an interior nobility of character and grace of action; there is the confirmation of the necessity of commune profit for human society. All of these practical lessons are there, as well as the teaching about Providence, which remains by assertion if undermined by feeling. The consequence is a recognition of the dilemmas associated with teaching and the human capacity to understand, to interpret teaching. It is not that we can learn nothing; we learn many home truths in the tale and are even persuaded that in some way the abstraction that the Clerk propounds has validity even if it defies human comprehension. What the Clerk has done is to recognize the limitations of our power to interpret the operations of God and spiritual truths because they seem so counterintuitive when human realities cannot help but intrude. The human instruments of interpretation are frail, made inadequate by the human feelings that always prevent us from becoming all Mind. What the Clerk has managed to do is to teach through the impossibility of teaching, to interpret by means of the ragged impossibility of interpretation made necessary by our human existence in a Divine world. Interpretation is confounded, but learning prevails.[10]

As we have seen in the "Clerk's Tale", to know nothing is not to know nothing at all; that is, glimpses of truth in human relations are possible and moral exhortations can be efficacious even in a world that defies thorough philosophical understanding. The "Merchant's Tale", embarked upon without connective tissue immediately after the conclusion of the "Clerk's Tale" even though they are consistently tied together in the manuscripts, purports to offer in practical terms a clarity of vision about the way the world is. Its vision is unambiguously one of the bleakest in the whole of the *Canterbury Tales*.[11] The fable trashes marriage as an institution, gentilesse as a human possibility, human relations as anything but a tangle of self-deception and manipulation. It is a cautionary tale about the moral vacuity of the human world, which uses marriage as its vehicle in a scathing and relentless indictment of human nature. The Merchant's views are bitter and clear; what is harder to see is why he holds such views and how they compare to alternative views, more or less flawed, that provide its context in the *Canterbury*

Tales.

Because of its juxtaposition with the "Clerk's Tale", its setting in Lombardy, and the self-willed marriage of a noble to a woman of lower birth, it has sometimes been seen as a companion piece or a counterbalance to the "Clerk's Tale".[12] If so, it is a reversal in several important respects. January is no scheming Walter, May has none of Griselda's patience, the "resolution" is not even superficially salvific or edifying. Although the Clerk's world is only factitiously abstracted into a transcendent vision, and that ambiguously, the Merchant's world is clear, brutal, and relentless in its devastation of any sense of idealism in human relations. The problem here is not the interpretation of what the Merchant's vision of the world is; the problem is in the interpretation of the sources, accuracy, and efficacy of that vision as an understanding of marriage, virtue, and idealism. Thus, the echoes of the "Knight's Tale" may call to mind the Knight's idealism and highlight the Merchant's jaundiced views as a bitter quiting rather than the more simply comic quiting in the "Miller's Tale".

The presence of the Merchant in his tale is intense; he never wants to let us see the actions in any way other than in the bitter context of his own assessment. The savagery of the Merchant's irony is apparent from the opening lines. A sixty year old man who decides to marry after a life of "bodily delit" seems fair game for satire; we are ready for foolishness and prepared not to sympathize. Thus does the Merchant use conventions of the fabliau as the foundational structure of his narrative. But this is a more ruthless and analytical presentation of the fabliau than we have seen in Chaucer. It is fabliau expanded by contexts that reflect on and expand the internal givens of fabliau; it is fabliau without the spareness that allows the comic to thrive, if superficially at least without relentless analysis. It is fabliau brought into the full light of day in order to excoriate the underlying dispositions implied but ignored in that much more benign genre.

January's doltishness is explored rather than assumed and the result is a ferocious indictment of his intellectual and moral failures, all presented with an irony that gives no relief. The Merchant's view is clear from his arch introduction of January's desire for marriage: "Were it for hoolynesse or for dotage/ I kan nat seye . . ." (IV, 1253-4). The depth of January's self-deception is also clear in his purported desire

> . . . to lyve under that hooly boond
> With which first that God man and womman bond.
> "Noon other lyf," seyde he, "is worth a bene,
> For wedlok is so esy and so clene,
> That in this world it is a paradys." (IV, 1261-5)

The confounding of marriage as a paradise on earth is a recurring bludgeon used by the Merchant in establishing his rancorous context for the behavior of January. Already the Merchant's ironic assessment of January's wisdom is clear: "Thus seyde this olde knyght, that was so wys" (IV, 1266). The old, rich, but disingenuous "gnof" is put under a spotlight as the Merchant proceeds with a perverted paean in praise of marriage:

> And certeinly, as sooth as God is kyng,
> To take a wyf it is a glorious thyng,
> And namely whan a man is oold and hoor;
> Thanne is a wyf the fruyt of his tresor.
> Thanne sholde he take a yong wyf and a feir,
> On which he myghte engendren hym an heir. (IV, 1267-72)

The blisses of marriage are blistered in the mockery of the holiness of January's intent and the solace that marriage can provide.

The Merchant turns to authorities and uses them as much to his own purposes as ever the Wife of Bath did. The Merchant narrator seems to be speaking directly to us as he cites Theophrastus's indictment of marriage and reminds us of the Miller's view: " 'And if thou take a wyf unto thyn hoold/ Ful lightly maystow been a cokewold' " (IV, 1305-6). In his ironic certainty the Merchant simply dismisses the views of Theophrastus.[13] The double irony here is that under other circumstances we would condemn the anti-feminism of Theophrastus and approve of the Merchant's skepticism. But in this morally inverted world we know that the Merchant's dismissal is foolish, or intended to be taken as foolish. Similarly, the import of the Biblical exempla is inverted by the heavy irony in the Merchant's inverted vision. That Eve was created as a comfort to man tempts us to recall, almost embrace for the purposes of the Tale, the traditional anti-feminist view of Eve. Likewise with other examples. Once we start seeing things from the Merchant's perverse perspective, the virtues of Rebecca, Judith, and Abigail become murder and trickery.

Yet, the indictment of women is merely propaedeutic to the Merchant's harsher treatment of the self-deceptive behavior of January. He clothes his desire in marriage, in a veil of holy aspiration, but his intentions, realized or not, are self-indulgent stupidity:

>"But o thyng warne I yow, my freendes deere,
>I wol noon oold wyf han in no manere,
>She shal nat passe twenty yeer, certayn;
>Oold fissh and yong flessh wolde I have fayn." (IV, 1415-8)

His goals are shallow as revealed in his version of the Wife of Bath's proverb: "For sondry scoles maken sotile clerkis" (IV, 1427). His confidence in his idealism and sexual prowess are intertwined in such a way as to make painfully clear a self-culpability that simple fabliau ignores:

>I feele my lymes stark and suffisaunt
>To do al that a man bilongeth to;
>I woot myselven best what I may do.
>Though I be hoor, I fare as dooth a tree
>That blosmeth er that fruyt ywoxen bee;
>And blosmy tree nys neither drye ne deed.
>I feele me nowhere hoor but on myn heed;
>Myn herte and alle my lymes been as grene
>As laurer thurgh the yeer is for to sene.
>And syn that ye han herd al myn entente,
>I prey yow to my wyl ye wole assente." (IV, 1458-68)

If the painfully applied insight into blindness and self-deception is not enough, the appeal to counsellors reinforces the venomous probing. The sycophancy of Placebo is revealed as transcendent stupidity or obstinate blindness in its ignorance even of the conventional wisdom of fabliau:

> "And trewely, it is an heigh corage
> Of any man that stapen is in age
> To take a yong wyf; by my fader kyn,
> Youre herte hangeth on a joly pyn!
> Dooth now in this matiere right as yow leste,
> For finally I holde it for the beste." (IV, 1513-8)

Justinus is not any better. His advice is more prudent and "correct," but it too is based on anti-feminist assumptions and becomes as much an indictment of women as a caution to January, who dismisses Seneca as easily as the Merchant has ironically dismissed Theophrastus. Placebo confirms January in his self-deception. He is confident in his fantasies and selects a wife who reminds us of Griselda in everything except any mention of natural gentilesse. The apex of his self-delusion is his expectation of heaven on earth, his fear that he may endanger his salvation by having his Paradise on earth. Justinus's caution, though an appropriate corrective to January's fantasy, comes, sadly, only from a reliance on the anti-feminist tradition: " 'Paraunter she may be youre purgatorie!' " (IV, 1670). There is no high ground in this narrative. Justinus's curious reference to the Wife of Bath, who, as a pilgrim, is on a different level of reality than Justinus, a character in a tale, recognizes none of the glorious ambiguity in the Wife's triumphant transcendence of anti-feminist platitudes.

The bitterly ironic indictment of January's self-deception is pursued ruthlessly throughout the description of the marriage and consummation. January's prideful eagerness for the marriage bed is, from a narrative point of view, suspended while the Merchant describes the Nicholas-like courtly attraction of Damian for May. The snake is already in January's paradisal garden. But we return to the even more devastating representation of January, coked to the gills on aphrodisiacs, in his marriage bed, epitomized by the contrast between his deluded joy and May's perception:

>But God woot what that May thoughte in hir herte,
>Whan she hym saugh up sittynge in his sherte,
>In his nyght-cappe, and with his nekke lene;
>She preyseth nat his pleyying worth a bene. (IV, 1851-4)

So our attention turns to the love of Damian and May, but here we find no more to admire than we do in January's self-deception. As January has been subjected to an elaboration of the fabliau, Damian and May are discredited as participants in a romance. Damian is quickly sketched as a suffering courtly lover who writes his complaint and hangs it in a silken purse on his breast. He does not have to wait as long as Palamon, hardly longer than the more enterprising and decisive Nicholas because, unknowingly, he can rely on January to act as unwitting pander by sending May to check on his health when, presumably as a result of love-sickness, he has been absent from court. With unromantic quickness Damian gives her the purse with the message, and she leaves. We are familiar with abrupt transitions, but the romantic connection beginning between Damian and May is bluntly undercut by the Merchant's harsh and arch: "Ye gete namoore of me" (IV, 1945). And certainly the dignity of the "derne love" is quickly compromised by May's disposal of the note in the privy. The undignified disposal of the note is the beginning of a courtly love degraded and compromised, but given its only sympathy by the culpably unconscious complicity of January. The idealism of the "Knight's Tale" provides an echoic context for this wholly compromised world. May loves Damian "by destynee or by aventure" (IV, 1967) and more accurately by lust. The seaminess of their love is made prominent by the fact that her submission to love occurs in January's bed and is because "pitee renneth soone in gentil herte." (IV,1986). May is given little more understanding than January by the Merchant as "fulfilled of pitee" she readily realizes: "Ther lakketh noght oonly but day and place" (IV, 1998).

Once again, and even more dramatically, opportunity is provided by

January. In a continuation of the paradise theme, he builds a garden of delight which is conflated by the Merchant with a courtly garden more beautiful than anything that could be devised by the writer of *The Romance of the Rose*. A bitter multiple irony. In the first instance, the garden is rather a prison for May, as January keeps custody of the key. And it becomes not only a romance garden prison but a romance garden perverted by the most uncourtly behavior of May and Damian. It is another example of the blindness of January and the crassness of the ostensible "courtly lovers." It is a garden of ironies and absurdities, with Pluto and Proserpina, the deities of the underworld its tutelary spirits.

When, in this intellectually and morally garbled context, January suddenly and inexplicably goes blind, his condition is attributed to Fortune. But the apostrophe to Fortune only undercuts the notion of Fortune itself because the blindness is so clearly the physical reification of January's pre-existent moral condition. The behavior of January, Damian, and May in the garden is simply an acting out of what already obtains. The Merchant is relentless in his pursuit of January as we see him absurdly keeping a constant hand on May, and the Merchant exclaims:

> O Januarie, what myghte it thee availle,
>
> Thogh thou myghtest se as fer as shippes saille?
>
> For as good is blynd deceyved be
>
> As to be deceyved whan a man may se. (IV, 2107-10)

The simultaneity of January's fatuous love as he gives May financial sovereignty in the garden with May's planning and execution of the adultery is devastating. The black paradox reaches its nadir as May feigns pregnancy to rationalize climbing the tree, and January provides the perfect visual emblem of his instrumentality when he becomes, unwittingly and eagerly, a stepping stone up to the pears and to Damian. When she asks, he complies: " 'Certes,' qoud he, 'theron shal be no lak,/ Mighte I yow helpen with myn herte blood' " (IV, 2346-7). The visual impact and pace are brutal as January hugs the tree and May embraces the waiting Damian. The physical and symbolic climax is immediate: "And sodeynly anon this Damyan/ Gan pullen up the smok, and in he throng" (IV, 2352-3). The absurdity of January and the vulgarity of May come together with the resounding poignancy of John's cry "Water" in the "Miller's Tale".

But what has come together here is not two fabliaux, coarse but comic, but the moral self-delusion of January and the courtly parody of May's love, coarse and degrading. That January gets the worse of it at the narrative hands of the Merchant is clear. When January regains his sight (by an act of Fortune degraded or by the frivolous interference of Proserpina and Pluto), his moral blindness continues and deepens as May convinces the culpable gull that he has not seen what he has seen and that he can expect to see such "illusions" again as his sight improves. The mixture of fabliau and romance is complete. We look beneath the surface of fabliau and find that January is its logic carried to absurd conclusion. We look beneath the surface of romance and find it to be glamorized fornication.

Damian and May are bogus courtly lovers and are blameable, but the treatment of January in this tale, his exposure and ridicule, is the main burden of the Merchant's fable. Damian and May, corrupt as they are, are merely clever recipients of crass opportunities offered neither by chance nor Fortune but by the unrelenting, self-inflicted blindness of January. It seems implausible to take January as an alter-ego of the Merchant who has used fabliau and romance to expose invincible self-delusion. If Damian and May come off more sympathetically, it is not because they are moral ideals. We know them for the shabby adulterers they are; the point is that January does not and will not. The Merchant is not recounting autobiography but a vision of the human condition.

Our focus has been on Chaucer's preoccupation with the process of the interpretation of fiction as a metaphor for our attempts to interpret reality. How does the "Merchant's Tale" function in this context? In one sense, there is no problem of interpretation in the broad outlines of the "Merchant's Tale". That January lives in a tawdry world that may masquerade as romance is abundantly clear. But that tawdriness is not the object of the Merchant's "sentence"; his target is the failure of January to understand his world and himself. The world represented is without a redeeming feature: it is corrupt and all the seedier for the fact that a dose of anti-feminism is the only defense proposed against self-destructive blindness. So our interpretation of the tale itself is not the issue in the larger drama; it is our, and Chaucer's, interpretation of the interpretation. Is the world like this? Is it without honor, altruism, or idealism? Is it without amelioration in marriage, gentilesse, or commune profit? Are we trapped always and everywhere by self-inflicted moral blindness? And, if so, is human interpretation of the world impossible? The vision of the Merchant is not so much a vision of the corruption of the world palliated by salvific human values as it is a vision of a world in which human beings are forever in an epistemological and moral prison that is self-imposed. What can we make of a world that offers no exit because we ourselves make it impenetrable by forfeiting the capacity to interpret and aspire?

The Franklin may not be a philosopher-king, but his narrative does provide a foundation for climbing out of the self-entrapping hell depicted by the Merchant. Who the Franklin is and what he stands for may be more difficult to tell than the apparent simplicity and good will and good nature his narrative and self-characterization imply. At least since Kittredge associated these tales as "the marriage group," there has been a strong critical tendency to see the tales as related even when to marriage is added the question of "gentilesse" and "troth." And there has long been a tendency to see the "Franklin's Tale" as, somehow, the culmination or summation or resolution of the sequence, even when questions about the character of the Franklin have complicated the issue.[14] It is true that more recently many critics have noted that the narrator and the tale are not above criticism, suspicion, or ambiguity, that in many ways the tale is at odds with itself, and that indeed internal conflicts in the tale reflect and are informed by the character and opinions of the Franklin himself.[15]

The Franklin's character itself is not easy to pin down. The portrait in the "General Prologue" is hazier than many would like to believe. A man of property, just below the level of the aristocracy, conscientious in fulfilling his county duties, and the very model of generosity, he has been seen both as the straightforward exemplar of these virtues and as a social climber whose generosity is wholly material. We are left to take him at face value, though a nagging doubt cannot be entirely suppressed. As is so often the case with portraits in the "General Prologue", there are not enough definitive words to make the matter conclusively decideable. We look to the tale and its surrounding materials to clarify our judgment and, once again, these turn out not to be definitive either. Still, I would argue that no matter what we make of the Franklin himself, the issues that he consciously takes on in his Tale go beyond him, imply issues that he ignores or is not aware of, so that in the end he is not in control of his Tale and the moral implications inherent in it. Consequently his Tale, appealing as it is, is not a resolution of the issues that have occupied the preceding Tales in the group.

Recent criticism has focussed on the incommensurable aspects of his Tale in and of itself, and that seems fair enough.[16] The very disagreements that form the history of criticism of the Tale, as in so many other cases in the *Tales*, are prime indicators of inconclusiveness. Chaucer has presented both the Franklin and his Tale in such a way as to ensure that we cannot be sure of him or of the tendency of the Tale itself. The fact that he is very present to his Tale does not answer the kinds of questions that narrator and Tale itself imply; indeed it complicates them.

I would extend this controlled confusion to the relation of this teller and Tale to the preceding Tales in the sequence and to the moral and philosophical issues they raise. No matter what the Franklin and his Tale are, they are not "the right answer" to questions that have been raised, partly because the problems raised in his Tale are only tangentially related to matters that are themselves only superficial, or nominal, issues in prior Tales. Thus, marriage, gentilesse, and troth, all mentioned and played with in the preceding Tales, are no more the primary concentration of the "Franklin's Tale" than they are of the preceding Tales. For the problems raised in this group, important as they are, are in fact subsidiary to the question of interpretation that pervades them; the "Franklin's Tale" is summative not in that it approves or condemns moral opinions espoused in those tales, but rather as a coda on the problem of interpretation itself. To construct this argument, I will first confront, particularly in the context of the insights of the Tale's most recent critics, the ineluctable in the Tale, and then relate this to the larger problems of interpretation that characterize this group of Tales.

The uncertainty that I have referred to in the portrait of the Franklin in the "General Prologue" surfaces as he speaks his first reported words on the pilgrimage:

> "In feith, Squier thow hast thee wel yquit
> And gentilly, I preise wel thy wit,"
> Quod the Frankeleyn, "considerynge thy yowthe,
> So feelyngly thou spekest, sire, I allow the!" (V, 673-6)

Praise for how the Squire has acquitted himself as a sign of his gentilesse, but perhaps some condescension? The problem, as frequently noted, is that the Squire has not completed his Tale. Is the "Squire's Tale" simply unfinished? That seems the least likely of possibilities; the manuscripts do not leave a space for matter to be discovered later as they do for the more problematically unfinished "Cook's Tale". Does the Franklin genuinely think that the "Squire's Tale" is over? Possibly (we are not told the answer), but the presence of the first two lines of "Pars Tercia" at least arouse suspicion that this is an interruption, though we cannot be sure that the Franklin is not simply in error. Does the Franklin interrupt because he has had enough of the "Squire's Tale"? The Tale is a fanciful romance in the popular manner and a little bit of this goes a long way; the "Knight's Tale" it is not, and the Franklin prudishly or for appearances' sake may just wish to get on with something of more sentence. Is the Franklin magnanimously saving the young Squire from himself? That Tale, if continued, would certainly extend to at least four or five thousand lines, twice the length of any Tale told thus far. If this is the case, we have a very admirable Franklin who graciously rescues the Squire from the youth's own lack of self-restraint. Finally, might the Franklin simultaneously be eager to have the chance to display his own "finer" sense of the moral and social issues raised in the preceding Tales? Each possibility has its critical adherents and there are some critics who ignore the matter entirely.[17] It seems that we cannot decide the purpose of the interruption definitively; this indeterminacy must hover over and pervade the "Franklin's Tale".

The tone of the Franklin's interruption, regardless of his intention, is graceful. There is the criticism of his own son: who does not find favor with others by granting the limitations of his own offspring? The focus is on gentilesse, but it would be hard to characterize the Squire's narrative as particularly "gentil" except by the definition of gentilesse as a matter of birth or station, a notion we are already skeptical of. Yet, the Franklin seems to have a more moral idea of gentilesse in mind whether he fully understands the idea or not: gentilesse as human behavior, as a moral grace. The Franklin's ingratiating softness continues into his brief prologue where he modestly disclaims knowledge of rhetoric, a disclaimer belied by his Tale where he either does know some rhetoric or wants to appear to. So we may well look to the "Franklin's Tale" to better understand the teller as much as to discover his formulations on marriage, gentilesse, and fidelity.

The Tale itself is a self-proclaimed Breton lai, for reasons that are mysterious: the Franklin, practical man that he is, is careful to explain that the supernatural elements are simply there because such were the beliefs at the time of the tale he is telling. He distances himself, as he does in other ways as the tale proceeds. Moreover, the frame of his Tale has to do with marriage rather than courtship; the only courtship in the Tale is Damian's illicit and prosaically frustrated attempt.

Marriage is the opening focus of the Tale and perhaps it is an answer to the Wife's views of sovereignty, the Clerk's disclaimed views of submission, and the Merchant's savaging of the institution. Indeed, marriage is presented as potentially idyllic. In the summary treatment of the courtship, the courtly is abbreviated if not ignored as it is in several ways later in the Tale: this is about marriage, and about gentilesse. The accord that Dorigen and Aurelius achieve suggests a mutuality that answers some views presented in preceding tales. The sermon on marriage (V, 761-90) admirably and generously condemns "maistiye" and enjoins patience since we all have faults. So much for the Wife, the Clerk, and the Merchant (simply understood.) There are, however, two troubling lines in the original accord: "Save that the name of soveraynetee/ That wolde he have for shame of his degree" (V, 751-2). Although Dorigen commends Arveragus's gentilesse, there is an unseemly concern for external appearances in his reservation. And appearances are to become a non-trivial issue as the Tale unfolds. Our niggling uncertainty is sustained not only by the fact but also by the nature of Arveragus' temporary departure. After a year, he departs for "a year or tweyne" to do undefined, but apparently admirable knightly things which within four lines turns out to take two years. Arveragus cannot really be faulted, but the result for Dorigen is as fraught with danger as if he had been more explicitly culpable in dashing off to do "knight stuff": she is alone; their marriage and its mutuality is disrupted and must survive on gentilesse and troth.

Her initial suffering is a laudable marital correlative of courtly love-longing. However, she begins to cope, as we must learn to with what cannot be changed, and Arveragus's letters provide a confirmation of continuing troth. Her friends provide, or attempt to, the kind of sympathy and community that gives us the human support we require in adversity. But their ministrations are confounded just as she is learning to live with her sadness and anxiety. The world is not cooperating with Dorigen. The apparently harmless occupation of a soothing seaside walk perversely becomes the source of the distress that overwhelms her:

> But whan she saugh the grisly rokkes blake
>
> For verray feere so wolde hir herte quake
>
> That on hire feet she myghte hire noght sustene. (V, 859-61)

Initially, her prayer seems to spring from domestic love and suitable piety, but she takes her prayer too far. The prayer becomes a challenge to the perfection of God's creation:

> "But, Lord, thise grisly, feendly rokkes blake,
>
> That semen rather a foul confusion

> Of werk than any fair creacion
>
> Of swich a parfit wys God and a stable,
>
> Why han ye wroght this werk unresonable?" (V, 868-72)

This leads to her questioning of God's providence and a wish that the divine creation be changed:

> "I wot wel clerkes wol seyn as hem leste,
>
> By argumentz, that al is for the beste,
>
> Though I ne kan the causes nat yknowe.
>
> But thilke God that made wynd to blowe
>
> As kepe my lord! This my conclusion.
>
> To clerkes lete I al disputison.
>
> But wolde God that alle thise rokkes blake
>
> Were sonken into helle for his sake!
>
> Thise rokkes sleen myn herte for the feere." (V, 885-93)

It is selfish and dangerous to question divine order and providence. She is punished condignly by a disruption of that order and interference with providence. The nature of her offense is clear in its consequences.[18]

Her friends, still seeking to comfort her, take her to a garden where we, if not she, know she ought to beware. It is a courtly garden that might be mistaken for a "verry paradise" (reminding us of the "Merchant's Tale") and it contains Damian, a conventional courtly lover. In this larger world the courtly garden and the artificial Damian are the real enemies, but Dorigen, steadfast in marital devotion, is not deceived by these trappings of love. Her rejection of Damian is swift and summary. The problem is her residual rebellion against the order of God's creation. Although her "promise" is a folk-motif afterthought, it is rooted in this desire to alter God's reality, and thereby she makes herself vulnerable to the artificiality of Damian and the appearances that can be contrived by magic.

Damian's suffering, in courtly terms and with prayers to underworld forces, is at odds with the marriage, gentilesse, and troth of Dorigen's Christian world. The Franklin virtuously dissociates himself from Damian's excesses. The foolishness of Dorigen's questioning of God (more than the thoughtless promise to Damian which directly gets her in trouble) is mirrored in the triviality of the world of magic in which Damian gets himself involved. That world is made all the more absurd, as Dorigen's lapse in faith is made all the more apparent, by the return of Arveragus even before Damian's plot gets under way. It is then that Damian's brother, knowledgeable about the arts of magic (which gives the Franklin a chance to show off a bit of his learning), thinks of an answer from which the Franklin dissociates himself by reminding us that the Tale is set in a superstitious past. But that past is the reality of this fiction, and Damian's brother can help. Their lack of concern about whether the solution is real or apparent becomes even clearer in his brother's statement than it was in Damian's prayer:

> "My brother shal be warisshed hastily;
> For I am siker that there be sciences
> By whiche men make diverse apparences,
> Swich as thise subtile tregetoures pleye. (V, 1138-41)

Magicians are, of course, serious sinners because they interfere, by false appearances, with God's creation. But Damian's brother is unconcerned:

> "For with an apparence a clerk may make,
> To mannes sighte, that alle the rokkes blake
> Of Britaigne weren yvoyded everichon,
> And shippes by the brynke comen and gon,
> And in swich forme enduren a wowke or two.
> Thanne were my brother warisshed of his wo.
> Thanne moste she nedes holden hire biheste,
> Or elles he shal shame hire atte leeste." (V, 1157-64)

He, and eventually Damian, does not care whether the request is met in reality, only in appearance. And he betrays a curious notion of where shame should lie. The magic they resort to is further discredited by the behavior of the Clerk of Orleans to whom they appeal. He provides a Beelzebubian magic show that trivializes his arts. It is enhanced by the insistence that this is appearance not true accomplishment of Dorigen's wish, which in any case has been made irrelevant, though still blameworthy, by Arveragus's return. The Clerk of Orleans is discredited in other ways. He is a hard dealer on his Ł 1000, and they return home not in a courtly May, but a cold, real December. The Franklin later shows the clerk up for the cheap trickster he is, but takes the opportunity to display his own learning. (Is he showing off or is the Franklin?) By the time Damian presents his case to Dorigen, his suit is contemptible and his reaction extravagant.

Dorigen's lament, with many classical examples that the humble Franklin is happy to supply, expresses the extremity of her distress. There seems to be no alternative but suicide: death before dishonor. But there is a striking anti-climax to her rhetorical outburst. As soon as Arveragus returns, after a couple of days away, she blurts out her predicament. In a way she is blameless, but she is also comical. She has not been unfaithful, but she is quick to appeal to Arveragus. Silly, but right for a solidly married couple. His reaction, however, complicates the narrative in a darker way. Is it admirable that he tells Dorigen to keep her part of the bargain? That would be to keep her word, one of the highest ideals in the poem, but surely this is a flawed moral world where Arveragus, even if he is pained to do so, can bring himself to counsel his wife to infidelity, even if it is a matter of keeping truth. Surely, principle is called into question in a world where it leads a husband to countenance the prospect of adultery. And the moral universe is made even murkier when Arveragus mentions that in keeping her word (clearly a sin, clearly a word that has no imperative to be kept) she should guard appearances: " Ne make no contenance of hevynesse,/ That folk of yow may demen harm or gesse" (V, 1485-6). The moral world of the Tale has become clouded if not compromised. The Franklin's promise that things will turn out better than we expect is a shallow misapprehension of the moral dilemmas that obtain:

> Paraventure an heep of yow, ywis,
> Wol holden hym a lewed man in this
> That he wol putte his wyf in jupartie.

> Herkneth the tale er ye upon hire crie.
>
> She may have bettre fortune than yow semeth,
>
> And whan that ye han herd the tale, demeth. (V, 1493-8)

The Franklin's shallowness comes under further suspicion in the sequence of events that leads to the climax of his concluding question. Damian's release of Dorigen from her promise, which he has only fraudulently fulfilled, is attributed to Arveragus's nobility in insisting that Dorigen keep her word. In any case it is hard to credit Damian with "compassion" or "routhe" or even to admire his respect for Arveragus's murky holding of "troth." It is impossible to see it, as Damian does, as "gentilesse" (V, 1527). But, Damian, a squire who is as "gentil" as a noble, releases her and Arveragus and Dorigen live happily, if factitiously, ever after. Damian's debt is, upon appeal, forgiven by the Clerk of Orleans, who summarizes:

> This philosophre answerde, "Leeve brother,
>
> Everich of yow dide gentilly til oother.
>
> Thou art a squier, and he is a knyght;
>
> But God forbede, for his blisful myght,
>
> But if a clerk koude doon a gentil dede
>
> As wel as any of yow, it is no drede!" (V, 1607-12)

But how laudable is this commercial generosity for not collecting on a fraud?

Thus, what are we to make of the Franklin's concluding question: "Which was the mooste fre, as thynketh yow?" (V, 1622). Is it a *demande* which, conventionally, should open up polite discussion? Or is it a rhetorical question which the Franklin thinks has no answer because the liberality, a prime feature of gentility, of each of the three is equal? In either case, the Franklin is inadequate to his task. He has raised issues which go beyond *demande* or rhetorical question into realms of conflicting morality: imperfect marriage, appearance and reality, fraud and cynicism. The "Franklin's Tale" is not an adequate definition of ideal marriage, gentilesse, and "troth." Whether the Franklin is a decent fellow or a sham, his story has gotten out of control; it cannot be the key to the issues that this group of Tales has raised. Indeed, he has compounded the confusion raised by the

Wife, Clerk, and Merchant by showing an honest effort, whether made for altruistic or selfish motives, inadequate to confer unexceptionable meaning on human moral affairs and relationships, and the complexities of how life should be lived. He has, thereby, raised the level of our epistemological perplexity.

The so-called "marriage group" is not so much an approximation of the truth, like Fragments I and II, as it is an encirclement of the truth with regard to fundamental issues of human relations. The Wife of Bath's comments on marriage and gentilesse are neither answers nor deceptions. The Clerk intends to teach on these issues but both his genre and the context of his Tale make definitive precision impossible. The Merchant's bitter perspective, no matter how caused, and the relentless self-deception of January provide a model neither of knowledge nor of behavior. Each does, however, raise the issues and attack them with varying and more or less sympathetic results. We look to the Franklin for a more balanced view, a sorting out of the self-deceptions and indeterminacies of the preceding narrators, but the Franklin cannot provide an ultimate solution. Like the "Man of Law's Tale," the "Franklin's Tale" is a kind of "provisional palinode." It seems to embrace comprehensively the issues that have troubled his predecessors and separate wheat from chaff. But his vision is itself inadequate or at least opaque. While excesses and absurdities are noted, the Franklin cannot provide authoritative guidance. Our means of communication and the limitations and vagaries of our own perceptions do not admit of human generalizations that bring closure and confidence to our moral lives. Yet, we do learn some things about marriage itself and marriage as a metaphor for human relations, about gentilesse as a kind of spiritual generosity which can be salutary, and about "troth" which, if hard to determine and live by, is the foundation of commune profit. As I have said before, not to know is not to know nothing.

Chapter V: The Limitations of Teachers

As we move towards the end of the *Canterbury Tales* in Fragments VI and VII, Chaucer turns his and our attention more explicitly to the limitations and reliability of teachers—not of authorities, but of *viva voce* interpreters of spiritual questions. I am assuming, once again, that the order of the Ellesmere Manuscript has some authority.[19] The Bradshaw shifters have moved VII to a much earlier position and, indeed, VI could go almost anywhere. But I am again accepting that the Ellesmere is the order in which generations have received their Chaucer and that the *Tales* are complete if unfinished. There is some reason to believe from revisions in VII that Chaucer had already moved it and this is where he wanted it. In any case, the order of the whole is not critical to my interest in VI and VII. What is important is that we have a series of teachers: the Physician, the Pardoner, the Prioress, Chaucer as character, the Monk, and the Nun's Priest. And they all turn their attention to questions that are more explicitly spiritual: various perspectives on how to gain everlasting salvation. But because of who they are (whom Chaucer has made them) and the world they live in, their insight and reliability are called into question. All, except perhaps Chaucer[20] (though he is a different case entirely), have some legitimate claim upon our credence, but none is able to disentangle the almost ineluctable realities of the spiritual life as it must be lived in this world. Sometimes the problem is with them, sometimes with their doctrine, but none is to be dismissed out of hand.

The "Physician's Tale" is a slight and familiar narrative.[21] The Physician has some claim, as a learned man, to authority and credibility, and the ostensible morality of his tale is so commonplace as to be easily accepted by virtue of its sheer familiarity. Physicians are learned men and, although a vague suspicion of greed hovers about them, as in the portrait in the "General Prologue", they are well educated and men of experience in this world. Notice, for example, the authority accorded to them by Prudence in the "Tale of Melibee".

Though slender, the tale is emotionally powerful. The lewd intentions of Apius towards the blameless Virginia portray a bald assault on the moral integrity of the helpless virtuous. The decision of Virginius to sacrifice his daughter rather than permit her sexual violation (death before dishonor) is a familiar motif; it is an even more poignant version of the dilemma Dorigen wriggles through. Moreover, the implacability of Virginius in preserving her chastity, though perhaps extreme to relativistic modern eyes, is here a familiar literary problem and his killing of her and taking her body to Apius is merely an intensification of a common motif, but one that adds to the poignancy and pathos of the circumstances. Folk-tale alone would persuade us that Virginius is no ogre and Dorigen's lament would provide authority. But this situation is even worse because Virginius kills out of a pious conjunction of his love of God and his love of his daughter.

Apius's lechery is the focus of the Physician's moral blame, but it is not finally the focus of our moral attention. The canker in his spiritual life is something more pernicious because of his use of his position for moral coercion. His collaboration with Claudius and his civil power are the greater corruption, and this may be overlooked as we concentrate on the pathetic sacrifice of Virginia for the preservation of chastity. What is at stake becomes clearer as the Tale comes to its end: Apius's crime is a crime against the whole community, not simply against the virtue of Virginia. Indeed, it is the people who rise up against Apius:

> The peple anon had suspect in this thyng,
> By manere of the cherles chalangyng,
> That it was by the assent of Apius. (VI, 263-5)

because it is the abuse of his judicial power, his civil authority, that is his greater crime. Certainly there is pity for Virginia and Virginius, but the populace arises because the civil order has been overturned by Apius's abuse of power. Apius, cast in prison, commits suicide and the Physician fashions this into the moral of his tale:

> The worm of conscience may argyse
> Of wikked lyf, though it so pryvee be
> That no man woot therof wot but God and he. (VI, 280-2)

But Apius' suicide is swift; what we see is not his repentance but his escape from moral consequences, and it is the people who bring about his separation from the body politic. Claudius, to save him from certain execution by the aroused populace, is exiled, separated from the body politic. Thus, despite the Physician's interest in the pathos of Virginia and the unbridled lechery of Apius, it is the people who purge the city and protect commune profit. It is not that the Physician obscures or fails to see the nature of the resolution; it is rather that he has concentrated so vigorously on the commonplace and the pathetic that he has missed the kernel of the resolution. The Physician is not a bad man, or stupid, but he has missed the more profound lesson in favor of the more dramatic manifestations of the moral evil. He is, at least partially, a flawed though not a blameworthy teacher. And it is the Host who, with typical superficiality, focuses on the pathos and even provides indiscriminate analysis. He convicts the "fals justise," but he also sees her beauty as the cause of her death. There is not much moral insight here. To him the story is pathetic and an example of the workings of Fortune. He has not seen the nature of the resolution any more than the Physician apparently has. But if the Physician misses, or lets slide, the formidable implications of the conclusion in favor of the pathetic and sensational consequences of lechery, there is a hope that the teaching remains in the narrative. Perhaps the structure of the narrative itself goes beyond the limitations of the didactic perspective of the narrator.

This issue is raised more explicitly and even more complexly in the narrative of the Pardoner which follows, for here is a narrator who is not inadvertent but who teaches a very familiar lesson with an overriding agenda of his own.[22] It is important that our distrust of the Pardoner be ever present, from the very beginning of his tale. The gentles worry, even before he starts, that he will tell of some "ribaudrye." But the Pardoner turns out, as teacher, to be both more and less clever than their expectations. That he means to be playful is evident from the moment he accepts: " 'I graunte, ywis,' quod he, 'but I moot thynke/ Upon som honest thyng while that I drynke' " (VI, 327-8). But the question of his honesty and his uses of honesty will become critical.

He is, by virtue of his profession, a teacher, but a very ambiguous one. His granting of indulgences requires that he preach in order to edify his audience and motivate them towards virtuous action, the seeking of indulgences for past sins. So the Pardoner must expound on the nature and consequences of sin: that is his job. But we already know from the "General Prologue" and from the uneasiness of the gentles when the Host calls upon him that this is no simple, disinterested teacher, no man of virtue committed to the spiritual welfare of his audiences past and present. What we get is a virtuoso performance and much more, even more than the Pardoner, who prides himself on his intelligence and cleverness, bargains for, because in the end he betrays a larger lesson than the one he teaches so effectively and self-servingly. He lacks the wisdom and self-awareness that might enfold him in the human community and effect his own salvation.

In one sense, the Pardoner, as teacher, is entirely straightforward and orthodox. He promises that he will give the pilgrims a sample of the lesson that is his constant text: "*Radix malorum est cupiditas*" (VI, 334). What he intends further is to show off, not only to teach but to provide an example of the virtuosity with which he teaches. His motive may be simple pride or it may be an attempt to overcome or disguise the physical limitations that separate him from the human community and its generative power. But there is no doubt that in the presentation of his familiar text he is a teacher of extraordinary ability. I will not repeat the many and various ways critics have, quite rightly, extolled his skill and effectiveness as the hammer of cupidity.[23] Whether the tale follows the form of the sermon precisely, his deft use of authorities and argument, and his priceless and potent exemplum identify him as a preacher/teacher of unparalleled expertise.[24] The interesting aspect of his teaching, and eventually of his relation to the rest of the pilgrims and to this world and the next, arises in the meta-text of his sermon. On the question of cupidity, he is orthodox and effective; he is a good teacher. But much more is at stake, and it is in these complexities that the larger issues of teaching and learning, of expertise and community arise.

For the Pardoner, perhaps disingenuously, makes two things very clear at the outset: he is not considering this audience as identical with his ordinary unsophisticated auditors, and he is going to be candid about the nature and intentions of his pedagogy. He makes it quite plain that his accomplishments as a preacher are more than they might seem. He is candid about his usual motives:

> For myn entente is nat but for to wynne,
> And nothyng for correccioun of synne.
> I rekke nevere, whan that they been beryed,
> Though that hir soules goon a-blakeberyed. (VI, 403-6)

The examples that he gives of his teaching are clearly better suited for a lower class audience than is generally the case among the pilgrims: lechery, gambling, blasphemy, and especially gluttony. It is not really until he gets to his main exemplum that his main theme, greed, dominates. Masterful in his demonstration of his abilities in his "Prologue" and early in his "Tale", he delights in directly calling the attention of this audience to his expertise. When he gets to the exemplum he rolls forward powerfully with the momentum of his cautionary tale regarding his consistent "main text."

It must be remembered that what the Pardoner teaches about the "tavern sins" and especially about greed is not a profound or sophisticated message. The lesson is a commonplace; the Pardoner is much more a rhetorician than a moralist. His performance, fraudulent as his motives are, is an attempt to change behavior with regard to commonly shared beliefs. His "goal" is to change action, not thought, and that fits his larger motive: to motivate his audience to do things.

Here his performance is quite sophisticated. His purpose is to prod his audience to give money, not to reform their moral lives. He is a familiar type in selling indulgences.[25] He is a teacher who does not care if the moral lessons are learned and lived, only whether his own greed is satisfied. Thus he is no teacher at all: he can preach a moral tale, but the moral consequences are irrelevant to him and, in any case, he has no moral news. His whole performance is a perversion of rhetoric. Of course, there is a lesson here about the dangers of empty or perverted rhetoric, but the moral is platitudinous and the method is instrumental. Do his usual hearers reform? We don't know. Do they come across? They clearly do.

Now, what is the dynamic of the Pardoner's relationship with his present audience? He has nothing moral to teach them; his immediate goal is to show off his virtuosity. What then is added by his pitch to the pilgrims? Has the Pardoner been transported by his own rhetoric to the point where he forgets the distinction between this audience and his "lewed" audiences? Or is he carried away by his own virtuosity to deceive himself that his rhetorical abilities are so great that he can deceive even this audience, or at least Harry Bailly to whom he directs his pitch? Either is possible in that it is not contradicted by evidence in his "Prologue" and "Tale": certainly his pride is enormous. And in either case rhetoric would remain paramount over doctrine, and it would be a toss-up as to whether his judgment was overpowered by his pride or his greed; in either case he is a corrupt and ineffective teacher, indeed not a teacher at all.

The interchange between the Pardoner and the Host, however, suggests that, even if the above is true, there is more to the Pardoner's attempt than pride or greed. Assume for a moment that the Pardoner is not out of control in either of the ways described above. His concluding attempt could have another motive that would fit with what we know about him from the "General Prologue" and his interruption of the "Wife of Bath's Tale", as well as with the self he presents in his own "Prologue" and "Tale". His pitch to Harry Bailly could be an attempt to join the human community of the pilgrimage at least on a superficial level. It could be that he sees Harry Bailly as the most vulnerable and that to ensnare him would put himself in the human community of the rest of the pilgrims (those who understand.) If such is the case, the Pardoner has made a miscalculation. Harry may not be as stupid as the Pardoner thought. At least he has the innkeeper's eye for a fake. Harry's angry reaction thwarts the Pardoner's attempt to insinuate himself into the fellowship of the more perceptive pilgrims at Harry's expense. We know from the "General Prologue" that the Pardoner is a eunuch and thus separated from the human community of generation. It may be that his greater interest in bonhomie is a pathetic attempt to be one of the boys (so often accomplished by picking on one of the boys and enjoying the joke with the majority.) If so, the Pardoner has seriously misread at least one member of his audience. Harry Bailly sees right through the scam, if a bit coarsely:

> "Nay, nay!" quod he, "thanne have I Cristes curs!
> Lat be," quod he, "it shal not be, so theech!
> Thou woldest make me kisse thyn olde breech,
> And swere it were a relyk of a seint,
> Though it were with thy fundement depeint!" (VI, 946-50)

He has been unaffected by the rhetoric and has seen clearly what the Pardoner has professed to demonstrate: that he is a supreme con-man. So much Harry can see, and this is jarring, but what Harry does not see is the even greater need that the Pardoner has to become a full member of the pilgrim community. It seems more likely that the Pardoner has assessed well his immediate rhetorical situation, that he never expects Harry to be taken in, and that Harry is to be incorporated among the cognoscenti by recognizing the Pardoner's ploy. This would make more sense if the Pardoner's driving ambition, and ultimate self-delusion, were to bring everyone together as insiders into a delicious enjoyment of his rhetorical *tour de force*. The Pardoner's hubris would then seem pathetic in a much more poignant way when the Host exclaims:

> But, by the croys which that Seint Eleyne fond,
> I wolde I hadde thy coillons in myn hond
> In stide of relikes or of seintuarie.

Lat kutte hem of, I wol thee helpe hem carie;

They shul be shryned in an hogges toord! (VI, 951-5)

This is exactly the fact that the Pardoner wants to obscure (that he has no testicles) in his quest fully to join the group. Harry is not stupid enough to fall for the rhetorical ploy, but he is not clever enough, or perhaps he is too angry, to avoid direct mention of that which the Pardoner most wants to hide. The Pardoner has tried disguise before when he mentioned his desire to marry during the "Wife of Bath's Prologue". The Wife "went along," even though the Pardoner's physical situation is painfully obvious, and the general good feeling remained uninterrupted. Here the Host out of anger, an anger that comes from pride, has crossed the boundary of spiritual generosity and highlighted the very thing that the Pardoner was trying to obscure. The Pardoner is so angry that he is silent; he loses the human power of speech that is his stock in trade, his pride. Rhetoric is muzzled; it cannot accomplish the ultimate human community towards which the Pardoner has aimed.

It is possible that Harry's outburst was without malice; his language is characteristically coarse, but others, like Chaucer when the Host rudely interrupts the "Tale of Sir Thopas," ignore his outbursts. The Pardoner cannot ignore the Host in this instance because Harry has publicly, that is, in the presence of the whole community that the Pardoner wishes to join, adverted to precisely what he had used his rhetorical skill to overcome or submerge. At least a superficial peace is restored by the intervention of the Knight; at least life (the pilgrimage) can go on, but the desperate attempt by the Pardoner to overcome reality with rhetoric is a failure. Rhetoric has its limitations. Human ingenuity has its limitations. Neither can change the reality of the created world. The Pardoner's rhetoric cannot make good men and it cannot grow the Pardoner testicles. Rhetoric is impressive but it is as impotent as the Pardoner as an instrument for changing reality. The Pardoner is perhaps, as Kittredge thought, the only damned pilgrim.[26] Rhetoric cannot bring him within the human community: the only thing he seems to want more than wealth. As with his preaching, rhetoric in itself cannot teach if its core is as empty as the Pardoner's exhortations are of virtue and his scrotum is of testicles. The accord that the Knight effects, though necessary if the pilgrimage is to go on, cannot alter the underlying realities any more than the Knight's resolution to his own Tale can. Once again, the story not the teacher bears the truth.

The next teacher, the Prioress, shows that pious simplicity can be as ineffective in teaching as devious rhetoric. The "Prioress's Tale" is a traditional genre for religious teaching and moral edification. We do not expect in such a tale that the complexities of how life is to be lived will be resolved. The world of the Prioress is not the setting for epistemological complexity or sophisticated interpretation. It is a world of devotional commitment that teaches by edification. Her tale, "a miracle of the Virgin," endeavors to make the simple point that Mary will protect virtue, and its Prologue is a simple and innocent paean to the Virgin, full of humility and devotion. The lesson will be a straightforward demonstration of the power, mercy, and love of the Virgin for the virtuous. The tale is simple and pathetic and its ostensible lesson is clear. But the way of the world is not so empty of questions as the "Prioress's Tale" would have us believe. It is not that the Prioress is fraudulent or deceptive. On the contrary, she is, if we remember the "General Prologue," simple to the point of fatuity (though in the "General Prologue" a very charming kind of fatuity it is.) Recall how, in her portrait, she seems so innocent or morally unself-conscious as be unable to make moral distinctions. Her courtliness becomes confused with her vocation; her pity and tenderness are indiscriminate. She does not seem inclined to trouble herself with hard moral questions. But just as her simplicity raises questions (if gentle ones) in her portrait, the simplicity of her tale, despite its intended pathos and piety, teaches nothing of the way the world is or should be; it may be a kind of simplicity that is more dangerous and destructive of human community than the hollow rhetoric of the Pardoner.[27] The Prioress does not have much on her mind. That might suffice as an object lesson in Christian edification, but Chaucer calls the simplicity into question in several places. The tale is familiar and conventional, but in the mouth of the unselfconscious Prioress can be devastating rather than elevating. Her moral unconsciousness in the "General Prologue" invites us to examine her Tale with a sharper eye than we might ordinarily cast upon a piece of devotional fluff, innocuous if insubstantial. But the "Prioress' Tale" emerges from a simplicity that borders on the culpable. Perhaps she can live in her own ambiguous world, where sentimentality can stand for morality, but when she tries to teach, the limitations, even brutality, of simplicity emerge.

The tale is full of pathos, but as we have seen in the 'Physician's Tale", pathos is not enough. Her invocation to the Virgin demonstrates as well as states her limitations. The foundation of Christian understanding in the Tale is thin. The little boy learns "O Alma Redemptoris" by heart; he learns and loves it without knowing what it means. To his credit he asks an older boy to translate for him but the explanation is vague:

> "This song, I have herd seye,
>
> Was maked of our blisful Lady free.
>
> Hire to salue, and eek hire for to preye
>
> To been oure help and socour whan we deye.
>
> I kan namoore expounde in this mateere.
>
> I lerne song; I kan but smal grammeere." (VII, 531-6)

The boy still has only a rudimentary notion of the meaning of the hymn; it is in another language and he gets only the gist of it from the slightly older boy whose Latin is limited. That is not to say that his understanding is incorrect, but it certainly is tenuous: he depends on a language he doesn't know, explicated by someone who knows it only a little better. The doctrine is not incorrect, but it is a mirror of the way we all understand spiritual mysteries through a glass darkly. This is no blame to the boy; the doctrine is sound and such "miracles" were common and popular stories. It is the grasp of larger moral imperatives that is missing, and this seems a metaphor for the Prioress' limited comprehension of her religion and her vocation especially in the context of her unconsciousness in the "General Prologue". The situation of the boy may actually represent the situation of all Christians who, rejoicing in a limited knowledge but full of simple devotion, set forth among the evils which surround and threaten them. If there is a lesson here, it is not the one that the Prioress means to teach. Her purpose is edificatory not analytical or cautionary.

The evils that the boy faces are even more revealing: the Jews, through whose ghetto he daily passes singing his faith. The portrayal of the Jews clearly characterizes them as evil incarnate, the very essence of the dangers the faithful Christian faces, a cultural disposition that Chaucer uses to make his point in the Tale. They are a useful conventional symbol of the evil that the Christian inevitably encounters. A stereotypical presentation of the evil and cruelty of the Jews certainly does fit into the horror of the murder that the Prioress means to emphasize. That Chaucer shared contemporary anti-Semitism seems at least doubtful. It does not appear anywhere else in Chaucer except in the "Parson's Tale" where it is simply a formulaic presentation of common belief, the sort of thing that is merely true and accepted uncritically by a pilgrim.[28] The Prioress, however, focuses on the anti-Semitism; it is central to the martyrdom and described vigorously. But the revenge of the Christians is no less bestial:

> With torment and with shameful deeth echon,
> This provost dooth thise Jewes for to sterve
> That of this mordre wiste, and that anon.
> He nolde no swich cursednesse observe.
> "Yvele shal have that yvele wol deserve";
> Therfore with wilde hors he dide hem drawe,
> And after that he heng hem by the lawe. (VII, 628-34)

This comparison suggests that the anti-Semitism is not Chaucerian, but a convention that is useful when put into the refined sensibility of the Prioress.

I am not trying to make Chaucer politically correct, but it seems much more probable that anti-Semitism is a vehicle, a readily identifiable symbol of the evils and dangers that surround the Christian, but no more barbarous than the vengefulness of the Christians. Such would fit the moral consciousness of the Prioress much better than that of Chaucer. The evil Jews are useful for the

Prioress. It should not be surprising that the corresponding cruelty of the Christians is, for her, a highly satisfying resolution, which leads on to the miracle that happily and neatly, for the Prioress, completes her conventional Tale. There are truths embedded in the Tale. On earth our understanding of the spiritual is as limited as the boy's understanding of the hymn and as admirable as his simple devotion. But there is a problem in the Prioress's unconscious coupling of pathos and brutality. The simplicity of her highly conventional tale and conventional views of Jews are a playing out, with the help of a correspondingly simple genre, of the dangers of the precarious piety we saw in her in the "General Prologue". It is hard, indeed impossible, to condemn her of anything more than childlike simplicity and unself-consciousness in her spiritual life. But the consequences of such a sensibility are perilous: in the "General Prologue" her spiritual life is on a knife's edge between charm and ignorance; in her Tale the spiritual lives of us all hang in the balance. She does not have the wisdom or self-knowledge to teach, though her Tale is intended to be didactic. The dangers and uncertain consequences of her sensibility are made manifest: human knowledge may not suffice, but Christian simplicity can generate a sanguinary vision of the universe in which we must work out our salvation. When she is done, the pilgrims are "sober"; we are not told why. I doubt, however, that readers of the Tale can find much comfort in the concluding miracle.

The Host quickly turns to Chaucer, the character in the *Tales*, for the next story, and we embark upon a complex section in which the matters of self-conscious fiction and levels of reality are as prominent as anywhere in the *Canterbury Tales*. Who is this self-characterized character and what can we expect of him, especially after the hollow rhetoric of the Pardoner and the ominous simplicity of the Prioress? The Host's address is comic, familiar, perhaps even condescending:

> "What man artow?" quod he;
> "Thou lookest as thou woldest fynde an hare,
> For evere upon the ground I se thee stare.

> "Approche neer and looke up murily.
>
> Now war yow, sires, and lat this man have place!
>
> He in the waast is shape as wel as I;
>
> This were a popet in an arm t'enbrace
>
> For any womman, smal and fair of face.
>
> He semeth elvyssh by his contenaunce,
>
> For unto no wight dooth he daliaunce." (VII, 695-704)

Ironies abound in this modest but "elvyssh" self-portrait—and self-placement in the *Tales*.

Despite the playful presentation, it is inevitable that we recognize him as the creator of this whole world, and tempting to suspect that he is a teacher to whom we can look for a clearer and more complex vision of spiritual life. Yet his position, simultaneously inside and outside of the world of the *Tales*, complicates our expectations. From what cosmological and fictional perspective will Chaucer speak? The ambiguity would have been even more acute if Chaucer the poet were reciting the tales to the court, as he almost certainly sometimes did. The Host sees him, of course, entirely as pilgrim, and asks for a tale of mirth to relieve the bitterness and gloom that have descended on the narratives. Chaucer's response seems to identify him as a humble pilgrim for now, not omniscient fabricator of the whole:

> "Hooste," quod I, "ne beth nat yvele apayd,
>
> For oother tale certes kan I noon,
>
> But of a rym I lerned longe agoon." (VII, 707-9)

He seems to be a different character from the literary figure referred to in the "Introduction to the Man of Law's Tale", and he refers to himself as "I". This scene presents the very essence of self-conscious fiction, and the poet Chaucer does not clarify the situation. The epistemology of the situation is more complex than simply whether this is playful poet or simple pilgrim. Chaucer has been recognized as a prolific writer yet this person, "Chaucer", speaks like a simple pilgrim to those who should know better. He both is and is not Chaucer. It is a world of total mystification in identity. Should we listen up? Is this the voice that will make all things clear? The answer is a resounding yes and no because it is here that the interpenetration of the two Chaucers is most complete, the character I call "Chaucer" because Chaucer will not allow us to have it simply one way or another. We can only look at what he says to try to discover what he means.

The "Tale of Sir Thopas" is a parody of the popular tail-rhyme romance: boring, inept, and all too familiar.[29] It is a debasement of tales of chivalry, a sing-song popularization all too familiar. Riotously funny with its clumsy formulae, repetitions, improbabilities, and bathos, it is a brilliant literary satire, the sort of thing where you point to lines and laugh helplessly rather than explicate. What is Chaucer-the-poet up to in inserting this clever and sophisticated parody into Chaucer-the-pilgrim's mouth, and thereby instating "Chaucer"? It is not an indictment of chivalry. It is a send-up of bad poetry that makes us laugh, but must be interrupted on the pilgrimage if only for the practical reason that it is funnier stopped than if allowed to limp to a predictable conclusion. It does not bear re-telling; suffice it to say that it ridicules all that is silly in the worst of romance. It does not bear explication, but we should all stop here and re-read it to put us into the frame of mind that can make its appearance at this point in the *Tales* intelligible. It is cosmic comic relief; it is the best, the only thing, that "Chaucer" can do as a fiction: it is all he knows. It is hilarious; and not interpretive but human, and that may be its heuristic function at this point. "Chaucer" is stymied in fiction: in one way as pilgrim, in another as creator.

The Host does not get the joke. When he interrupts and assesses the Tale, brusquely and contemptuously, he asks for a tale of "som murthe or som doctryne," and "Chaucer" meekly complies. The dynamic of this interchange is critical in understanding the whole enterprise of the *Canterbury Tales*. Keep in mind that the Tale is both a joke and not a joke if the idea of "Chaucer" is to be sustained. "Thopas" is enjoyable in itself and in the ambiguities connected with the presence of "Chaucer" and its reception, but, while it must be savored for the playful interlude that it is, it must also be seen in the context of the "Melibee," the tale that "Chaucer" decides to tell at the Host's behest. For in the combination there is the representation of Chaucer's refusal to "tell the truth." "Chaucer" preserves his mask by attempting to merely please rather than to teach and please, but that is not good enough for a world that includes people with the limited moral sensibilities of the Host.

"Chaucer" has already said that he knows only one poem, so his reaction is to say (coyly?) that he will tell a simple, well-known, virtuous tale in prose.[30] The "sondry folk" can hardly help but turn their minds back to their garrulous interlocutor at the Tabard. What follows is a relatively long and well-known allegory in prose. There are those who would have us believe that this is Chaucer the poet's revenge on the blunted sensibilities of the Host: having been thwarted in his literary cleverness, he will now tell a tale that will bore the whole company. I find this hard to accept as a literary or moral strategy. To bore your audience is not a satisfactory revenge for a literary artist. We can turn over the page and choose another Tale, but auditors of the *Tales* could not, and if we did turn over the page we would be missing something. But what are we to make of this Tale, told by "Chaucer" in the process of simultaneously teaching and removing himself as a final authority? The main alternative to "the boring joke" theory is to argue that people in the fourteenth century, accustomed to long sermons and "ponderous sentence" would have found something much more pleasurable and salutary in "Melibee" than is accessible to a modern sensibility.[31] However, this too would obfuscate "Chaucer's" purpose in his introduction of himself. Remember, as author he does not have to intrude himself at all. But as "Chaucer" the combination of "Thopas" and "Melibee" provides an opportunity in the larger didactic of the *Tales*. In any case, I find it hard to believe that 600 years could have wrought such a massive change in our capacity to enjoy, or prepare ourselves to enjoy, what might entertain and instruct a fourteenth century audience. After all, we must know something about tail-rhyme romance even to find "Thopas" funny. The question should be: what do we need to know in order to find

"Melibee" satisfying?

First, I would suggest, we must see it in the whole context of the *Tales*. It is told by "Chaucer", who must instruct as well as please, while preserving himself from moral and intellectual dictatorship. The tale, as "Chaucer" indicates, was common in many versions and well thought of: the many versions imply this. "Chaucer" simply has translated, quite closely, the most accessible version, Renaud de Louens' *Livre de Melibee et de Dame Prudence*. And he makes no substantial changes in his original because it already has what he wants in this context. "Melibee" fits "Chaucer's" complex plan because it is a necessary, though not sufficient, assay of moral understanding and action. Moreover, it echoes scenes and attitudes that have had prominence in the *Tales* thus far. If its moral simplicity is seen in this context, then it is both satisfying from a literary point of view and successful in teaching accurately but not more than "Chaucer" would have us believe is possible, even for him. It squeezes out of traditional pedagogy what "Chaucer" needs without overstepping the bounds of the personal authority he is willing to claim for his pilgrim self.

The Tale is a moral allegory of the sort that makes its lessons explicit rather than "teasing us out of thought." Melibee is a young man, but he is married to Prudence. The fact that their daughter, Sophie, is wisdom should give us some confidence in the efficacy of their experience. A line by line, *topos* by *topos*, explication of the tale need not detain us here. The overall tendency of the work is crucial. The literal situation is that, while Melibee is out, old enemies enter his house, beat his wife, and grievously injure his daughter. The rest of the Tale is Prudence's explanation of how he should react to this outrage. Now, this is an important and general situation: how ought we react to the palpable evil inflicted by others. Prudence instructs, and she is the right teacher. She is the first and foremost of the four moral virtues: prudence, justice, fortitude, and temperance. As with the other gatherings of sins or virtues, there is one foundational one (charity among the theological virtues, pride among the seven deadly sins.) Prudence, as is demonstrated in the Tale, is the underlying energizer of all the other moral virtues.

The rhetorical circumstance in the Tale is that Prudence teaches and Melibee has his objections satisfied. Her doctrine is consistently and profoundly grounded on classical and biblical authority. The rhetorical situation is contrived so as not to admit of contradiction. Melibee's reservations are always satisfied by elaboration; the authorities are never subject to the kind of scrutiny that they endure in the "Wife of Bath's Tale": their truth is self-evident; they only need elaboration. She is a wise and gentle wife with the well-being of her husband at heart. Here is no problem of sovereignty; there prevails the natural sovereignty of moral good sense and human good will. How many of the Tales could have been resolved under Prudence's rubric! Hers is a general remedy that applies to all human conflicts, and the rhetoric of the Tale, built around the structure of "objection raised-objection resolved," does not allow her authorities to be called in question. One could imagine such, but it is not possible in the rhetorical tendency of this Tale. Her teaching is simply so overpowering and makes such sweet, good sense.

A major section of the Tale deals with the wise use of counsellors: a powerful reminder of the self-will of January and an object lesson in the achievement of commune profit, for the well-being of the entire society is at stake, not just the moral life of Melibee. In any case, Prudence always has an answer and wedded to the well-intentioned, if often misguided, disposition of Melibee, the result is wisdom. To every objection raised by Melibee tending towards retribution or unwise means of proceeding, Prudence's response, as appropriate to her name, is just stop and think about it, especially in the context of the best moral examples. And the universal answer is forgiveness, human and divine, as Melibee demonstrates in his concluding speech to those who have sinned against him. Human forgiveness is the answer to strife and contention and is the pre-condition for living the moral and salvific life. It is important to remember that the repentance of the offenders is also necessary. Then, however, Melibee can act with a magnanimity that prefigures the circumstance we aspire to with our Final

Judge. We, if we take the lesson, will be doing the divine in human life, and thereby can have an expectation of condign treatment by God when our Last Judgment comes.

Why, then, is this not, conventional as it is, the last and final resolution to the moral dilemmas that human beings face? It would resolve most of the conflicts that have arisen in the *Tales* so far. The problem is, as the familiarity and conventionality of the Tale suggest, that "All this the world knows well . . ." Amidst this most edifying teaching, "Chaucer" reminds us that there is a disparity in human life between the moral truths that are simple and efficacious and the reality of the way human beings behave. The teaching of Prudence could order the world morally, but this is not the way the world works as the many previous Tales, which cannot be ignored, have demonstrated. It raises a profound epistemological problem in the living of the moral life: "The evil that I would not do, that I do. . ." If we are to understand the world around us, simple, moral sense is apparently not enough: this is the mystery and reality of human life. This is a truth that brings concordance but not stasis. It is, in a way, merely true.

The Host loves the story as an example of a good wife, but fails to see it as a model for living. We do see, but we are as aware as "Chaucer", who has told us the truth, that knowledge and virtue are not the same thing. Nevertheless, the counsels of Prudence to the moral virtues that issue in forgiveness are a gratifying interlude before we return to the more complex attempts to teach and understand that human beings force upon themselves. And in any case, the plain counsels of simple moral truths do not explain the muddle that is the world in which we work out our salvation. That is to say, we still want to understand more about our human condition, especially *sub specie aeternitatis*, and it is to this sort of question that the Monk, our next teacher, wrenches us back.

After the simple, moral sobriety of Dame Prudence, the Host is ready for a merry, perhaps scurrilous tale, so he turns quite reasonably to the Monk. The "General Prologue" has identified the Monk as manly and worldly, anything but what his religious vows would call for, but the Host goes too far in establishing the secular and sexual qualifications of the Monk. Chaucer is again asking us to distrust our expectations. In the "General Prologue" Chaucer gave us a Monk who violated our ideal notion of his vocation and gratified our sense of what to expect in a contemporary monk. The narrator had admired him, if misguidedly, for being what he is, even though one of the things that he is is completely unmindful of the rule of St. Benedict. However, the Host's prelude is too frank for the Monk, who does not want his religious failure openly stated. Thus it is that the Monk rebels and turns himself hypocrite as well; he will not have his monastic failings played out in public.

He stutters at the beginning; his first insistence is that:

"I wol doon al my diligence,

As fer as sowneth into honestee,

To telle yow a tale, or two, or three.

And if yow list to herkne hyderward,

I wol yow seyn the lyf of Seint Edward." (VII, 1966-70)

But he turns to the idea of tragedy. He will, in his rush to morality, first tell a series of tragedies, which he defines:

Or ellis, first, tragedies wol I telle,

Of whiche I have an hundred in my celle.

Tragedie is to seyn a certeyn storie,

As olde bookes maken us memorie,

Of hym that stood in greet prosperitee,

And is yfallen out of heigh degree

Into myserie, and endeth wrecchedly. (VII, 1971-7)

This sounds like a threat or boast pushed forward in self defense. Whether this definition is consistent with other Medieval definitions of tragedy or of Chaucer's own is a matter of some debate.[32] What is more important is whether the definition is consistent with the foundation of monastic *contemptus mundi*. The Monk seems to think so and embarks on a catalogue of examples of famous and prosperous men who have been brought low by Fortune. There is a way in which the Monk is learned; he does know all these *exempla*. But his mind and his moral sensibility are disordered. That the tales are not chronologically narrated, as the Monk freely admits, is less important than whether they are ordered or relevant at all.

Most are interesting stories, though some are so brief as to be trivial except as mere example. All are familiar. The Monk's intention seems simple and pointed: to demonstrate the instability of this world by showing that regardless of how powerful and wealthy one might be, there is a pattern of Fall. The Monk, however, seems to be exemplifying the operations of the Roman goddess Fortuna more than teaching any moral lesson. Now it is true that the ubiquity of the pattern he describes is a demonstration of the instability of this world: the disposition that leads monks to withdraw from this world and pray for it seems to mark the limit of the Monk's moral and spiritual understanding. The lack of order makes the tales seem like one damn thing after another. Not only is there no chronological order; there is no dramatic order; the tales do not seem to be building in any informative or instructive sequence. Nor do the tales make any distinction between whether or not moral culpability is involved.

This is a crucial absence. The fall of Lucifer and Adam are moral punishments brought upon themselves by disobedience to God. Sampsoun and Hercules are, on the other hand, good men who are not morally culpable. The pattern continues throughout the Monk's collection. Nebuchadnezzar, Balthasar, and Holofernes are all culpable; Alexander and Julius Caesar are not. Julius Caesar is a particularly good example of the absence of moral discrimination because the Monk pauses to mention the fall of Pompey within the story of Caesar without making any distinction. Cresus is a good example of another kind. His story could be, and indeed in Herodotus and other versions is, a prime example of pride going before a fall. But that is not the way the Monk tells the story. In the Monk's version Cresus's fortune has no moral significance. These confusions, or failures to make moral distinctions, are what is most suspect in the catalogue of tragedies. For catalogue it is, and the only lesson is the capricious and formidable destructive power of Fortuna. In themselves, these narratives could be seen as a radical criticism of the instability of this world. Even that would teach the primary monastic lesson of *contemptus mundi* and could serve as a caution. But the Monk offers no instruction as to how this life ought to be lived in view of the instability. The indiscriminate nature of the stories could be a reflection of God's use of Fortune as a tool of Providence inaccessible to human understanding, but there is no sign of the Monk taking advantage of this potential lesson. He is stuck with the goddess Fortuna and has not baptized her. The obvious discontinuity in the morality of the stories makes what could be a simple monastic counsel into a moral and epistemological hodge-podge. True, misfortune comes to good and evil alike, but is there nothing beyond this bleak insight? Where is the operation of God's Providence in the falls? Pagan and Christian alike fall victim to a blind force; there is no Christian application. The prominent mixture of innocence and culpability, again without comment or gloss, suggests that the Monk has a radically limited moral vision. He can teach the harsh pagan lesson that underlies monasticism, but he is a poor teacher of the moral imperatives that flow from the Christianization of Fortuna. His definition of tragedy has trapped him in a meaningless exposition of suffering.

That he should be interrupted by the Knight, who has tried, if only with limited success, to show how Fortune is to be understood and met, is instructive. The Knight simply finds the tales too sad; he would like to hear of "joye and gret solas" when a man climbs to the height of Fortune's wheel. This evidences no greater moral insight than the Monk's stories, but it is a reminder of the moral poverty of the Monk's examples. Without hope, without even significance, they are oppressive rather than edifying. There is even some truth in the Host's admonition that no matter what the moral intention, if the stories are boring and repetitive, the audience will fall asleep and fail to profit. In either case, they are the bleak foundations of withdrawal, which the narrator has himself not undertaken and they neither elucidate the moral life nor tell us how to live in view of spiritual realities.

It is notable at this point in the *Tales* that our attention has been gradually shifting epistemological ground. The focus has become increasingly spiritual. Fragments I and II explored the nature and structure of our world; Fragments III-V reflected on the moral life, how we are to live in this world; in Fragments VI-VII we have been moving towards an examination of the spiritual life, an examination of how we ought to live in this world in view of the next. For the most part, our teachers have not been good. Blindness and self-interest have obstructed the way with an ineffectual rhetoric. Only "Chaucer" has kept us on task, but we still await a true preceptor.

In view of this context, there is a tendency to look to the "Nun's Priest's Tale" for some kind of resolution or enlightenment.[33] That expectation is reinforced by the introduction of the Nun's Priest as a simple, modest character. The fact that he has not been characterized in the "General Prologue" intensifies our sense that he bears some kind of mysterious authority that is perhaps the voice of Chaucer, the poet, speaking more profoundly even than "Chaucer" who lives both inside and outside the *Tales*. The Nun's Priest gets right to his task without a revelatory prologue. His is a disembodied voice that tempts us to see him, despite his modesty, as "a man of gret auctoritee."

He turns out not to be the portentous kind of "man of gret auctoritee" who fails to appear at the end of the *House of Fame*, but rather a man of great practical wisdom who will speak of barnyards and fowl, the lowest order of birds according to the *Parliament*. That he is a disembodied voice enhances his authority because he is not burdened with baggage from the "General Prologue". That he speaks wittily and wisely is balanced by the fact that he speaks plainly and of barnyards; sophistication and erudition belong to the birds about whom he reports. That he is a man of great practical wisdom is emphasized by his disembodied yet playful and sympathetic voice. Even his use of the beast fable is a splendidly useful choice for his project. His voice provides a human commentary on a lower order of creation. Kind, sympathetic, but superior, he thereby raises the question of human limitations in the great order of divine creation. It is not that he is God interpreting the world (a simple shift from man-beast to God-man), but he blurs nicely the distinction between man and beast to tell a useful and pertinent tale. As we approach the end of the *Tales*, frustrated by philosophical uncertainty and disappointed by flawed teachers, the Nun's Priest's lesson is just what we need. As the *Tales* move from the theoretical and epistemological examination of the human condition to a more practical and spiritual quest to understand what is most necessary, *i.e.*, what is most needful for salvation, the Nun's Priest is the right narrator, in the right genre, with the right tone to teach sensibly but not condescendingly, perceptively but not definitively. He puts courtly love, rhetoric, and philosophical predestination in their place, and he puts us in our place, a not entirely disagreeable one.

The distress in which Chaunticleer begins the Tale is an emblem of the situation that we human beings find ourselves in: lacking confidence and tortured by phantasms, many of our own making. The story is embedded in the hoary question of the reliability of dreams as a source of knowledge. Chaunticleer's dream is an admonition:

> "Me mette how that I romed up and doun
> Withinne our yeerd, wheer as I saugh a beest
> Was lyk an hound and wolde han maad areest
> Upon my body, and wolde han had me deed.
> His colour was bitwixe yelow and reed,
> And tipped was his tayl and bothe his eeris
> With blak, unlyk the remenant of his heeris;
> His snowte smal, with glowynge eyen tweye.
> Yet of his look for feere almoost I deye;
> This caused me my gronyng, doutelees." (VII, 2898-2907)

His distress becomes the stimulus for his extended disputation with Pertelote about dreams. What should be noted first is the ambiguity in Chaunticleer's initial reaction. He is distressed, but he does not understand his dream in any practical way: he does not realize that he has dreamed of a fox, a recognition that should be critical for his order of creation, roosterdom. Instead of understanding (not necessarily that this is a prediction of the future but that foxes are, for roosters, worth worrying about), he gets involved with Pertelote in a highly philosophical disputation about dreams. This is the first of a series of reminders of motifs that have run through the *Tales* and suggests that this Tale has some summative authority.

Pertelote's first response is to assert what women want: in this case not sovereignty in marriage but masculine courage in their husbands. A simple view reflecting the courtly values that permeate their relationship; but the birds proceed to a learned disputation about the authority of dreams. She, a woman, is practical and gives a learned medical solution that ends in practical advice: " 'For Goddes love, as taak som laxatyf' " (VII, 2943). But this homely advice is wrapped in 48 lines of philosophical and medical learning. Impressive, but if we remember the simple dream, beside the point. Like a good rooster/human being, Chaunticleer takes up the argument. He insists that both experience and authority, our two ways of knowing, show that dreams are to be attended to. He even adds learned exempla to defend his position. Within his exempla the mention that "mordre wol out" and of the seven-year-old St. Kenelm cannot help but remind us of the Prioress. But the whole debate is a mnemonic animadversion on themes that have preoccupied the pilgrims. The major themes are iterated or acted out: fate and free will, experience and authority, rhetoric and reason. Even less profound motifs (what women want, dream lore, anti-feminism) are adverted to. But the disputation is left inconclusive. No one wins the argument on these abstract grounds.

Chaunticleer is distracted from abstract considerations by the sexual attractions of Pertelote. When he attempts to be learned (*"In principio/Mulier est hominis confusio."* VII, 3163-4), he mistranslates the caution into praise: " 'Womman is mannes joye and al his blis' " (VII, 3166). This could be a clever ploy, but at this point his sexuality seems to have greater potency than his intellect. It is the henly beauty of Pertelote that distracts him; both have already been introduced in courtly terms although that itself has included a reminder that they are chickens. So much for the dignity of courtly love. Here his distraction is more explicitly sexual (VII, 3168-9), but his language is still exalted. The red around her eyes overwhelms his roosterly passion and occasions a major blunder. His tribute in Latin, a familiar anti-feminist tag, is ironically and disastrously misinterpreted. It is not my point that what follows is Pertelote's fault, but that Chaunticleer is confused and distracted by sex, sex with some courtly forms, but sex after all. And he steps out "in al his pryde" and lust and self-deception.

The Nun's Priest's interruption of his own narrative here is instructive. He gives it the weighty implication of potential tragedy:

> But sodeynly hym fil a sorweful cas,
> For evere the latter ende of joye is wo,
> God woot that worldly joye is soone ago. (VII, 3204-6)

Then, he playfully reduces it to the reliability of the world of romance:

> This storie is also treww, I undertake,
> As is the book of Launcelot de Lake,
> That wommen hold in ful greet reverence.
> Now wol I turne agayn to my sentence. (VII, 3211-4)

He proceeds to a mock-serious disquisition on fate and foreknowledge, laying a mantle of seriousness and authority on a story which he quickly acknowledges for what it is: "My tale is of a cok, as ye may heere." (VII, 3252). He playfully dismisses the implication, which reminds us of the Wife of Bath, that woman is at fault in putting man in jeopardy. And indeed, it is not Pertelote's counsel that puts Chaunticleer in danger, but his own sensuality and lack of self-knowledge. The light hand of the Nun's Priest is ever present as profound human issues are worked out and confounded in the barnyard.

It is tempting to fall into a line by line explication of this Tale, so deftly does it remind us of the preoccupations of most of the preceding tales, so exquisitely does it use these motifs with a combination of criticism and sympathy without condemnation or ridicule. Chaunticleer and Pertelote are us as we have revealed ourselves in the substance, controversies, and perplexities of the preceding Tales. I must return to my first matter: the temptation, the fall, and the salvation of Chaunticleer.

The first of the simple lessons that follows is that pride goes before a fall. It is Chaunticleer's inflated sense of self, in the context of the blindness that has been followed by an obscuring barrage of rhetoric and authorities, that puts him at risk. The fox, Satan if I or any Medieval bestiary-maker ever saw him, uses Chaunticleer's pride-beclouded sense of self. The temptation calls upon Chaunticleer to put himself in a ridiculous and vulnerable position:

> This Chauntecleer his wynges gan to bete,
>
> As man that koude his traysoun nat espie,
>
> So was he ravysshed with his flaterie. (VII,3322-4)

The consequence is swift and predictable. The Nun's Priest's 36 line apostrophe compounds the drama and the absurdity of the situation. Man and chicken are made one in folly.

Chaunticleer gets another chance, as do we in our follies, because the Tale includes an order of creation higher than the barnyard fowls. The widow, her daughters, her whole household, described in modest terms at the beginning of the narrative, fly into action. It is easy, too easy, to see the widow as God intervening to provide Chaunticleer another chance as God did for man with Redemption and repeatedly does with actual grace. That would, I think, be too simple a view of the frame the Nun's Priest has created. Yes, in one sense it takes the intervention of the widow and her household to give Chaunticleer another chance. As such it can be seen, from the animals' point of view, as an inscrutable force of Providence. But the widow's household is both a higher order of creation which the Nun's Priest can intrude into the barnyard and also a household of specific virtues: prudence, justice, fortitude, and temperance. The four cardinal moral virtues, urged by the "Tale of Melibee" and issuing in forgiveness, are human instruments that contribute to redemption from sin and folly. The widow is perhaps not God, but humanity in a higher more ordered state capable of rescuing our lower selves from self-destruction.

My intention is not to exhaust the possibilities of the Tale, but to take one plausible reading, consistent with the pattern of pedagogy that I have been discussing in this chapter and the interpretation I have been discussing in this book, and to show how in these contexts the Tale can be seen as the most profound, if not definitive, teaching we have seen so far, and that it is a counsel to practical wisdom in the living of our spiritual lives.

Simply and modestly, the Nun's Priest, at the end of his Tale, notes that his narrative has been, in itself, a mere beast fable, that it might be mistaken for a "tale of folye/As of a fox, or of a cok and hen" (ll. 3438-9). But he pointedly charges us to take the "moralite," the spiritual significance of the allegory:

> Taketh the moralite, goode men.
> For Seint Paul seith that al that writen is,
> To oure doctrine it is ywrite, ywis. (VII, 3440-2)

Here is that familiar and challenging admonition again. It echoes the counsel in *The House of Fame* and the "General Prologue" where we are warned that we should not overlook any writing–the familiar counsel from St. Paul, Gower, and Chaucer himself. If we were to ignore his sentence, modestly but firmly stated, we would be in the same danger as if we turned over the leaf and read another Tale, as in the case of the Miller and Melibee. We might miss an element of the whole interpretation of the world that we are continually asked to make.

In the sequence of Tales in VI-VII, we have a series of pilgrims who would be teachers. None tells us the meaning of life, but by negative example or positive exposition, these pilgrims shape the view that supersedes the kind of inquiries that have engaged us earlier in the *Tales*. True, we must: "Taketh the fruyt, and lat the chaf be stille" (VII, 3443), but that is the process of interpretation that we are called upon to engage in and that the pedagogical weaknesses and strengths of the narrators lay before us. The pious simplicity of the Prioress is as misleading as the cunning rhetoric of the Pardoner. The ignorance of the expert, as in the case of the Monk, must be put aside in favor of moral imperatives, like prudence and forgiveness, humility and resilience. If a rooster can learn, so can we. Our two disembodied teachers, Dame Prudence and the Nun's Priest, existing as they do in different orders of reality, can, if not explicate the complex significances of the central theological enigmas and human constructs, tell us what it is needful to know for salvation. The varying shapes of these Tales conspire to the practical wisdom which empowers us in a world we cannot fully understand, and all tend towards the proclamation of a transformation that is necessary if we are to achieve an everlasting life which we cannot fully understand, but can and must aspire to. But, as we shall see, not all transformations are efficacious or equal. Again, not to know is not to know nothing. To know what is necessary for salvation—that is concrete, practical, and God's obligation to make accessible. To know abstractions, to know the nature of the universe and the mysteries of the human heart—that is another matter entirely.

Chapter VI: The Tellable Truth

Many have pondered the justification for seeing connections among the Tales in Fragments VIII-X.[1] Some have questioned, on practical as well as thematic grounds, whether the "Canon's Yeoman's Tale" is an afterthought, stuck in where possible, and whether the "Manciple's Tale" belongs here at all.[2] Others have made a persuasive case for the connectedness, even the unity of this sequence, as tales of transformation.[3] The resolution of such disagreements, however, does not bear much on the exploration of knowing in the *Tales*. It is true that the Tales have turned more towards the question of practical wisdom as in "The Tale of Melibee" and "The Nun's Priest's Tale", but I would not argue that there is a climactic order that issues in "The Parson's Tale" and "The Retraction", though there is a strong sense that "The Parson's Tale" is the end of the exploration that the *Tales* make. The idea of a pilgrimage may indeed suggest direction, but it would be premature and misleading to see the movement as a linear progression to the rejection of reason in favor of faith and the replacement of speculation with practical wisdom, even though something like that does occur in the clearly final "Parson's Tale".

The Second Nun has her own contribution to make which, while integral to the whole of the *Tales*, need not be forced into a prelude for the Parson.[4] Like the Nun's Priest, the Second Nun is a disembodied voice in that she is not described in the "General Prologue". Her Tale is a simple recounting of a familiar saint's life, but the Second Nun does have a prologue in which she gives us more perspective than we get on the Nun's Priest and more insight than we get in the Prioress's own "Prologue". The "Second Nun's Prologue" is not idle piety. In fact, idleness is the first vice that the Second Nun deplores and what she has to say amounts to little more than that "an idle mind is the devil's workshop." Her condemnation of idleness is an injunction to use our minds, not in intellectual speculation but in contemplation of the truths of revelation. Her moral tale is her work and should engage our attention.

In addition, the invocation to Mary is more than the simplistic, childlike piety of the Prioress, because the Second Nun emphasizes the instrumentality of Mary as the mother of Christ, who has redeemed us. Thus, moral regeneration is made possible, but for the Second Nun Redemption involves more than the simple acceptance of the redemptive act. There is still our part to do:

> And, for that feith is deed withouten werkis,
>
> So for to werken yif me wit and space,
>
> That I be quit fro thennes that most derk is! (VIII, 64-6)

Faith must live in works. The Second Nun is wholly orthodox in her union of faith and works and her work is to teach concerning the transformation of the soul to God and salvation. She claims no originality, only industry in the service of Christ's redemptive act. And that, as we shall see, is the simple but powerful message of her Tale. No irony here, only honest work that uses intellect for spiritual purposes.

If such is the case, it may seem odd that the Second Nun tarries to speculate on the meaning of the name Cecilia. Her etymologies are fanciful, but the fourteenth century did not view language, especially names, with the eyes of twentieth century linguistics. What the Second Nun engages in is meditation on the potentialities of the name for spiritual enlightenment and edification. The truths of historical linguistics are something neither she nor Chaucer would have thought of. And though it is a fanciful process, it is an exercise of the intellect in the service of devotion. Or rather it is an exercise of the informed imagination in trying to wring all of the salvific meaning possible out of the things of this world. Her exercise is a familiar devotional one with names, objects, and scenes as objects of contemplation, a spiritual discipline in which intellect blends with imagination in the making of meaning. The process is, on a small scale, analogous to allegory where, according to St. Augustine, the anagogical meaning is not a closed system but an arena for devotional imagination, an opportunity to wring truths from narrative. Far from being a charming digression, the meditation on the name Cecilia is itself a spiritual practice. It leads to truths, not of syllogistic demonstration, but of insights which invest the simple tale that follows with an imaginative richness. Cecilia is heaven's lily (virginity) and holiness and busyness linked in a way that suits the Second Nun's insistence on faith and works. All of the definitions reinforce the importance of a faith that lives in action.

That is exactly the ideal of the life of St. Cecilia. Indeed, her virginity is merely a pre-condition of self-denial. Her work is conversion and, with the help of God, she is a conversion machine. Her virginity a sign of her renunciation of this world, her activity is wholly directed to the transformation of this world into the next. When she faces her final test, that is exactly what is at issue. The terms of her argument with Almachius are instructive. In one sense, their conversation is not an argument so much as a confrontation between two different ways of looking at the world. Almachius is the embodiment of a secular view which is incompatible with and, in this case, impervious to the confident spiritual assertions of Cecilia.

Almachius accuses Cecilia of pride, and she turns the accusation back on him. It really is a matter of where one vests power and authority. Cecilia has been successful in her other conversions because she has been able to bring revelation, a new spiritual vision for receptive minds and hearts. The task with Almachius is intrinsically impossible because of the radical difference in views of what constitutes the world. For Almachius, power over life and death is ultimate authority. For Cecilia it is trivial:

>	Thou seyst thy princes han thee yeven myght
>	Bothe for to sleen and for to quyken a wight;

> Thou, that ne mayst but oonly lyf bireve,
>
> Thou hast noon oother power ne no leve. (VIII,480-3)

Her spiritual profession is confident and "spiritually true." It is worth citing at length because it is the foundation of her Christian view of the world:

> "There lakketh no thyng to thyne outter yen
>
> That thou n'art blynd; for thyng that we seen alle
>
> That it is stoon—that men may wel espyen—
>
> That ilke stoon a god thow wolt it calle.
>
> I rede thee, lat thyn hand upon it falle
>
> And taste it wel, and stoon thou shalt it fynde,
>
> Syn that thou seest nat with thyne eyen blynde.
>
> "It is a shame that the peple shal
>
> So scorne thee and laughe at thy folye,
>
> For communly men woot it wel overal
>
> That myghty God is in his hevenes hye;
>
> And thise ymages, wel thou mayst espye,
>
> To the ne to hemself mowen noght profite,
>
> For in effect they been nat worth a myte." (VIII, 498-511)

But her analysis is impotent in the face of what theologians would call Almachius's invincible ignorance. The source of that ignorance is clearly understood by Cecilia: it is a pride that makes it impossible for Almachius to imagine a world larger than his own imagination, his secular philosophy.

This is a broader issue than the familiar question of the two truths: faith and reason. This is an extension of reason to the rejection of the possibility of imagining a larger context than its own. It is significant that St. Cecilia is both glorified and unsuccessful. Almachius is not persuaded, so the end of Cecilia in his world is death. But in the larger world that Cecilia's mind and heart inhabit her death is life everlasting. There is no doubt in the Second Nun's mind about who is right, but Almachius's intractability in his confrontation with Cecilia is as instructive as her martyrdom. It is simply impossible for Almachius to see, to comprehend Cecilia's arguments because they depend upon an act of faith that he is incapable of making. It is interesting that the argument should be in terms of authority. Almachius can understand his own political authority, but the tale's tone and tendency identify that as blindness. It is not that Almachius is irrational or that reason is to be condemned. But it is necessary that reason, as in the case of Cecilia, be informed. For now, Almachius does not suffer because of his reliance on secular wisdom. In "the Canon's Yeoman's Tale", Chaucer will explore the human consequences of such reliance. It is not that reason must be left behind, but that the formation of practical wisdom depends upon right reason, reason informed by faith and a consequent recognition of important and inevitable human limitations. Some applications of reason are dead-ends and ultimately self-destructive irrationality.

In the "Canon's Yeoman's Tale", the Yeoman is given the opportunity to transcend the constraints, intellectual and moral, of simple secular reason, and thereby to free himself to join the human community.[5] That the Canon and his Yeoman should intrude into the *Tales* like no one else and that the Canon should flee and the Yeoman should remain are further invitations to investigate the limits and capacities of reason and imagination and the nature of human community and commune profit. The approach of the Canon and his Yeoman is, in itself, enough to cause suspicion. Their shabbiness and dishevelled appearance after a hard ride to catch the pilgrims and join the company identify them as outsiders. The narrator has to figure out from appearances that the canon is a canon. Yet despite their bizarre approach, they are welcomed and invited to join the community as it proceeds towards Canterbury, *i.e.*, they are invited to become part of the pilgrimage and to join also in the serious game of tale-telling. The talkative yeoman enters into the spirit immediately and disingenuously with praise of his canon.

At once the ambiguities in the situation of the Yeoman appear. It will be clear that the canon and yeoman have been devoted to alchemy. What remains more obscure is the relation of the Canon to the Yeoman, and the underlying nature of the enterprise they have been engaged in. While the Yeoman is in some ways quite candid, there is a dark side. On the one hand the Yeoman praises the Canon: " 'He is a man of heigh discrecioun;/ I warne yow wel, he is a passyng man' " (VIII, 613-4). And he proclaims:

> "That al this ground on which we been ridyng,
> Til that we come to Caunterbury toun,
> He koude al clene turnen up-so-doun,
> And pave it al of silver and of gold." (VIII, 623-6)

Now, clearly this is not true and the yeoman knows it; he must admit, at the Host's questioning, that they are poverty-stricken, and the yeoman quickly pours out a less attractive picture of the life they have been leading. He enjoins secrecy and admits their failures, though at first he tries to excuse the Canon on the basis of the excesses of great intelligence. He is aware, however, that the Canon, a man of great gifts, has in a kind of madness gone beyond the possible. The result has been failure, poverty, and secrecy. They must hide like robbers and thieves: " 'As they that dar nat shewen hir persence' " (VIII, 661). He admits too that they have gulled many: " 'To muchel folk we doon illusion' " (VIII, 673), and that this is the cause of the discoloration of his face. As described by the Yeoman, the Canon's behavior is obsessive, but it is not dishonest; it was not for personal financial gain, at least not successfully: " 'It wol us maken beggers atte last' " (VIII, 683). The canon, a shadowy character, hears what the yeoman is saying and warns him:

> "Hoold thou thy pees and spek no wordes mo,
> For if thou do, thou shalt it deere abye.
> Thou sclaundrest me heere in this compaignye,
> And eek discoverest that thou sholdest hyde." (VIII, 693-6)

The Canon is not clearly a charlatan. A true charlatan might well be more successful than the canon. It is his secret quest for knowledge that he does not want betrayed (and perhaps some incidental misdemeanors.) The slander that he expects from the Yeoman seems more a matter of fear of discovery. He is secret and driven and, when the Host urges the Yeoman on, he flees.

The reaction of the yeoman, when the canon departs, is curious. Somehow he feels liberated. The Canon has exercised some kind of power over him and now, in the company of the pilgrims, the Yeoman feels free to tell the truth as he knows it. Simple accounts of the relationship between the Canon and the Yeoman will not suffice. There is no definitive evidence that the Canon is deliberately dishonest. It is his compulsion that has distorted his personality and driven him into secrecy. There is no sign that his tricking of other people has been for material gain. Indeed, that would have been a much easier enterprise. The guilt lies in his compulsion and his failure. He is an intellectual zealot foolishly and hopelessly committed to the discovery of forbidden knowledge.

The "science" of alchemy was, we should remember, in disrepute. Based on pagan sources, Greek and Arabic, it had not only been a suspect enterprise but had been explicitly condemned by Pope John XXII.[6] Since its aim was to change the substance, not just the appearance, of materials in God's created universe, it was as wrong as Dorigen's wish and the clerk of Orleans's magic. Although interest in it had been growing since the twelfth century, it was already clearly defined as off limits. Thus, the Canon's secrecy. If there is a simple moral failure on his part, it is the gulling of the innocent to feed his own uncontrollable compulsion. Thus, the Canon is by definition a guilty outcast and his shadowy appearance and hasty departure are confirmations of his recognition that he is living beyond the pale. The Canon seems beyond salvation, recognizing his sin but unable to do anything about it, unable even to join the pilgrimage of imperfect Christians to Canterbury.

The situation with the Yeoman is more complex and more difficult to assess, and I think we are supposed to be left with a blending of confusions about him. If his initial praise of the Canon is sincere, what then are we to make of the candid revelations that ensue? Indeed, why does the Yeoman feel liberated when the Canon flees? The Yeoman passes from praise of the Canon to outright admission of continual failure. Out of the presence of the Canon, he is able to admit that he was never able to put credence in the endeavors of the Canon and indeed hates him for having trapped him into the whole enterprise. The Yeoman's recognition may be a rewriting of history, but it is what he thinks now.

The structure of the Canon's Yeoman's sequence is odd. What is called the "Prologue" acts rather as what might be called an "Introduction" as in the "Man of Law's Tale". The first part of the Yeoman's "tale" is a long prologue, reminiscent of the Wife of Bath and the Pardoner. The second part of the "tale" is indeed the Tale proper. The "first part" is a description of his life with the Canon and it is, in one sense, confessional, but we should already be wary of the ambiguities that can exist in confessions. The Yeoman admits that his association with the Canon and alchemy has been his ruin. That is the burden of his prologue: the exposition of the Canon's obsessions and their deleterious effects on him, and the admission that all of their labors have come to nothing but financial ruin and an enforced habitation of the fringes of society. The Yeoman even generalizes to how alchemists are dehumanized by the process:

> And everemoore, where that evere they goon,
> Men may hem knowe by smel of brymstoon.
> For al the world they stynken as a goot;
> Hir savour is so rammyssh and so hoot
> That though a man from hem a mile be,
> The savour wole infecte hym, trusteth me.
> Lo, thus by smellyng and by threedbare array,
> If that men liste, this folk they knowe may. (VIII, 884-91)

They also have a harmful effect on those they dupe which is greater than the simple loss of money, because the audience/participants are drawn by their own greed into a desire to believe that leads them to make excuses, but the Yeoman is well aware that there is a difference between appearance and reality: "But al thyng which that shineth as the gold/ Nis nat gold, as that I have herd told" (VIII, 962-963).

All this seems like confession leading to a clearer vision, but some ambiguities remain. In the Yeoman's condemnation of the Canon's activities, he cannot help but show off his own knowledge of the complex techniques. Even if he is free of the influence of the Canon, he is not free of the fascination with the "secret" processes that he has been privy to. Even as he condemns the intellectual pride and stubbornness of the Canon, he is not able to free himself entirely from a certain pride in the knowledge, fruitless as it is, that he has become privy to. The Yeoman's "confession" is an indictment of the Canon, of alchemy, and of the shady dealings that the Canon's obsessions impel him to. There is, however, a simultaneous betrayal of the Yeoman's own fascination that has trapped him with the Canon for so long. It is only by entry into the company of the pilgrims that his regeneration can begin, but the regeneration is not complete. To renounce sin and error is not necessarily to fully recognize it for what it is or to renounce its attractions. The joining of the pilgrimage is a first step in the opportunity it provides. The confessional first part of the Tale is a next step towards condemnation of the sin primarily on the basis of its ineffectiveness and self-destructiveness; the quest for the philosopher's stone is seen as a futile enterprise for human beings. But there is a final stage that the Yeoman must pass through and that comes in the telling of his Tale. At the end of Part One he is able to say the right thing:

> He that semeth the wiseste, by Jhesus,
>
> Is moost fool, whan it cometh to the preef;
>
> And he that semeth trewest is a theef. (VIII, 967-9)

Human wisdom is illusory, especially as it aspires to more than the proper sphere of mankind. But what that means for the moral life is an interpretation and application that the Yeoman, at least at this point, can only make in a significant fiction: a fiction that tells the truth more clearly than the apparently intellectual world of the canon can ever hope to do.

The Yeoman insists that the clearly evil and self-consciously duplicitous canon in his Tale is not the Canon he has served:

> This chanon was my lord, ye wolden weene?
>
> Sire hoost, in feith, and by the hevenes queene,
>
> It was another chanoun, and nat hee,

>That kan an hundred foold moore subtiltee. (VIII, 1088-91)

Why is there this insistence which raises rather than lowers our sense that there is some connection, even if only metaphoric, between the yeoman's Canon and the canon in the tale? What is the yeoman doing, and what does he mean to be doing? Where is he in his own spiritual regeneration, and what does his experience have to tell us about alchemy and the limits of human knowledge?

The Canon in the Yeoman's Tale proper is clearly evil in that he is a conscious deceiver whose goal is gain rather than the proof of an erroneous (heretical) theory. And the Yeoman clearly tells the Tale as a parable of the uses of pretended alchemy for deception. That it is a priest who is duped by the fraudulent alchemical trickery of the canon is in itself significant: the clergy are as vulnerable as the laity, because of their greed; the chicanery of the evil canon is merely a method to turn gold into nothing for the dupe. The significance of this simple moral tale that condemns alchemy as a means of fraud is intensified by the Yeoman's vigorous outbursts against the practice (*e.g.*, VIII, 1402-24), though it is further complicated by the subsequent citation of authorities, which add a "literary" flavor. Still, the vehemence of these lines suggests that the incident may be out of personal experience, even though the Yeoman has insisted that the canon in the Tale is not his own Canon and has decorated his anger with learned references. Again Chaucer has made a suggestion, neither proved nor insisted upon, but not clearly controverted by the Yeoman. And later, when the Yeoman rails against the canon in his tale (VIII, 1299-307), one suspects an underlying source for the warmth of this condemnation as he proceeds to detail the "fictional" canon's means of deception. This explanation itself is peppered with antipathy to the canon. At VIII, 1402, the Yeoman turns his attention directly to the question of the emptiness and perversity of alchemy. Then in VIII, 1388-1401, he modulates from the criticism of fraud and greed back to alchemy itself. The Yeoman confronts alchemy directly, cites philosophers, and concludes with conventional Christian doctrine:

>Thanne conclude I thus, sith that God of hevene

> Ne wil nat that the philosophres nevene
> How that a man shal come unto this stoon,
> I rede, as for the beste, lete it goon.
> For whoso maketh God his adversarie,
> As for to werken any thyng in contrarie
> Of his wil, certes, never shal he thryve,
> Thogh that he multiplie terme of his lyve. (VIII, 1472-9)

The source of the Yeoman's final condemnation is clear, unassailable Christian doctrine. To engage in alchemy is to attempt to understand "Goddes privitee," that which God would not have us understand, that which ought to remain beyond human reason because it is beyond human powers.

We are left with several key loci of perplexity in the Yeoman's whole presentation. Why does he praise the Canon but feel liberated by his disappearance? Why does he describe the trials and tribulations of himself and his own Canon with such relish even as he is ostensibly demonstrating the futility of alchemy and personifying its dehumanizing effects? Why does the Yeoman combine his exposure of alchemy as fraud with a condemnation of the greed of the "canon in the tale" that is so intense as to make us wonder whether this indeed is his own Canon and he is denying it? Why does he return at the end of his fiction not to the moral thereof, strictly speaking greed, but to a condemnation of alchemy itself on traditional theological grounds? He shifts from a demonstration of fraud to a condemnation of the means of the fraud.

All of these uncertainties can be rationalized. Yet I suspect that solving the uncertainties is exactly what Chaucer would not have us do. The disorder of the Yeoman's presentation is illuminating in itself and may illustrate a psychological quirk that blends indeterminacy of human understanding with a clarity of theological truth. Is the Yeoman frightened of his Canon and relieved to take refuge with the pilgrims? This is possible. But it is also possible that his situation is more ambivalent. He knows that his Canon is engaged in self-destructive behavior; their repeated failures prove this. And he is apparently frightened by his shadowy and ominous controller who is exorcised by the openness of the pilgrims. In Part One the Yeoman confronts his own demons, his own entrapment in his Canon's world of futility, yet its fascination remains. What the Canon has done is abstractly sinful but is not done with the intent to defraud. He is his own main victim. This is an analogue of the way we stand in relation to sin: trapped, fascinated, yearning to be free. In running off from the pilgrimage, the Canon is pursuing his personal ruin and theological damnation. The Yeoman has a chance like Chanticleer's to rescue himself, but the process is not easy. When he tells his tale, his fiction allows him to put the flaws of alchemy into a clearer moral context. However, the relation of the Yeoman's Canon and the canon in the tale remains intriguingly ambiguous.

When the Yeoman tells his Tale and puts alchemy in a concrete moral context, the effect is much like that of a dream. The abstractions of the first part are given a substance, a concrete moral habitation that is more intelligible to us and to the Yeoman. The Yeoman is learning through his Tale somewhat as we are, but his relation to it is necessarily different because he made it. This is not a simple process whereby the Yeoman is freed and reflects freely. His internal evolutions are more complex, and perhaps less complete. The condemnation of alchemy, given moral substance in the dream-like world of fiction, does not so much provide a rational dissection of the intrinsic evils of alchemy as an offense against God and his power over creation as it provides an epiphany for the Yeoman which he, through the concretions of the moral tale, can articulate even if he cannot fully understand. In the process, alchemy is made manifest as the fraud it necessarily is in the exemplum, so that we may understand that it is indeed a metaphysical fraud. Thus the Yeoman is able to articulate, at the end of his tale, doctrinal truths about the human condition which he himself may not fully understand, and the exemplum is the instrument that makes this possible.

Like the "Nun's Priest's Tale" and the "Second Nun's Tale", the "Canon's Yeoman's Tale" is oddly disembodied. Without auctorial commentary before or after, we are left to make sense of the theological, moral, and psychological experience of the Yeoman on our own. The Yeoman knows from experience a great deal of alchemy and at the end of his tale he is able to express, through authoritative philosophers and his own words, what is wrong with it. But his whole presentation suggests that he is in that ambiguous epistemological position that we all share as human beings, a state of knowing and not knowing. He also shares with us an ambiguous moral position. He can speak the theological truth, feeling it in concrete example, knowing what is wrong (that alchemy is fundamentally and necessarily a fraud) but it remains doubtful whether doctrinal clarity has been internalized. St. Cecilia, in her simple faith, has no doubt; Almachius, in his trust of the philosopher's stone, has no clue. The Yeoman is in that middle world that real human beings inhabit, neither wholly free nor enslaved, neither wholly ignorant nor wholly knowing even though he can speak with clarity the orthodox truth. For there is no doubt in Chaucer's fiction that alchemy is wrong and wrong in a very fundamental, perhaps *the* fundamental, way. It is the arrogating of God's power and certainty to ourselves. Whatever else may be in doubt, it is not for us to put ourselves in the place of God. And thus our dilemmas flow in knowing and doing. Yet it must be said that the Yeoman is, like us, on the pilgrimage, with his chances for welcome into the new Jerusalem alive.

It might have been well to move from the psychological and moral complexities of this representation of the ambiguous nature of the human condition directly to the transformation that is effected in the "Parson's Tale". But Chaucer intrudes the pesky "Manciple's Tale", which seems neither summative of our dilemma nor exemplary of the broadest ranges of the human condition. But we are not viewing the movement of the *Tales* as climactic. There has not been an inexorable placing of one building block upon another until we come to the summit of the "Parson's Tale". That in itself would be a falsification of Chaucer's project by means of macro-structure. So we are left to deal with this troubling little tale of transformation which is more than it seems to be. Nevertheless, the Yeoman has had his epiphany and, as Traugott Lawler indicates, "After such knowledge the poem [*Canterbury Tales*] seems less able to turn away from the solemn spiritual issues that have seemed deferable but never finally dismissable."[7] What does the "Manciple's Tale" explore, and where does it fit into Chaucer's metaphor of the indeterminacy of knowing? The "Manciple's Tale" takes us into a world of apparent sentence but underlying moral confusion.[8] The moral of his Tale fits the kind of verbal discretion that he must maintain if he is to be successful as the clever cheat described in the "General Prologue". The final advice, put into his mother's mouth, calls into question the whole purpose and efficacy of speech and its relationship to human action. "The Manciple's Tale" is a chaos that is continually at odds with itself. It is an example of how fiction and report can issue in self-destructive nonsense.

Phebus is a man of honor and talent, but he has taught his pet crow to speak. This is a capacity beyond the nature of the crow, a point that becomes more poignant when the Manciple goes on to point out, at great length, the impossibility of changing nature. Phebus is jealous of his apparently virtuous wife, but the Manciple insists that a good wife is a good wife and a bad one bad: you can't change the moral nature of a woman any more than you can change the nature of a caged bird that wants its freedom or of a cat that wants to eat a mouse. Nor can we change human nature, of which carnal desire is a salient feature. But the Manciple follows with an odd and quick juxtaposition. He claims that he is speaking of male behavior, then immediately reveals the infidelity of Phebus's wife with a man of lower degree. He speaks of her "lemman", and then justifies the use of this low word by insisting that words must be appropriate to the facts, that villainy should not be hidden with euphemism.

What commentary does the Manciple mean to make on nature and language? The crow, who has been raised beyond his animal nature, speaks the simple truth to Phebus. Phebus reacts with an intensity that causes him to murder his wife and destroy his own instruments, a separation of himself from his nature as maker of song. His subsequent repentance is as powerful as his initial anger, but in his emotional outburst he blames the crow and exculpates his wife. Now, this is simply wrong. The crow, speaking beyond his nature, has told the truth and

Phebus has angrily believed what he would. He punishes the crow, paradoxically, by taking away his power of speech, which has conveyed truth, and turns him a symbolic black because he is in Phebus's disordered view a traitor.

This leads into the extended advice from his mother, with which the Manciple concludes his Tale. The advice is long (IX, 317-62) and pious, but it is full of apparent moral confusion. While this extended maternal admonition is sprinkled with Biblical references and "home truths" about discretion, it is, after all, just a comprehensive "Keep your mouth shut." It is not troubled with moral complexities or discrimination. It may have served the Manciple well in his profession, but does it serve us well in the living of our spiritual lives?

Let us look at what is covered by the blanket teaching that concludes the Tale. The Manciple begins by insisting that we are all trapped by our natures: we are what we are, and this remains unquestioned within the Tale. Phebus raises the crow beyond its limited animal nature, an almost blasphemous God-like act, but the crow does tell the truth. The Manciple extols the virtues of calling a thing what it is, but then decries the consequences of candor. The narrative details an adulterous affair engaged in by a woman, counter to the immediately previous attribution of lechery to men. The calling of a thing by its name leads to passionate murder, and murder leads to self-deluded repentance (for Phebus rejects the truth that the crow has spoken) and unjustified retribution. What then, does the extended moral of the Tale teach, if anything? That we should beware of speech. So far so good, and there are good Biblical and classical examples for taking care about speech. But the advice goes too far in suggesting a practical rather than a moral course of action: never speak, whether from good or ill intentions.

In a very short space the "Manciple's Tale" has created both a moral chaos and a confusion about the uses of speech. The Tale is a rhetorical, metaphysical, and moral mess, mixing doctrine and expediency in a way that frustrates human potentiality and moral vision. Are we trapped like birds, cats, and wolves in our natures or is there a possibility of transcendence? Should we speak the truth regardless of consequences for ourselves and others? Are we capable of repentance? Phebus is not, or at least he is not shown to be in the Tale because he ignores his own culpability and falsely puts responsibility on the crow, who has in fact gone beyond his innate crowlike capacities by offering Phebus a vision of the moral truth. Phebus makes a hash of it. And the concluding counsel is not only shallow but beside the point of what has occurred in the Tale, except on the most superficial level: all it would accomplish is a kind of tranquility that would come from condoning adultery. The crow, who has been raised beyond his nature, simply tells the truth about the moral situation. It is Phebus who reacts with immoral violence and it is Phebus who fails to accept moral responsibility for his actions.

Now perhaps the concluding advice is good policy for the Manciple in his own life, but it is blind to the capacity for rising above our nature, blind to merciful reaction to sin, and blind to genuine repentance. As a whole enterprise, it calls into question whether fiction has the capacity to tell the truth, as well as whether man has the capacity for Redemption. It raises issues, in its thoroughgoing moral confusion, about sin, Redemption, and fiction which are very dangerous if we do not see them for what they are. The antidote, of course, awaits in the extended exposition that the Parson is about to give, but the "Manciple's Tale" offers a worrisome memento of the mixture of truth and error that fiction conveys. It is an amusing tale, but it is potentially a subversive one for the whole of the *Canterbury Tales*. Indeed, it makes us wonder how so much moral confusion can be packed into such a short, simple, and entertaining fiction.

Although the "Manciple's Tale" is replete with self-delusion, the fictions of the *Tales* are, after all, a reality of Chaucer's creation. Chaucer, on the other hand, lives in the reality of his own life. And we all live in a reality that transcends our capacity to confidently interpret the human fiction in which we live. What the Parson is about to tell us, and how he tells us, is a transcendent antidote to the deceptions of the multiply-layered fictional worlds in which we live. He speaks the incontrovertible truth, but as we approach his exposition that brings the fictional pilgrimage to a conclusion, we must also be careful not to assume that he has all of the answers to the fictions and narratives of our human lives as they are lived in this sublunary sphere.

When the Host calls upon the Parson, it is clear that we are not only coming to the end of the day, but are most assuredly coming to the end of the pilgrimage.[9] No matter what Chaucer's original plan may have been, no matter what changes he may have made or foreseen, the "Parson's Tale" is definitively presented as a geographical and fictional closure. The Host says:

> "Lordynges everichoon,
> Now lakketh us no tales mo than oon.
> Fulfilled is my sentence and my decree;
> I trowe that we han herd of ech degree;
> Almoost fulfild is al myn ordinaunce." (X, 15-19)

It may be odd to note its fictionality, because the Parson insists that he can communicate only unadorned sentence.[10] It is essential to remember, with Lawler, that "The Parson's job is to save souls, and in his Tale he shows us how he does it: like the Pardoner, he gives an exemplary sermon. He also teaches us the art of repentance."[11] Yet the Parson cannot avoid the fact that his straight talk is in the context of the grander fiction of the *Canterbury Tales*. Plain speech within a fiction cannot avoid being part of that fiction. This placement complicates his plain-spoken doctrine.

The sentence of the "Parson's Tale" falls into clear segments. The topic of the whole is Penitence and, in a completely orthodox way, he divides Penitence into Contrition, Confession, and Satisfaction. The second element, however, Confession, incorporates the Parson's extended commentary on the Seven Deadly Sins. Meditation on the Seven Deadly Sins is a necessary prelude for auricular confession, a discipline which has been prescribed by the Church since the twelfth century though probably practiced for a long time before.[12] The innumerable parts of the exposition could be recounted in detail but it is sufficient to our purposes that they are of unexceptionable orthodoxy. What is more to the point of the "Parson's Tale" is an examination of where and how this highly orthodox exposition fits with the diversity of the preceding tales: how its subject matter, method of presentation, and placement relate to the whole of Chaucer's metaphoric pilgrimage.

We must go back to the Parson's introduction to his own contribution. It would be, in his view, wrong to call it a "tale," except that it has been made by Chaucer into one of the *Canterbury Tales*. The Parson says that he will not tell a "fable" though he does characterize his presentation as a "tale." The distinction is important. In fact, he condemns "fables" on the authority of St. Paul:

> "Thou getest fable noon ytoold for me,
>
> For Paul, that writeth unto Thymothee,
>
> Repreveth hem that weyven soothfastnesse
>
> And tellen fables and swich wrecchednesse." (X, 31-4)

Thus will be *his tale* as opposed to a fable. This sets him apart from all the other pilgrims. He eschews both alliteration and rhyme in favor of a simple prose that will suit his sentence. And he immediately states his intention:

> And therfore, if yow list—I wol nat glose--
>
> I wol yow telle a myrie tale in prose
>
> To knytte up al this feeste and make an ende.
>
> And Jhesu, for his grace, wit me sende
>
> To shewe yow the wey, in this viage,
>
> Of thilke parfit glorious pilgrymage
>
> That highte Jerusalem celestial. (X, 45-51)

He is going to tell a tale, but not a fable, but he cannot escape living within the Chaucerian fiction. He sees what he has to say as the last word, the most important words that must be said, and most appropriate to the conclusion of the ultimate pilgrimage. No matter at this point that he is part of Chaucer's whole metaphor; he is going to instruct us in how things are in their most important sense, and do it in a clear and straightforward way. This is what we would expect of the humble and learned Parson of the "General Prologue", who is presented as an eager teacher of ultimate sentence. He distances himself from the fables that have preceded because he is going to present the simple truth. His is a completely spiritual exercise based on that most practical of all wisdoms, the wisdom that leads to salvation. Fables are fictions, metaphors for human experience; this is to be not a metaphor but the thing itself with regard to the most important issue, salvation. The Parson distrusts fables because they are subject to interpretation and may be misleading, and not all fables are conducive to salvation. The Parson is going to bring a resolution to the pilgrimage in its most spiritual sense. I would contend, however, that the ultimate practical truth that the Parson has to offer, in and of itself undeniable, is not a solution to the human issues and epistemological dilemmas that have accumulated in the course of the *Tales*. In an Ockhamite resolution for Chaucer's fable, the Parson explains what we know by faith and what we must do in light of that faith. It is eminently practical despite the fact that its epistemological foundation is faith rather than reason. Everything preceding has been in the realm of reason. It may seem odd to speak of fables as within the domain of reason, but tales, fiction, and metaphor are the human literary constructs by which we attempt to understand the world around us. True or false, they are instruments of human reason rather than the divine inspiration of faith. And thereby the Parson brings us back to the two truths, of faith and reason, of Ockham. The perceptions that can come of fabling, the human attempt to give significance to the perceptions of experience, give way in this last tale to the authority of faith. But the sublime, and necessarily true, insights of faith do not obliterate the human enterprise of rational understanding that the fictions have as their aim. As in Ockham our perceptions of the world, here multiple representations of the real world in fables, do not lose their relevance. They co-exist with the ultimate truths of faith and retain their value because human attempts to transform perceptions into meanings, which is what fiction and Ockhamite philosophy do, are not annihilated by the other truth. They co-exist in a human world that is harder to understand by reason than by teleology. As in Ockham, faith is the ultimate answer, but it does not solve the confusions and dilemmas that arise in our exercise of reason, here represented by the human attempts at fiction.

The truths, or rather indeterminacies, of fable/reason remain. The Parson does not answer, point by point, the rational arguments (the epistemological sallies and excursions) that the Tales have raised by means of fable, but he does present the other truth, the truth of faith, that is the key to the ultimate mystery: salvation, the coming together of the human and the divine, or rather the coming of the human to the divine.

To see better how this works, it is necessary to look at the characteristics of the doctrine that the Parson expounds in relation to the fabling that has come before. It will also be necessary to reconcile the odd position of the "Parson's Tale", both inside and outside of the whole metaphor of pilgrimage of the *Canterbury Tales*. Penance is fundamental to salvation, but, like all sacraments, it is a curious thing: it is both retrospective and prospective, and it is in reality what it symbolizes, a fundamental difference from human fables. Penance is retrospective because it calls upon us to look back, honestly and steadily, on how we have lived our lives. Contrition, genuine sorrow, at first felt but unspecified, must be applied to what we have done and not done. For contrition to become actualized, it is necessary to face directly what we have done and to confess it to God's representative, the priest. In order to do this it is necessary to examine our conscience; and meditation on the Seven Deadly Sins was, by the fourteenth century, one of the primary systematic ways to conduct this examination.[13] This is the crucial part of Penance, because it leads to self-knowledge. That is why the Parson devotes the bulk of his Tale to it.

Meditation on the Seven Deadly Sins, as the sources of all other sins, is the practical way to ensure that we have examined every aspect of our spiritual lives so that confession and contrition can be complete. The Parson allows for the traditional distinction between mortal and venial sins and with admirable and orthodox charity allows that the latter cannot be entirely avoided by human beings. But we must face up to the comprehensive moral inventory of the serious sins, the deadly ones, the ones that destroy spiritual life and lead to damnation.

The process is also prospective because Penance is incomplete without satisfaction, the retribution due God for our offenses, all of which are ultimately against Him. This is an important point: sin is ultimately something between the individual and God, even though acted out on a human stage. This is one of the truths that lie beneath the phenomena of perception and experience. Because Penance is also prospective, the Parson includes his very practical remedies for each of the Seven Deadly Sins. Penance is about conviction of ourselves of our sins and sorrow that comes from this recognition; it is equally a look forward, a determination about how we are going to live the rest of our lives. This interior disposition and determination is essential for valid Penance, for the achievement of its goal which is absolution.

Now, Penance is a sacrament. It is a process that not only represents forgiveness but in fact is the thing itself: forgiveness. It is in the nature of sacraments that we find the basic difference between the knowledge of fables and the knowledge of faith. Sacraments are indeed symbols, but they are simultaneously the spiritual reality itself; there is not the disjunction that exists in fables and in human epistemology. Penance is the precondition for the ultimate sacrament, the Eucharist, where the bread and wine do not simply symbolize the body and blood of Christ but are *in fact* the body and blood of Christ. Penance enables this union with God, which is the goal of human life, of human pilgrimage, of spiritual experience culminating in salvation. Thus the Parson's world is not a world of fables but a world of realities, a world in which the signifiers are the realities. The Parson is not answering, at least not *directly*, the doubts, difficulties, ambiguities, and tentative understandings that the preceding Tales have raised. He presents a world in which symbol is reality not instrumentality, leaving a necessary disjunction between what can be known by faith, and what can be known by reason which must rely on fictions, fables, metaphors, perceptions which are generalizable into that imperfect and honorable thing we call human knowledge but are not identical with it.

Thus, the truth of faith has a fixity that the truth of reason, however potent and necessary, can never have. In this extreme assertion, which is at the heart of

Christianity and especially of an Ockhamite view of human understanding, the Parson remains humble and puts himself "under correccioun/ Of clerkes, for I am nat textueel" (X, 56-7). This is the Parson's attempt to tell the truth that is tellable.

The *Tales* end after the "Parson's Tale", and presumably the pilgrims arrive at the final stage: the shrine of the martyr, the new Jerusalem, the Eucharist. Thus the Parson is set apart, in his enterprise, from all the other pilgrims. No matter how high-minded their intentions have been, their means have been proximate or instrumental rather than direct. That is to say, human doctrine, the doctrine of fables and metaphor, must all be seen in the psychological context of their tellers and in their heuristic means. Even if the teller is unexceptionable, and often he or she is not, the means are fictions and fables. And even if the genre is "legend," a saint's life, the metaphoric foundation of fiction and fable remain.

This world of metaphor corresponds to reason in an Ockhamite view of human faculties, because the world of human perceptions, which must be generalized into rational truths, operates like metaphor. What we perceive with human epistemologies is a world in which there is meaning, but the discovery of meaning depends upon the comparisons and arrangements of things into meanings. This process is valid and distinctively human and indeed it can lead to truth. But it is not the same as the truth of faith, the world of faith that the Parson lives in where the truth is the thing itself not something that the thing represents, and therefore not subject to the kind of interpretation that fiction and fable require. We will never find the "man of gret auctorite" to endow our fictions with authority, but that does not make the enterprise less human or less urgent. Indeed, to live entirely in the Parson's world of faith would be to deny the world of fictions and fables and metaphors, in which we engage in the essentially human attempt to figure out who we are and where we are. Faith merely has ultimate answers; reason and its handmaidens make the world in which we live and aspire to faith and salvation. But the ultimate answers are inextricable from the "commune profit" that is the closest thing that we will know on earth to salvation, and an instrument of divine reconciliation. Lawler makes clear that "The Parson's Tale is a vision of perfect community or oneness, on two levels: here on earth and in heaven. Both are brought about by a double communion, between men and men and between men and God."[14]

Nevertheless, the "Parson's Tale" does provide an "ultimate" answer. Even if it does not resolve the issues that the *Tales* have raised about the perplexities of living in this world, the Parson can show how to live in order to have a hope of the next. In this juxtaposition of worlds, terrestrial and heavenly, the placement of the "Parson's Tale" is significant. Certainly, its location at the end of the *Tales*, as the pilgrims, ready or not, are about to enter Canterbury, gives it pride of place, and Chaucer emphasizes the atmosphere in which it is presented with its strong "sense of an ending." Still, the "Parson's Tale" is within the *Tales*. It may have a view beyond, but it is, in the structure "Chaucer" has created, a view from within and it is important, both philosophically and metaphorically, that within the *Tales* the pilgrims do not actually enter Canterbury.

At this important juncture, I again refer to the maker of the whole as "Chaucer", that inseparable amalgam of poet and pilgrim, maker and participant, because the ambiguity of this persona is relevant to the placement and meaning of the "Parson's Tale" within the whole. In the "General Prologue", in the "Introduction of the Man of Law's Tale", and in "Thopas" and "Melibee" the interpenetration of those two identities, the fusion of two different levels of reality, has been most prominent, although it is maintained throughout. It is within the compass of this blended vision that the "Parson's Tale" must finally be appreciated. The blended sensibility of "Chaucer" is at the heart of the fusion that would simultaneously place the resolution by faith in the context of human condition, not outside it as a magisterial force. The Parson is last and true, but is also among the *Tales*, appropriate to a narrator who places himself inside and outside his narrative not alternatively but as a single, indivisible entity.

The complexity of that Chaucerian "identity" becomes clearer when we apply to the "Parson's Tale" as well as to all of the *Tales* the perspective of the "Retraction". Obviously the "Retraction" is troubling in some ways, and many critics have wished that it would go away or be easily dismissed; others see it as Chaucer's sincere renunciation of a large part of his own work. This latest opinion has been extant since Thomas Gascoigne's suggestion (1434-1457) of a death-bed conversion by Chaucer.[15] This is absurd on the face of it, no matter how many death-bed conversions can be cited. The "Retraction" is connected to the "Parson's Tale" and thereby connected to the whole of the *Canterbury Tales* in twenty-eight manuscripts. Thus it seems an integral part of the *Tales*, as much as the "General Prologue", not a guilt-ridden, eleventh hour addition. It is, paradoxically, integrally connected with a work that includes some of the very narratives that it renounces. It is difficult even to see the "Retraction" as an epiphany occasioned by the penitential doctrine so fully detailed by the Parson and apparently alluded to in the "Retraction" (X, 1089). It is equally difficult to see the "Retraction" as Chaucer's clever way of incorporating a record of his bibliography; if true, this is unimportant.

The real question is in the language of renunciation of a large part of a literary career, including a work to which the renunciation is inextricably linked. Neither internal nor external evidence supports the notion that the "Retraction" is an awakening by Chaucer. The idea that Chaucer is protecting himself from retribution by the Church is nonsensical. There is nothing in Chaucer that would attract such attention and little motive for the Church, especially in its confused late fourteenth century state, to pay attention to or single out a privileged person like Chaucer. So sincere death-bed conversion and nervousness about the Church seem highly improbable.

Similarly, an epiphany based on the "Parson's Tale" seems improbable, at least in any simple, literal way. After all, Chaucer apparently made no attempt to suppress any of his works that he "indicts." The composition of the *Tales* was a long process that Chaucer worked on, off and on, throughout his own life. That roughly eighty-three manuscripts could be produced after his death does not suggest any attempt on his part to suppress the narratives that are condemned in the "Retraction". And this is in the context of a Chaucer who seems to have been tinkering with the *Tales* up to the time of his death. The inconsistencies in the *Tales*–the change from four tales to one, the change to a one-way journey (or if one believes the Bradshaw shifters, the reverse), the reference of the Shipman and Manciple to themselves as women, the slippery placement of Fragment VI–all suggest that the *Tales* were being refined, reshaped, revised, not abandoned. Benson's comment,"The Retraction leaves us in no doubt that, unfinished, unpolished, and incomplete, as *The Canterbury Tales* may be, Chaucer is finished with it," is not conclusively borne out by the apparent continuation of tinkering.[16] Thus there seems to have been no reason to expunge the offending narratives and no disposition on Chaucer's part to do so.

Indeed, evidence within the *Tales* suggests that the "offending matter" was very much embraced by Chaucer. The "Introduction to the Man of Law's Tale" cites approvingly, if enviously, some of the "offending matter." And back in the "General Prologue" the narrator has warned us that as a matter of accuracy he must report exactly, to the best of his ability, what each of the pilgrims said. Although the excuse is playful and to some extent disingenuous, it is also a statement of the kind of accurate record the *Tales* will be. There is a moral obligation to truth in recording that the "Retraction" conflicts with if it is taken too literally or somberly. In any case, there is no possibility that the "tales that sounen into sin" could be taken as moral ideals or injunctions to sin in the whole context of the *Tales*. This responsibility to truth is asserted at the beginning of the "Miller's Tale":

> And therfore every gentil wight I preye,
> For Goddes love, demeth nat that I seye
> Of yvel entente, but for I moot reherce
> Hir tales alle, be they bettre or werse,
> Or elles falsen som of my mateere.
> And therfore, whoso list it nat yheere,
> Turne over the leef and chese another tale. (I, 3171-7)
> Blameth nat me if that ye chese amys. (I, 3181)

It is the last line that is most devilish when we try to consider what should or should not be censored. We may indeed be making a mistake if we pass over the Miller's obscenity. Finally, there is the repeated injunction that "al that writen is,/ To oure doctrine it is ywrite, ywis" (VII, 3441-2). Of course, it is especially tantalizing that this saw, familiar from St. Paul, to St. Augustine, to "moral Gower," should also be inserted into the "Retraction".

The possibility that the "Retraction" is wholly ironic, perhaps to the point of cynicism, is at least equally unattractive. What, then, is Chaucer doing in the "Retraction", if it is neither wholly ironic nor a repudiation of a large number of his fictions? I think the answer lies in the way that Chaucer can take advantage of the very literary mode that the "Retraction" is, a palinode, that most conventional of conventional endings so popular in the Middle Ages and to be used again by Chaucer in *Troilus and Criseyde*. In considering the "Retraction" precisely as a palinode, the question must be addressed as to who is the speaker. Is it Chaucer the pilgrim (as character or ironic *ficelle*)? That would be impossible because that voice literally cannot exist in the world of this palinode. Is it Chaucer the poet (maker of the *Canterbury Tales* as creator of the pilgrim or ironic voice)? Perhaps, but if such is the case, this is a very odd way for this Chaucer to speak. Is it "Chaucer", the compounded and interpenetrated entity which makes distinctions between poet and pilgrim, ironist and *ficelle*, impossible? This, too, seems unlikely because the compound has life in the *Tales* not in the abstracted world of the "Retraction".

I would suggest, rather, that the "Retraction" is the voice of Chaucer, *in propria persona*, beyond even Chaucer as poet. If that is the case, what is he doing with the "Retraction" as palinode? The answer I believe is in the combination of the very artificiality of the palinode with the sincerity of the voice that speaks within it. Chaucer, speaking as himself here, as Chaucer the fourteenth century human being, concludes the *Tales* with a final ineluctable paradox: a statement that is both true and not true simultaneously, a self-contradiction that is the mirror of human beings living their lives suspended between time and eternity.

Somehow, the ultimate penance spoken in the "Retraction" cannot wipe out the experience of being human, as we are reminded by the inclusion of the "written for our doctrine" refrain. In one sense, the palinode is a proper response to the "Parson's Tale"; in another, it is inadequate to the *Tales* as a whole (or the corpus as a whole.) That is the advantage of a palinode: in its sheer conventionality it allows self-contradiction; it can be sincere and artificial simultaneously as it speaks of ultimate truths. And this paradox is a mirror of the human condition.

Chapter VII: Paradigm Lost—*Troilus and Criseyde*

It is a daunting prospect to write about *Troilus and Criseyde*. The poem has attracted the commentary of many learned critics. Almost all have something instructive to offer, but the poem is so rich and various, so full of contending ideas, that no generalization about it takes the poem fully into account. Hardly a scene has not received an abundance of commentary, often contradictory, and not an interpretation has been tried that does not, at least by omission, somewhat fail to grasp the whole. One is tempted to line by line explication, but that too would slight some theme, miss some nuance. This chaos is perversely comforting. I console myself that I will not attempt a comprehensive interpretation of the poem, but will concentrate on the poem as itself an artefact of interpretation consonant with my views on the dream-visions and the *Canterbury Tales*.[1]

The narrative is a story of the power of love, particularly of love as conceived through the conventions of courtly love.[2] But those conventions themselves, if not undermined, are made to seem precarious in our view even before the decline in Books IV and V. It is not that the conventions of courtly romance are ridiculed or even satirized, but that they are examined, their features played out in detail, in such a way as to give us cause for trepidation about the future. It is also a story of rise and fall in Fortune, a Medieval tragedy or some more complicated tragedy or, according to some, not a tragedy at all.[3] In some way, its conclusion seems to suggest an admonition to *contemptus mundi*, but as with the "Retraction" to the *Canterbury Tales* the palinode does not seem to have the power to cancel out the hopes, fears, and imaginations of the preceding fiction. The narrative is also a story, influenced by Boethius, of the operations of Fate, Fortune, and Free Will. Yet, even here, what is said in the tale cannot be unsaid, what is done cannot be wholly undone in the palinode, and consequently it is hard to see the whole simply as a cautionary tale. So it is a romance, a Medieval tragedy, and consolation, but it is also an unhappy romance, a thwarted tragedy, and scant consolation. Each mode is present in a way that is both potent and attenuated, thereby representing inconclusive visions and indeterminate ideologies that characterize the human condition.

If genre is used in such an effectively slippery way, it is all the more important to examine the consciousness that guides the unfolding of the narrative. This is a more complex enterprise than is ordinarily the case in romance or tragedy; the complexity of vision is the result of a multiplicity of perspectives and a modulation of voice that shape the narrative and complicate both the triumph of love and the fall from high place. The first person narrator intrigues and engages us as we try to better understand the story, even when we have reservations or suspicions about the narrative he recounts and his sense of the significance of it. He attributes his story to the fictional authority Lollius,[4] but his first reference to his source does not come until I, 394 and even there it is clear that the Song of Troilus is his own invention, meant to be in the spirit of the "sentence" of Lollius. Now, the existence of Lollius somewhere in the background, even if he is a fiction, gives an authority to the speaker's narrative. But it also calls our attention to the importance of the narrator himself as more than translator. His sensibility is present throughout in his generous sympathy for his characters in the exaltations and the agonies of their fate. Indeed, he seems more than a little in love with Criseyde himself, and that attachment is not trivial or comical. The greater problem, however, is in the transformation of the narrator from the persona clearly established at the beginning of Book I and sustained more or less throughout, the "servant of the servants of Love," to the moral speaker who at the end of Book V puts his work under the correction of "moral Gower" and "philosophical Strode."

It is possible to argue, I know, that the narrator is supplanted by another graver and more philosophical voice near the end of the poem. I will propose, however, that it is impossible to identify such a radical shift. If such were the case, we would be left with a narrator who has himself had a remarkable epiphany during the course of the story or with a very perplexing discontinuity indeed. I will approach the narrator of the eighth spheres of Gower and Strode later. Here let us take a look at how he presents himself as he sets out upon his narrative. In his self-styled capacity as "the servant of the servants of Love," he identifies himself as both above and below the pains of lovers. In one sense, as the Pope of Love, fitting the spiritualization of the secular tradition of the Religion of Love, he is above the experience and not in fact a participant. In another sense, simply as servant, he takes on the role of doing the bidding of lovers. But he also sees himself as some kind of teacher, reliable or not, about the joys and pains of love.

His role, however, is as Pope and servant of courtly love, not just of love. We will leave courtly love, for now, undefined, for it has been amply defined and re-defined, even if never lived in the Middle Ages. His narrative is not of the triumph of Love, but of the pains of Love. The opening stanza is loaded:

> The double sorwe of Troilus to tellen,
> That was the kyng Priamus sone of Troye,
> In lovynge, how his aventures fellen
> Fro wo to wele, and after out of joie,
> My purpos is, er that I parte fro ye.
> Thesiphone, thow help me for t'endite,
> Thise woful vers, that wepen as I write. (I, 1-7)

His story is a tale of sorrow, indeed of double sorrow: the pain of the courtly lover and the pain of the noble fallen from grace. He melodramatically claims that his verses weep as he writes, a powerful pathetic fallacy, and in the succeeding stanza he invokes the fury Thesiphone as the ambient deity of his narrative. He himself is not a lover, a pose that Chaucer's narrators have used before, but he addresses both those who are currently in love and those who have lost love. His primary audience is lovers and his focus is on loss, loss so great that he hopes that suffering lovers will, for their pains, be rewarded with heaven (I, 22-42). But can the pain of love merit heaven? Can it even be prayed that God would solace forsaken lovers with death? There is a confusion of worlds here: the artful, if agonizing, pains of conventional love are entwined with a heavenly reward. There is a rational confusion between worlds and there is an emotional confusion in this narrator, devoted to the exaltations of love and devastated by love's transience. Whatever we are to make of the narrator's sensibility, and sometimes he seems sympathetic and sometimes arch, it is clear that it is more full of sentiment, perhaps even sentimentality, than of sentence. He is emotionally overpowered by the joys and pains of love, but he is an observer, not a participant.

Therefore, no matter how great his sympathy, his role in the poem is, whether we find him reliable or not, that of interpreter rather than experiencer. Crudely put, he is an interpreter of the Lollius narrative, but one whose sensibility is drenched in rivers of sorrow and sympathy. Even when he knows he is not putting the most sympathetic cast on events he is reluctant to do so, so great is Love's splendor and devastation to him, the outsider. He may mention refuge in heaven, but his pathetic energy is devoted entirely to the human experience of Troilus. It is with this mind and heart that he sets out to enshrine the courtly passion and unfortunate fall of Troilus, for from his perspective the fall *is* unfortunate, and heaven in his overwrought emotionalism is a consolation prize. To accomplish what he has promised he must first use the conventions of courtly love to establish the ideal, even if it is transitory, and then use the philosophical tradition of consolation to deal with the sharp pains of IV and V. He has the power to move us as the pain of love moves to the joy of love and the joy of love recedes into a greater still pain of love. There is, however, something about the way he describes pain and exaltation that has within it the implications of its own inadequacy. Thus as courtly love reigns, he repeatedly, if unintentionally, implies its limitations; and when ultimate pain must be born his consolations seem no more adequate. It is a version of the approximation of truth of the Knight's and Miller's

"Tales". Neither is adequate in itself; together they are as much of a vision as is given to human beings.

So let us begin with the triumph of love even though we know from the Introduction that it is human and impermanent, perhaps even a doomed attempt to make the human permanent. That ambience must not, in itself, destroy our capacity to enjoy the triumphal movement of I-III. The problem is that that joyful movement, as wrapped in the conventions of the courtly love tradition, is presented with recurrent reminders of its vulnerability. We know Troilus will fall, but we must see his rise from pain to pleasure with all the enthusiasm of the tradition. Such seems the intent of the sentiment-crammed narrator, even when this upward movement betrays cautions amid the glories.

It is significant that the whole story plays itself out in the fated context of the Trojan War (I, 57-63). Troy is doomed in this war that is being fought over the abduction of Helen. Calcas's pragmatic decision to leave Troy exhibits both prudent foreknowledge of the disaster that will come upon Troy and unfeeling treachery in his abandonment of Criseyde. This is the wrong universe for a romance. Except for the late highly self-conscious narratives like the *Alliterative Mort Arthur*, the *Stanzaic Morte Arthure*, and *Sir Gawain and the Green Knight*, the world of romance is a joyful and, for the hero, a collaborative one; the romance hero is placed in a universe that is just right for him, one in which, regardless of trials and obstacles, he is certain to be happy and successful in the end. This is precisely not the world of Troilus. Not only is the collapse of his society "fated," but there are hints, lightly and sporadically made, that this is a morally tainted world: the protection by Troy of the lovers Paris and Helen is at least as morally ambiguous as the tacit acceptance of Guenevere's adultery in the *Mortes*. So this is an odd context for romance, even though the conventions and sentiments of romance are superimposed on the world of the poem.

If Troilus and Criseyde must pursue their love in this fragile world it is only, with respect to the fiction, by "conditional necessity." The narrator insists that he is working from a source, Lollius. Now, it is true that that source is fictional and Chaucer or Chaucer through the narrator could modify what is in an imaginary source. Indeed, Chaucer could even manipulate the real sources, especially Boccaccio and Benoit, as he has in other places, if he chose to. But the overarching story, once chosen, has a consequent necessity because it is, as the narrator reminds us on other occasions, embedded in the incontrovertible authority of Homer, Virgil, and Statius. Thus, we have Chaucer's choice of the universe exculpated by the woeful narrator's exculpation of self by means of reference to his fictional source. The narrator turns away from the full story (he refers us to Homer, Dares, and Dictys) for the more circumscribed story "found" in Lollius; but still this is the wrong world for a romance hero.

The narrator's project is, at least in Books I-III, to describe for us the evolution of the perfect courtly love and happiness. He flirts with the ambient world in Calcas's departure, but he concentrates on the progress of the love of Troilus and Criseyde by persistently applying his romance sensibility to the circumstances of the lovers. Thus, we have the full array of the paraphernalia of romance. There is a woman who is put in danger and is beautiful beyond compare, even heavenly:

> Criseyde was this lady name al right.
> As to my doom, in al Troies cite
> Nas non so fair, forpassynge every wight,
> So aungelik was hir natif beaute,
> That lik a thing immortal semed she,
> As doth an hevenyssh perfit creature,
> That down were sent in scornynge of nature. (I, 99-105)

The exaggeration is so great as to border on the blasphemous, or at least to tempt retaliation from the devalued rest of the created world. Here we see for the first time the infatuation of the narrator himself with Criseyde, which will play an important role in our view of her throughout.[5]

As in a traditional romance, we have a handsome and heroic young man who is at first contemptuous of Love but is brought under its power by the conventional artificialities of the Religion of Love. Indeed, the narrator blames him for his initial hostility towards Love and sympathizes increasingly as Troilus comes under the power of that irresistible force. Troilus then engages in the requisite love-longing and the association of love with a kind of secular salvation and consequent ennoblement: he fights all the more fiercely because of his romantic devotion. We have a go-between who assists in the ministrations that will help to overcome the obstacles of a love that is presented by the narrator as salvific, one of the more dangerous if familiar doneés of romance. And, finally, we have the consummation of the love in the overwhelmingly beautiful culmination of Book III. The power and beauty of that romantic idealism cannot be ignored if we are to understand the narrator's sensibility, but more importantly invest the story with the emotional complicity of us, as audience, that romance demands.

The first three books present the paradigm of successful courtly love with all of the major accoutrements of that artificial, ennobled view of human love. We build to a crescendo in Book III, but even on our way there is some scratching in the violins and burbling in the brass. Troilus himself does not pose much of a problem with regard to the flowering of the narrative: he is young, passionate, devoted, even simple in his observance of the niceties of the conventions of courtly love. The doubts and difficulties arise with Criseyde and Pandarus.

Superficially the two are suitable players for romance. Her beauty is celestial and Pandarus fulfills the role of go-between, which is essential to the progress of so many romances. But there the simplicity of the romance construct ends. First, Criseyde is a widow: no disqualification here, but odd. The narrator also disclaims any knowledge of whether she has children (I, 132-3). The narrator excuses his ignorance by saying that the information is not in his source. But his source is fictional, and anyway there is no need for him to bring up the question at all. Thus begins the narrator's ambiguous presentation of Criseyde, which, within the poem, cannot help but be seen to be colored by his own infatuation with the character he has created. She is the perfect object of Troilus's love, celebrated in Book III, but even before that transcendent scene, what are we to make of her? Is

Criseyde old or young, ideal, fragile, faithful, vulnerable, manipulative, self-conscious, inscrutable? The narrator is overwhelmed by her, but is she as simple as he wants to, but cannot quite, make her seem? When Troilus is agonizing in love-sickness, the narrator claims ignorance about whether she is aware of Troilus' love (I, 491-7), but he says, frankly or archly, that she did not *seem* to be aware. This is mysterious. Is she unaffected (in a chaste or a heartless way), or is she acting? Even more perplexing is the coyness and wit displayed in the conversation between Troilus and Criseyde early in Book II (II, 50-595). There is a sophistication, perhaps even a sly coyness, in her sensibility which raises suspicions, which are certainly not confirmed, about how neatly she fits the role of courtly beloved. Is she dissembling, in the face of Pandarus' specious but courtly arguments or is she fooling herself? It is hard to eradicate one's suspicion that she perfectly well aware of what she is doing:

> "And if this man sle here hymself—allas!—
> In my presence, it wol be no solas.
> What men wolde of hit deme I kan nat seye;
> It nedeth me ful sleighly for to pleie." (II, 459-62)

Of course, quite properly, she will love him chastely.

Is Pandarus himself overstepping the bounds of go-between? His presentation to Criseyde of Troilus's love-longing is true in substance but fictionalized in Pandarus's presentation in order to to persuade Criseyde more effectively. It is a fictional account of Troilus's love-longing, though the love-longing is real. The sentiment is authentic but the rhetoric of the presentation is self-consciously conventional. It is hard to say how much of this Criseyde understands, *i.e.*, to what extent she is complicit in transforming convention into reality, in making a virtue of necessity, which might be laudable in other circumstances where genuineness of feeling as opposed to manipulation of the conventions is not at stake. The wit and sophistication of the conversation of Criseyde and Pandarus may be more than the simplicity of romance can bear. And Pandarus can make a pragmatic pitch that the love-sick Troilus cannot. Is Troilus out of his league?

Criseyde's "falling in love" is instructive if inconclusive. As Fortune would have it, or chance, Troilus rides by as Criseyde is reflecting. Her ambivalence, as the narrator is eager to point out, is attractive, but it is also highly self-conscious. It uses the language of courtly dilemmas, but suggests an underlying calculus of goods that goes beyond the love-ideal. She descends to a garden where Antigone's song urges love and she has a violent dream about an eagle replacing her heart. The progress of the love for most of Books I and II seems so much in the hands of Pandarus that it is hard not to see the attachment as shaped by his pragmatic, non-courtly manipulations. He essentially writes Troilus's letter to Criseyde and composes her response. He instructs them both in how to act and how to feel. Even if we acknowledge the conventionalities of the courtly love tradition, his management of the progress of their love is far too present and practical for us to be unaware of its instrumentality.

Yet Troilus's passion even if dangerous and misguided is real, and Criseyde's gradual descent/ascent into love is given all of the trappings of genuine courtly engagement. Love comes in at her eyes; she has pity on Troilus's love-suffering; she is falling but circumspect. On the other hand, she is quite self-conscious about her vulnerability and displays a wit and playfulness in her banter with Pandarus that suggests a self-awareness alien to courtly love. Pandarus verges on the cynical, Criseyde verges on the self-interested, but the narrator will not allow our reservations about either; his emotional commitment to Criseyde is so great that we cannot but accept his admiration even while a small concern niggles in our minds about the path that courtly love should follow. It is no crime for a woman to be playful, even coquettish, but is this condign with the total passion of Troilus? Pandarus's final stratagem in Book II, involving Helen as it does so thoroughly, may be the most devious of all. He is stage-managing the affair, and he seems without conscience, religious or courtly. In any case, the stage is set for the consummation in Book III. The behavior of the characters in Book III, brought to love and bed by Pandarus, is central to my view of the ambiguous and shadowed courtly world where the love of Troilus and Criseyde plays itself out. Troilus lies in trepidation of their first encounter. It will be the movement from this first love encounter through their intervening behavior to their transcendent culmination that will form the complex business of Book III. In Books I and II we have observed the experience of Troilus and Criseyde through the prism of courtly love. Although there have been ambiguities in the presentation of that paradigm for the understanding of human love and joy, the model is useful if we are conscious as Chaucer is that it is a metaphor which does not translate one-to-one into human experience, and if we simultaneously become emotionally engaged as the limited narrator is. In Book III, we are presented with the apex of romantic love and secular happiness in the union of Troilus and Criseyde.

The book begins with their first confidential, face to face meeting and, although there is some apparent naivete on Troilus's part, some worrisome signs of experience on Criseyde's, and some intrusions by Pandarus, the love that has been developing, however artificially, is confirmed in its mutuality. The forms of their bliss are established and made manifest in the language of courtly love: they pledge secrecy and fidelity and the effect on Troilus gratifies our conventional expectations: he behaves more courageously and nobly in battle than even he ever has. Now insofar as there has been any hesitation on our part in Books I and II, unshared by the emotional and sympathetic narrator, it is because we have, perhaps, noticed too much of the machinery of the paradigm and have noticed where the joints squeaked. The Proem to Book III, however, prepares us for the triumph of Love and that is what we get, mostly. Even in Book III, though, there are reminders, before we are properly overwhelmed, of the limitations of the ideal paradigm. When Troilus, out of gratitude to Pandarus, offers him any one of his sisters (III, 407-13), one wonders whether Troilus' enthusiasm has gotten a bit out of hand. Nevertheless, Troilus and Criseyde speak cautiously while they await the physical consummation of their love in a state of anticipation that is spiritually ennobling and humanly delicious. That it will occur at Pandarus's house is a bit nervous-making, a bit of tarnish on the paradigm, but as the moment approaches we are caught up in the anticipation and splendor. Never mind that there are momentary snubs to our sharing in this ideal lust. Security is important, if a bit too obviously stressed. Fortune is present, even if she seems momentarily benign, even cooperative. Troilus, sympathetically, is both charming and silly (III, 722-35), Criseyde is both eager and hesitant for moral and practical reasons, but also because of a sympathetic trepidation as the momentous moment approaches.

But the time has arrived: the most delectable consummation in the history of human love-making. It is potent and charming and suspect that Troilus faints and that this is the means of bringing him into bed and physical contact with a somewhat more confident and aggressive Criseyde. But there is a tenderness in the scene that transcends quibbling. They pledge fidelity in the most persuasive and high-minded way. The actual moment of union is handled with a delicacy of passion that cannot help but entrance and intrigue. The narrator, whose passion we can credit if not his wisdom, stresses his position as observer /outsider (III, 1324-1337). He leaves their bliss to our imagination. How could we be more involved and complicit in the high moment of their love? The narrator transfers authority to us.

However, as readers we must enjoy the consummation with a divided consciousness because they are engaged in an act of imagination at least as much as an act of love, and we cannot but be aware of some danger signs that surround the moment of moments, the apex of human amatory bliss. We must keep in mind the ambiguities and possible self-deception involved in this Christianization of the sexual: "Thus sondry peynes bryngen folk in hevene" (III, 1204). Even more, and even closer to the consummation, speaking of the way sex assuages love's pains, the narrator advises: "For love of God, take every womman heede/ To werken thus, if it comth to the neede" (III,1224-5). This borders on narrator-as-pander. Aware as we are of the limitations of the paradigm that has informed Books I-III, we cannot but wonder and worry, even if we are soon distracted from our internally spoken discouraging words. Bliss prevails, we share, but, of course, asleep or awake, Pandarus is in our room. And the narrator is once again teetering between innocence and heresy.

When the triumphal union has been accomplished, the lovers bathe in the afterglow with conventional and complementary Ovidian laments: Criseyde about the passing of night and Troilus about the coming of day. The love will go on, secretly, joyfully, and triumphantly, for three years, but even before we leave the chamber of initial bliss, the specter of Fortune insinuates itself. Pandarus warns:

> "For of fortunes sharp adversitee
> The worste kynde of infortune is this,
> A man to han ben in prosperitee,
> And it remembren whan it passed is.
> Th'art wis ynough; forthi do nat amys:
> Be naught to rakel, theigh thow sitte warme,
> For if thow be certeyn, it wol the harme." (III, 1625-31)

And the narrator, who knows the ending, is even more ominous: "And thus Fortune a tyme ledde in joie/ Criseyde and ek this kynges sone of Troy" (III, 1714-5). We have just shared in a transcendent experience, but even in Book III, the book of joy, we are warned that what is human is transitory and, worse yet, may even be illusory.

Books IV and V are the books of human decline. The narrator loses no time in establishing the context of reality and consequence that will be played out in these books. He attributes it all to Fortune, and although we can search for and find the human rationalizations that describe the ensuing decline, Fortune is a useful concept, and a familiar one, for describing the changes in the human condition that seem undeserved and/or beyond our control. And in any case, the narrator wants to exculpate Criseyde. Indeed, much later, towards the end of Book V, he apologizes to women generally for having to portray Criseyde as faithless and false. But the narrator is stuck with his source; even more he is stuck with the subsequent reputation of Criseyde, though this too is a contingent constraint and indeed he is largely responsible for the reputation he laments.

It is tempting to follow the fading of Criseyde: the intrusion of Fortune in the form of Calcas's velleity, her protestations of fidelity (perhaps suspiciously overdone) before she leaves Troilus, her rejection of alternatives, her dangerous and over-confident commitment to a temporary visit, and her gradual submission to Diomed and abandonment of Troilus and courtly love. Criseyde's behavior is curious and indeterminate, but its primary importance is played out in the experience of Troilus. Criseyde drifts from the structural model that had given this world its temporary cohesion, but we have been aware all along of the tenuousness of that courtly paradigm. We can live by fictions only so long as we manipulate them well and circumstances do not intrude. When the inevitable in the form of Fortune or Fate does intrude, the conventions of romance become vulnerable and the formerly delicious can become painful. Only tatters of the ravaged paradigm remain in Books IV and V. Criseyde's courtly protestations of fidelity are futile; Pandarus's practical advice to find another love is not only futile but anti-human as well as anti-courtly.

The focus is on the pain of Troilus, and it is delineated with a power that equals or exceeds his former exaltation. Even before Criseyde has left, while they are painfully dithering about what to do, Troilus stops to meditate on Necessity and Divine Providence (IV, 958-1078). Concerned about what his future will hold, whether it is foreordained or simply foreknown by God, he agonizes in Boethian terms. His philosophical speculations are indeterminate or at least ineffective. He rejects the notion that God does not know what the future holds; that would be an "abusioun," an error or absurdity, in Christian terms a heresy, because it would place restrictions on God's knowledge:

> "And certes, that were an abusioun,
> That God sholde han no parfit cler wytynge
> More than we men that han doutous wenynge.
> But swich an errour upon God to gesse
> Were fals and foul, and wikked corsednesse." (IV, 990-4)

On the other hand, if God does have foreknowledge, does that necessarily imply foreordination and the consequent implication that human life is controlled by destiny? Troilus's example of the man in the chair (is he there because of destiny or is it his destiny because he is there?) does not solve the problem. Troilus concludes that there is a mutuality of causes. But that does not answer the question of free will, which Troilus knows, but cannot prove, he ought to maintain. For, if the operations of free will (that which will come to be) are determinative, then that is a limitation on God's power, also an "abusioun":

> "And this suffiseth right ynough, certeyn,
>
> For to destruye oure fre chois every del.
>
> But now is this abusioun, to seyn
>
> That fallyng of the thynges temporel
>
> Is cause of Goddes prescience eternel.
>
> Now trewely, that is a fals sentence,
>
> That thyng to come sholde cause his prescience." (IV, 1058-64)

The problem with Troilus's reflection is its incompleteness. Troilus accepts that we have free will and therefore God does not cause our misfortune. But he stops short of reflecting on how we should behave when misfortune comes. Troilus is not able to make a virtue of necessity. He is left with the dilemma of fourteenth century nominalist man. Ockham had argued that it was impossible to prove foreknowledge and divine providence rationally, although they, like free will, had to be accepted on faith.[6] Now Divine Providence is the Christian elaboration of the consolation of philosophy. However, Troilus's speculations do not, indeed from a nominalist point of view cannot, yield comfort, except in faith. His philosophical ruminations, Boethian or Thomistic, cannot provide a rational substructure for consolation and Troilus is left with a crisis of faith—or a crisis that can only be resolved by a faith that transcends the limitations of rational capability. It is possible to compose the arguments, but, as Ockham tells us, these arguments may be consistent in themselves but unrelated to the reality of intuited experience, our only source of certain knowledge.

For now, Troilus is trapped in a world where he slips back into faint hopes that all will turn out well, and foolish consolatory injunctions from Pandarus to forget Criseyde and thereby avoid the whole problem. Troilus's sadness and perplexity are undiminished by ratiocination or by diversion. It is only the capacity of faith to transcend that can provide spiritual equanimity, and Troilus does not have that vision until he gets to the eighth sphere. Of course, it is not faith at that point but knowledge. However, translated back into the context of human life, it would correspond to the capacity of faith to allow human beings to make a virtue of necessity. The implication is that, granted the power of emotion to limit our capacity to know, human beings do not have the capacity (or it is hard indeed) to know in a philosophically certain way. Troilus stops short of the only knowledge that can give him consolation in the world that we know he lives in but that he overpoweringly wishes were other.

Consequently, we return to the relentless suffering that dogs Troilus for the rest of IV and V. His counting of the days, his rationalizations when ten days have past, his painful exchange of letters, and his agonizing resistance to the dream of Cassandra torture him to a culmination in his recognition of the inevitable when he sees the brooch on the armor Deiphobus has captured from Diomed and knows that Criseyde must have passed his gift along to a new lover. What a poignant, fitting, and painful moment of recognition: there is now, indeed, no hope. Both of the paradigms have let Troilus down. Courtly love has collapsed and Christian consolation has been short-circuited by the nominalist dilemma. He fights on, hoping only to die. He has lost one consolation and foregone the other; his life is mercilessly left without meaning. He does not even have the poetic justice of a confrontation, win or lose, with Diomed but dies an inconsequential death at the hands of Achilles.

When Troilus dies, the transformation of the narrator is as great as the transformation of Troilus. The narrator who speaks from V, 1786 is radically different from the narrator, the servant of the servants of love, who has taken us from I, 1 to V, 1785. First of all, the narrator abstracts himself from the fiction he has created. By addressing his book, and characterizing it as a tragedy, he is placing himself on, and drawing us to, a different level of reality. He returns briefly to note Troilus's death, but the perspective of the whole concluding section is different. In a sense the old world remains, since Troilus's afterlife is consistent with the pagan context of the narrative; but even that is translated into Christian terms in the concluding admonitions. We find ourselves in a palinode, not by radical shift, as in the "Retraction", but by modulation in the narrator's voice. This is a moral voice that can speak of human affairs with spiritual authority. By the time we get to V, 1856, it is difficult not to see the voice as that of Chaucer, *in propria persona*, putting himself under the correction of Gower and Strode and enjoining us to turn our minds to salvation.

The abrupt shift is in itself startling and instructive. Only a few lines before, the narrator spoke sympathetically of Troilus's melancholy subjection to Fortune: "Gret was the sorwe and pleynte of Troilus,/ But forth hire cours Fortune ay gan to holde" (V, 1744-5). And he made the kind of excuses for Criseyde and disclaimer of his own responsibility (V, 1772-8) that one would expect from the voice that has carried the story. But at V, 1786, the voice becomes that of the maker of fiction: we are on a different level of reality. We are implicitly asked to see Troilus's experience as a fiction and by implication as we proceed to see Troilus's world *sub specie aeternitatis*, there is the suggestion that the terrestrial life we live is also a fiction: God's fiction, God's creation. Chaucer's relationship to his book is analogous to God's relationship to the human world that he has created. Troilus has been transported to the level of the fixed stars, where worldly mutability and the domination of Fortune no longer apply. This is the world of theological stability and clarity of vision that the speaker now inhabits. He is with God and "as God."

There is no doubt about to the orthodoxy of the narrative voice in these concluding lines; they eschew worldly vanity, counsel trust in God, and reject worldly "appetites." However, the abrupt transition and the discontinuous transformation of the narrator are troublesome. There is no sign that the narrator has had an epiphany; we have simply leapt to a different narrator on a different level of reality. The very abruptness of the change suggests that, although the concluding lines are ultimate truth, they are a surprise, not an answer to the human dilemmas posed in the poem.

Theological consolation is adequate to our system of belief, but it is not adequate to the joys and sufferings of the preceding narrative. No matter how devout we are, we simply cannot *suddenly* feel that way. Like Troilus, we have trouble generating the capacity really to see, *i.e.*, to make the consolation of philosophy work in our lives. Of course, epistemologically, human beings cannot really see, except through intermediate perceptions that may include phenomena like fiction, because there is a disjunction between the emotional and rational. A corresponding disjunction also exists between the rational capacities of our philosophies and the ultimate truth of the spiritual. The modulation in the voice, even in the nature or character, of the narrator is the jarring representation of this radical disjunction.

Human life and love are not to be condemned, I would suggest, despite the clarity of the conclusion. The conclusion cannot take away the terrestrial narrative that has engaged us for 8,000 lines any more than the "Retraction" to the *Canterbury Tales* can obliterate the stories that it would ostensibly condemn; and, in any case, who knows better than Gower that everything that is written is written for our doctrine. Of course, we do live in a dangerous world of artificial forms and seductive, misleading phenomena. That world can bring joy and pain when lived at the height of imagination, even when we must ignore its imperfections and ultimate insufficiency. The fragility of human joy and love does not negate its intensity or attractiveness; some of the most beautiful and compelling passages in *Troilus and Criseyde* are images of human life, regardless of its ultimate limitations. Even the pain of love has its beauty in the human imagination and the representation of the human dilemma is not to be made bestial.

The palinode in *Troilus and Criseyde* thus seems analogous to the "Retraction" of the *Canterbury Tales*. It is a manipulation of levels of reality so as to make it possible for us to have a vision of a world beyond our experience, an intuition of the world and the God we must ultimately trust in. Thus, this palinode leaves us with two truths embedded in our consciousness. We cannot deny the vision that comes, however abruptly, with death, the vision that is mirrored in the abrupt translation of the narrator as well as of Troilus to a different level of reality. But neither can we deny the reality and value of human experience because we do not live on the eighth sphere but in a world where we must live with two truths. To deny the glories of human experience, however limited from the perspective of spiritual truth, would be to falsify the complex and sinuous world in which we work out our salvation.

Chapter VIII: Epilogue

Critical exposition makes Chaucer's canon seem more systematic than it is. His fictions are, in fact, poetry not philosophy, insights not propositions, visions not conclusions. The language of philosophy can simplify and categorize what in Chaucer's narratives is imaginative wondering not definitive resolution. It is the immediacy and indeterminacy of Chaucer's vision that makes his works profound explorations rather than categorical solutions. Chaucer's narrative forms and structures are not explanations or attempts at answers to the perplexities of the human condition. Nor are they a search for an adequate form. They are the discovery of forms that correspond to our perplexities, to our odd location with regard to the geography of stable truth. Thus, the transformation of genres, the ambiguities of voice, and the creation of ironies that do not offer us an interpretive vantage between what is said and what is meant but suspend us between what is said and what is unsaid transform metaphysics and epistemology into human wonder. The result is not confusion but assay, most decidedly not dogma but imagination, not science but art. It is the art of giving human habitation to our most profound philosophical conjectures. It is not systematic and comprehensive but visionary and suggestive. Chaucer did not versify Ockham or the nominalists or anyone else; he found or created the poetic visions that imagine the world in as precarious a way as their propositions describe it.

In the dream visions Chaucer invites us to examine the nature of the world but does not allow conclusive definitions. *The House of Fame* challenges our very powers to understand, by experience and authority, the truths of the world we live in, but withholds the "man of gret auctorite." *The Parliament of Fowls* presents a world in which resolution is suspended, but the value of hierarchy is acknowledged and the value of community is affirmed, especially in that great metaphor of harmony and generation: marriage.[1] *The Book of the Duchess* looks deep into the human heart and finds no anatomy of grief intelligible and no remedy possible, for only in profound sympathy can we share the agony of others—and it may be our duty, even our terrestrial salvation, to try.

The *Canterbury Tales* probes these issues in broader and more expansive human contexts. In Fragments I and II, the truth is suspended somewhere between the insufficient world-views of the Knight and the Miller and is given only a provisional stasis in the conventional tale of the Man of Law. Fragments III, IV, and V anatomize "gentilesse," the foundational virtue of human community, Chaucer's version of Aristotle's magnanimity—the binding virtue that encompasses all others and for which marriage may be the best metaphor. In Fragments VI and VII, human teachers reveal truths and frailties, sometimes of the world around them, sometimes of themselves, but ultimately colored by Melibee's acceptance of forgiveness as the means by which we can, tentatively and imperfectly, bring order out of chaos and infuse the human community with a generosity of spirit. As I have said before, not to know is not to know nothing. Although the foregoing summary is more sequential and segmented than the reality of the *Canterbury Tales*, there seems little doubt that when we come to Fragments VIII, IX, and X, especially as we come to the Parson, we are coming to the end of the pilgrimage and the poem. And in these Tales, community and reconciliation emerge as the dominant features of the tellable truth, though a community that only reaches its ultimate intelligibility and efficacy when the human is joined to the divine. How appropriate, then, that within the compass of the *Tales*, after all their explorations and revelations, the pilgrims do not actually enter into Canterbury, the New Jerusalem of Chaucer's metaphor. The *Tales* can only, after all, point a direction; they cannot lodge us in our safe destination.

In *Troilus and Criseyde*, Chaucer takes love itself as his theme and shows how human love and its secular paradigm, courtly love, are beautiful and ennobling but finally fall short of the divine love that truly conquers all.

Thus does Chaucer invent genres: dream visions that do not provide answers, fabliaux that tease thought, romances that betray authorial self-consciousness. He speaks in multiple voices that are given fleeting and partial authority. He makes ironies that tell us more than we hoped to know but less than we might wish. Insight is here envisioned; certainty is somewhere else. And yet it is our responsibility to struggle to interpret, because our struggle with Chaucer's fictions is the imaginary recreation of man's struggle with the created universe. It is our poetic, as it is our human, duty to try.

The world is God's fiction. To interpret God's fiction Chaucer creates the human fictions that scrutinize all of the major paradigms his world offered for the understanding of the human condition: ideas such as chivalry and courtly love, Fate, Fortune, and Free Will, and Boethian consolation; heuristic devices like faith and reason, logic and rhetoric, science and literary structures. By making his fictions, Chaucer gives a shape to the Ockhamite nominalist approach to human understanding of the world. By interpreting Chaucer, we imitate his imaginative struggle to interpret God's fiction, known ultimately and fully only by faith. By attempting to understand Chaucer's fictions, we share in Chaucer's imaginative attempt at interpreting the passions and phenomena that surround and define the human condition and human limitation. As Chaucer's enterprise is necessarily limited and indeterminate, fraught with the undecidable, our interpretation of Chaucer's fictions becomes a metaphor for his interpretations of the splendors and imponderables of God's fictions. Only by faith can the leap to the truth of spiritual realities be made by man; only by the hermeneutics of fiction can we share in this enterprise, recognizing our last end, but struggling to understand the divinely constructed reality–rich and variegated, complex and opaque, joyful and painful–in which we strive towards salvation while suffering from and revelling in the world God has placed us in and which we therefore cannot help but long to know.

Interpretations of Chaucer's fictions, necessarily incomplete, lead us to the circumscribed human truth; we engage his intractable fictions as he has engaged God's. This is the never-ending game to be played in earnest.

NOTES

Foreword

[1] The intellectual ancestors are: Donald R. Howard, *The Idea of the Canterbury Tales* (Berkeley: University of California Press, 1976); Robert B. Burlin, *Chaucerian Fiction* (Princeton: Princeton University Press, 1977); Larry Sklute, *Virtue of Necessity* (Columbus: Ohio State University Press, 1984); Jesse Gellrich, *The Idea of the Book in the Middle Ages* (Ithaca: Cornell University Press, 1985); Robert M. Jordan, *Chaucerian Poetics and the Modern Reader* (Berkeley: University of California Press, 1987).

[2] Quotations from Chaucer are from *The Riverside Chaucer*, third edition, general editor Larry D. Benson (Boston: Houghton Miflin Company, 1987), by Fragment and line number.

Chapter One

[1] See especially Burlin, Howard, Jordan, Sklute, and, always in the background, the critical corpus of E. Talbot Donaldson.

[2] See Sklute, *Virtue*, and Sheila Delaney, *Chaucer's House of Fame* (Chicago: University of Chicago Press, 1972).

[3] Gower, for example, restricts his comments on the made-upness of fiction to the opening of the *Confessio Amantis* and Boccaccio speaks directly of "story" only in the Introduction to the *Decameron*. The self-consciousness is not embedded in their narratives.

[4] One may see Gawain as triumphant or as a failure in his dealing with the challenge of the green knight. It is also possible, however, that his real triumph is in doing the best that a flawed humanity can in a world no longer protected by a romantic ideal of chivalry. See A. C. Spearing, *The Gawain-Poet* (Cambridge: Cambridge University Press, 1970), 219-36; Ross G. Arthur, *Medieval Sign Theory and Sir Gawain and the Green Knight* (Toronto: University of Toronto Press, 1987), 128-58; and many others.

[5] *Chaucerian Belief* (New York: Oxford University Press, 1989), 1-5 and *passim*. This may be a good time to apologize for the critical and misguided review I wrote of this book when it was published.

[6] Gellrich, 199, 203.

[7] Gellrich, 233.

[8] Delaney, 1. The promise stated here permeates her book.

[9] The view of Chaucer as involved in a hermeneutical circle is offered by Judith Ferster, *Chaucer on Interpretation* (Cambridge: Cambridge University Press, 1985).

[10] Russell A. Peck, "Chaucer and the Nominalist Questions," *Speculum* 53 (1978), 745-60.

[11] Sklute, 3-4

[12] Sklute, 21-22 and *passim*.

[13] Burlin, 239.

[14] See D. W. Robertson, *A Preface to Chaucer* (Princeton: Princeton University Press, 1962) and D. W. Robertson and Bernard F. Huppe, *Fruyt and Chaf* (Princeton: Princeton University Press, 1963).

[15] The sometimes confusing terminology of Medieval epistemology and metaphysics must be kept in mind. "Realism" refers to the Platonic tradition that located reality only in the Forms or Ideas. Nominalists, on the other hand, solve the problem of universals by seeing reality in things, in the experience of the senses, while ideas are seen as categories in the mind. An old, but reliable and tidy, summary is in Gordon Leff, *Medieval Thought* (Harmondsworth, Middlesex: Penguin, 1958), 104-14. Leff's later work, *William of Ockham: The Metamorphosis Of Scholastic Discourse* (Manchester: University of Manchester Press, 1975) is a fuller and somewhat moderated treatment of the same topic.

[16] For a sampling of literary applications of Ockham, see *Literary Nominalism and the Theory of Rereading Late Medieval Texts*, ed. Richard Utz (Lewiston, NY: E. Mellen Press, 1995).

[17] Traugott Lawler, *The One and the Many* (Hamden, Conn.: Archon Books, 1980), 13.

[18] See the expositions of Leff cited above.

[19] Although Ockham's views on logic, epistemology, and metaphysics were troublesome to Church authorities, it was actually his opinions on the temporal authority of the Pope, as in *Breviloquium de principatu tyrranico*, that occasioned the summons to Rome by John XXII, which Ockham avoided by travelling in areas under the protection of the Emperor.

[20] Peck, "Nominalist Questions," 748.

[21] Peck, "Nominalist Questions," 749.

[22] Peck, "Nominalist Questions," 748.

[23] Peck, "Nominalist Questions," 756.

[24] Gellrich, 203.

[25] Gellrich, 203.

[26] Gellrich, 234.

[27] Peck, "Nominalist Qhestions," 745.

[28] Peck, "Nominalist Questions," 745.

[29] Peck, "Nominalist Questions," 748.

[30] Peck, "Nominalist Questions," 757.

[31] I have put "two truths" in quotations marks because Medieval Christian nominalists did not really adopt the strict Averroist notion of the two truths of faith and reason. Aquinas tried to accommodate the two; even Ockham allowed for separate but not incompatible lines of inquiry, that is, reason has its own proper area but, when it fails, truth can come only by faith. See Leff, *Medieval Thought*, 211-24 and 279-91.

[32] Peck, "Nominalist Questions," 758.

[33] See Russell A. Peck, "St. Paul and the Parson's Tale," *Mediaevalia* 7 (1981), 91-131. This is a splendid treatment of the influences of Pauline doctrine on Chaucer's fiction. Peck notes that the idea that "al that writen is, / To oure doctrine it is ywrite, ywis..."(VII, 4631-2) is based on Romans 15:4 while injunctions against fable, as in the "Parson's Prologue," are from the later Paul (1 and 2 Timothy.) The doctrine from Romans is also echoed in Gower's discussion of the virtues of books from the past and the importance of books to the present in *Confessio Amantis*, "Prologus," ll. 1-92.

See also Daniel Kempton, "The Nun's Priets's Festive Diction: Al That Is Writen...," *Assays: Critical Approaches to Medieval and Renaissance Texts* 8 (1995), 101-18.

[34] Gellrich, 203

Chapter Two

[1] John M. Fyler, *Chaucer and Ovid* (New Haven: Yale University Press, 1979), 25.

[2] Fyler, 20-24.

[3] Fyler, 26; James Winny, *Chaucer's Dream Poems* (New York: Harper and Row, 1973), 23-27; A. C. Spearing, *Medieval Dream Poets* (Cambridge: Cambridge University Press, 1976), 10.

[4] See the arguments of Sklute, Delaney, and Gellrich. Other explorations of the matter are: J. A. W. Bennett, *Chaucer's Book of Fame* (Oxford: Clarendon Press, 1968); John P. McCall, "The Harmony of Chaucer's Parliament," *Chaucer Review* 5 (1970), 22-37; Donald K. Fry, "The Ending of the *Hous of Fame*," in *Chaucer at Albany*, ed. Rossell Hope Robbins (New York: Burt Franklin and Co., Inc., 1975), 27-40; B. G. Koonce, *Chaucer and the Tradition of Fame: Symbolism in the House of Fame* (New Haven: Yale University Press, 1979), 25; Bernadette Vaskeerbergen, "Chaucer's House of Fame: A Journey into Skepticism," *Medieval Perspectives* 9 (1994), 158-69; Stephen F. Kruger, "Imagination and the Complex Movement of Chaucer's

House of Fame," *Chaucer Review* 28 (1994), 117-34; Kathryn L. Lynch, "The Parliament of Fowls and Late Medieval Voluntarism,"*Chaucer Review* 25 (1991), 1-16 and 87-95; Katherine H. Terrell, "Reallocation of Hermeneutic Authority in Chaucer's *House of Fame,*" *Chaucer Review* 31 (1997), 279-90.

[5] Both internal evidence and a marginal note, apparently by John Stowe, in the Fairfax Manuscript occasioned a long history of commentary, now subsided, on the "occasion" of the poem. For a useful survey see the notes by Colin Wilcockson in the *Riverside Chaucer*, 966 and 976.

[6] For an array of opinions on "hert huntynge," see Helge Kökeritz, "Historical Word-Play in Chaucer," PMLA 69 (1954), 951; Paull F. Baum, "Chaucer's Puns," PMLA 71 (1956), 225-46; Joseph E. Grennen, "Hert-huntyng in the Book of the Duchess," MLQ 25 (1964), 131-9

[7] Sklute, Winny, and Spearing all weave this problem into their discussions of the dream visions.

[8] The "divided self" is prominent in St. Paul (Romans 7) and St. Augustine (Confessions VIII, 5.) In both, the self is divided between the knowledge of the good and the appetite for evil. For both, the answer is in an act of will. Such an act of affirmation does not seem possible for the narrator at this point, so he must follow another route.

[9] See Dante, *Inferno* III, ll. 1-9. A less noted but possibly pertinent allusion may resonate in these lines to the gates of ivory or horn through which Vergil must pass to return from the underworld (*Aeneid* VI, 893-901). Vergil's much disputed choice is betwee the gates of ivory (false dreams) and horn (true dreams.)

[10] Cf. Boccaccio, *Teseid* 7.55 for substantial correspondences in personifications.

[11] See Jack B. Oruch, "St. Valentine, Chaucer, and Spring in February," *Speculum* 56 (1981), 534-65.

Chapter Three

[1] Speculation on the order of the *Tales* abounds. It ranges from those who simply accept the Ellesmere order, through those who argue on the basis of the *Tales* as a one-way or round-trip journey, through those who take into account length of historical Canterbury pilgrimages, through those who would emend the order on the basis of speculations about editors' influences or Chaucer's changing plans, to N. F. Blake's insistence on the authority of the Hengwrt manuscript (Blake, *The Canterbury Tales*, London: Arnold, 1980.) See Benson, *Riverside Chaucer*, 796-7.

[2] See Jill Mann, *Chaucer and Medieval Estates Satire* (Cambridge: Cambridge University Press, 1973).

[3] V. A. Kolve, *Chaucer and the Imagery of Narrative* (Stanford: Stanford University Press, 1984), 369.

[4] Though, obviously, we keep trying. See note II, 4 above.

[5] The commentary on the "General Prologue" is massive, from Muriel Bowden's old, reliable *A Commentary on the "General Prologue" to the Canterbury Tales* (London: Macmillan, 1973), through Mann, *Estates Satire*, to *Geoffrey Chaucer's "The General Prologue" to the Canterbury Tales*, ed. Harold Bloom (New York: 1988) and beyond.

[6] E. Talbot Donaldson, "Chaucer the Pilgrim," PMLA 69 (1954), 928-36. Donaldson's view has been questioned by, among others, Bertrand H. Bronson, *In Search of Chaucer* (Toronto: University of Toronto Press, 1960) and John M. Major, "The Personality of Chaucer the Pilgrim," PMLA 75 (1960), 160-2.

[7] See Chalres Mitchell, "The Worthiness of Chaucer's Knight," MLQ 25 (1964), 66-75 and Terry Jones, *Chaucer's Knight: The Portrait of a Medieval Mercenary* (London: Weidenfeld and Nicolson, 1980).

[8] See my "Humor in the Knight's Tale," *Chaucer Review* 3 (1968), 88-94.

[9] The Ellesmere and Hengwrt manuscripts have space after the "Cook's Tale" as if the scribe hoped to get additional material to complete it. Many manuscripts insert "Gamelyn," which is certainly not Chaucerian. Although Kolve (*Imagery*, 257-85) argues that a fablian may not have been intended, it seems most likely that Chaucer found himself at a dead end and abandoned the sequence.

[10] Almost everyone who comments on the *Tales* has an opinion of Harry Bailly. A few special perspectives are provided by Barbara Page, "Concerning the Host," *Chaucer Review* 4 (1969), 1-13; David R. Pichaske and Laura Sweetland, "Chaucer on the Medieval Monarchy: Harry Bailly in the Canterbury Tales," *Chaucer Review* 11 (1977), 179-200; S. S. Hussy, "Chaucer's Host" in *Medieval English Studies Presented to George Kane*, ed. Ronald Waldron and Joseph Wittig (Woodbridge: Brewer, 1988), 153-66.

[11] See Morton W. Bloomfield, "A Tragedy of Victimization and a Christian Comedy," PMLA 87 (1972), 384-90 and Thomas H. Bestul, "The Man of Law's Tale and the Rhetorical Foundation of Chaucerian Pathos," *Chaucer Review* 9 (1975), 216-26 on the question of tone and sympathy. For an Ockhamist view, see Roger E. Moore, "Nominalist Perspectives on Chaucer's 'The Man of Law's Tale'," *Comitatus* 23 (1993), 80-100.

[12] See Kolve, *Imagery*, 297-358.

[13] See Kolve, *Imagery*, 360-71.

Chapter Four

[1] See George Lyman Kittredge, *Chaucer and his Poetry* (Cambridge: Cambridge University Press, 1915), 185-211. The view has been taken up by many others, notably R. E. Kaske, "Chaucer's Marriage Group," in *Chaucer the Love Poet*, ed. Jerome Mitchell and William Provost (Athens, Ga.: University of Georgia Press, 1973), 45-65. There are many variations depending on the critic's view of the order of the *Tales*.

[2] An especially perceptive reworking of the "marriage group" is in Howard, *Idea*, 247-71.

[3] Cp. La Vieille and La Jaloux in the *Roman de la Rose*. On the tradition of the "old bawd," see Thomas J Garbaty, "Chaucer's Weaving Wife," *Journal of American Folklore* 81 (1968), 342-6.

[4] The critical extremes are apparent in the notes to Benson's *Riverside Chaucer*, 865. In recent years, critical attention has turned away from such characterizations of the Wife towards concentration on her sexuality. Historically, however, few of the pilgrims have elicited such extremes of contradictory passions.

[5] St. Jerome, *Epistola adversus Jovinianum*, but also Walter Map and Machaut. See Lee Patterson, "For the Wyves Love of Bathe: Feminine Rhetoric and Poetic Resolution in the *Roman de la Rose* and the *Canterbury Tales*," *Speculum* 58 (1983), 656-95.

[6] John Gower, "Tale of the Knight Florent," in *Confessio Amantis*, ed. Russell A. Peck (New York: Holt, Rinehart and Winston, 1968), 58-71. See also the romance "The Wedding of Sir Gawain and Dame Ragnell," in *Sir Gawain: Eleven Romances and Tales*, ed. Thomas Hahn, TEAMS (Kalamazoo: Medieval Institute Publications, 1995), 41-80.

[7] The story has a long history. Chaucer's source is Petrarch's *De obedientia ac fide uxoria mythologia*, a version of the story in Boccaccio's *Decameron*, 10.10., which is itself drawn from folkloric sources. Other fourteenth century versions exist. See J. Burke Severs, *The Literary Relationships of Chaucer's "Clerk's Tale"* (New Haven: Yale University Press, 1942), 3-37 and 135-180.

[8] The tale is full of the anti-feminism found in the Wife's and Merchant's Tales. The tale has been seen as everything from an edifying exemplum to a moral outrage. No wonder that some have felt that it contains an allegory in which the "sentence" is at odds with the literal meaning; see Elizabeth Salter, *Chaucer's "Knights Tale" and "Clerk's Tale"* (London: E. Arnold, 1962), 39-65.

[9] See John M. Ganim, "Carnival Voices and the Envoy to the Clerk's Tale," *Chaucer Review* 22 (1987), 112-27; Thomas J. Farrell, "The 'Envoi de Chaucer' and the Clerk's Tale," *Chaucer Review* 24 (1990), 329-36; H. Chickering, "Form and Interpretation in the Envoy to the Clerk's Tale," *Chaucer Review* 29 (1995), 352-72.

[10] The Clerk's Tale has evoked an especially large number of Ockhamist interpretations. See Robert Stepsis, "*Potentia Absoluta* and the Clerk's Tale," *Chaucer Review* 10 (1975), 129-46; David Steinmetz, "Late Medieval Nominalism and the Clerk's Tale," *Chaucer Review* 12 (1977), 38-54; Kathryn Lynch, "Despoiling Griselda: Chaucer's Walter and the Problem of Knowledge in the Clerk's Tale," SAC 10 (1988), 41-70; Elizabeth Kirk, "Nominalism and the Dynamics of the Clerk's Tale," in *Chaucer's Religious Tales*, ed. C. David Benson and Elizabeth Robertson, Chaucer Studies 15, (Cambridge: Cambridge University Press, 1990), 111-20; Rodney Delasanta, "Nominalism and the Clerk's Tale Revisited," *Chaucer Review* 31 (1997), 209-31.

[11] Attempts to see the tale as rather light or comic have been effectively dismissed by E. Talbot Donaldson, *Speaking of Chaucer* (New York: Norton, 1970), 30-45 and Norman Harrington, "Chaucer's Merchant's Tale: Another Swing of the Pendulum," *PMLA* 86 (1971), 25-31.

[12] The Merchant's Tale has sometimes been seen as a companion piece to the Clerk's Tale. Not suprisingly, it has also been seen as related to the Knight's, Miller's, Wife of Bath's, and Franklin's Tales. See, for example, Helen Cooper, *The Structure of the Canterbury Tales* (Athens, Ga.: University of Georgia Press, 1984), 124-54 and 227-30. Parallels to other tales are often based on the *senex amans* and "love triangle" themes.

[13] *Aureolus liber Theophrasti de nuptiis*, extant only in Jerome's *Epistola adversus Jovinianum* 1.47.

[14] This view is consonant with the idea of the "marriage group." It dates from George Lyman Kittredge, "Chaucer's Discussion of Marriage," MP 9 (1912), 435-67, but extends to Germaine Dempster, "A Period in the Development of the Canterbury Tales Marriage Group and Blocks B^2 and C," PMLA 68 (1953), 1142-59 and Paul Ruggiers, *The Art of the Canterbury Tales* (Madison: University of Wisconsin Press, 1965). For a broader view, see Brian S. Lee, "The Question of Closure in Fragment V of the Canterbury Tales," *Yearbook of English Studies* 22 (1993), 190-200.

[15] See R. M. Lumiansky, "The Character and Performance of Chaucer's Franklin," UTQ 20 (1951), 344-56; Donald Howard, "The Conclusion of the Marriage Group: Chaucer and the Human Condition," MP 57 (1960), 223-32; Robertson, *Preface to Chaucer*, 470-2; Burlin, *Fiction*, 197-207; Effie Jean Matthewson, "The Illusion of Morality in the Franklin's Tale," *Medium Aevum* 52 (1983), 27-37; Douglas J. Wurtele, "Chaucer's Franklin and the Truth About 'Trouthe'," *English Studies in Canada* 13 (1987), 359-74.

[16] See note IV, 15 above.

[17] In Donald Howard's excellent *Chaucer: His Life, His Works, His World* (New York: Dutton, 1987), 432-3, I keep hoping for a full explanation, but Howard dismisses the issue in a sentence as a tactful interruption by the Franklin.

[18] The views on Dorigen are various. See, for example: Judith Ferster, "Interpretation and Imitation in Chaucer's Franklin's Tale," in *Medieval Literature: Criticism, Ideology, and History*, ed. David Aers (New York: St. Martin's Press, 1986), 157; Mary R. Bowman, "Half as Were Mad: Dorigen in the Male World of the Franklin's Tale," *Chaucer Review* 27 (1993), 239-51; Carol A. Pulham, "Promises: Dorigen's Dilemma Revisited," *Chaucer Review* 31 (1996), 76-86; Francine McGregor, "What of Dorigen: Agency and Ambivalence in the Franklin's Tale," *Chaucer Review* 31 (1997), 365-78. After all, I find Burlin's view (*Fiction*, 200) of her "almost giddy femininity" most persuasive.

Chapter Five

[19] The Bradshaw shifters have moved VII to a much earlier position and, indeed, VI could go almost anywhere. But I am again accepting that the Ellesmere is the order in which generations of readers have received their Chaucer and that the *Tales* are finished, even if incomplete. There is some reason to believe, from revisions within VII, that Chaucer had already moved that fragment and wanted it where it is in the Ellesmere.

[20] See, *e.g.*, Donalson, "Chaucer the Pilgrim." The word "Chaucer" has multiple possible impositions: the naïve pilgrim-character, the self-conscious character, the poet, some conflation of these. The situation is more complicated than a dichotomy between poet and pilgrim. That is why, whenever one reads the *Tales* again, it is hard to settle on "poet and pilgrim" or "pilgrim" or "ironic poet" for the voice of the narrator. Then add the complexity of Chaucer reading these narratives to an audience (as he almost certainly sometimes did) and the ambiguities may not be capable of definitive resolution – and that may be the way Chaucer wanted it.

[21] Chaucer probably drew the story from the *Roman de la Rose* rather than Livy. It was a popular tale, appearing in Boccaccio's *De claris mulieribus* and Gower's *Confessio Amantis* 7:5131-306. The little commentary that the tale has attracted usually sees it, at best, as modest Chaucer. E. Talbot Donaldson, in *Chaucer's Poetry: An Anthology for the Modern Reader* (New York: Ronald Press, 1975), 927, stands as a balnced example of the limited estimation in which the tale has generally been held.

[22] The ostensible object of the Pardoner's "sermon" is the "tavern sins": gluttony, drinking, swearing, gambling. See Gerald R. Owst, *Literature and the Pulpit in Medieval England*, second edition (New York: Barnes and Noble, 1961). On the behavior and reputation of pardoners, see Alfred L. Kellogg and Louis A Haselmayer, "Chaucer's Satire of the Pardoner," PMLA 66 (1951), 251-77 and Bowden, *Commentary*, 274-90.

[23] The list is impressive. See summaries in Benson, *Riverside Chaucer*, 905-6.

[24] See Nancy H. Owen, "The Pardoner's Introduction, Prologue, and Tale: Sermon and *Fabliau*," JEGP 66 (1967), 541-9; Robert P. Merrix, "Sermon Structure in the Pardoner's Tale," *Chaucer Review* 17 (1983), 235-49; Alan J. Fletcher, "The Preaching of the Pardoner," *Studies in the Age of Chaucer* 11 (1989), 15-35; Paul Shannon, "The Tongue as Sword: Psalms 56 and 63 and the Pardoner," *Chaucer Review* 27 (1993), 396-400.

[25] Boniface IX condemned the abuses of the sale of relics and pardons (indulgences) in 1390. See Bowden, *Commentary*, 276-9.

[26] Kittredge, *Chaucer and his Poetry*, 22 and 211-8.

[27] Her education at the Benedictine convent of St. Leonard's (Stratford atte Bowe) would have been pious but slender; see John M. Manly, *Some New Light on Chaucer* (New York: Henry Holt, 1926), 204-6. The debate over whether she violates the rule of her order has been extensive but indeterminate.

[28] The whole subject of the Prioress's anti-Semitism is vexed. Even the Parson may show vestiges of anti-Semitism (X, 599) and the disposition may have simply been a pious reflex since the Jews had been expelled from England in 1290. Of course, the condemnation of the "perfidious Jews" remained in the Mass until the Second Vatican Council. If the Prioress's anti-Semitism is a thoughtless though brutal vestige of Christian piety, it would not have been complicated for her by the perfunctory and conventional education she was likely to have received. In any case, critical commentary has been various and persistent: see Harley Long Frank, "Chaucer's Prioress and the Blessed Virgin," *Chaucer Review* 13 (1979), 346-62; John Archer, "The Structure of Anti-Semititism in the Prioress's Tale," *Chaucer Review* 19 (1984), 46-54; Allen C. Koretsky, "Dangerous Innocence: Chaucer's Prioress and her Tale," in *Jewish Presences in English Literature* (Montreal: McGill-Queens University Press, 1990), 10-24;

Emory Stark Zitter, "Anti-Semitism in Chaucer's Prioress's Tale," *Chaucer Review* 25 (1991), 277-84; Steven Kroger, "The Bodies of Jews in the Middle Ages," in *The Idea of Medieval Literature: New Essays on Chaucer and Medieval Culture in Honor of Donald R. Howard*, ed. James M. Dean and Christian Zacher (Newark: University of Delaware Press, 1992), 307-23; Philip S. Alexander, "Madame Eglentyne, Geoffrey Chaucer and the Problem of Medieval Anti-Semitism," *Bulletin of the John Rylands University Library of Manchester* 74 (1992), 109-20; Denise L. Despres,"Cultic Anti-Semitism and Chaucer's Litel Clergeon," *MP* 91 (1994), 413-27.

[29] The Tale of Sir Thopas is a medley of motifs and meters from contemporary popular romances. See Laura Hibbard Loomis, in *Sources and Analogues of Chaucer's Canterbury Tales*, ed. Bryan and Dempster (New York: Humanities Press, 1958), 486-559.

[30] In fact, it is a rather close translation of Renaud de Louens' *Livre de Melibee et de Dame Prudence*. How Chaucer takes a ready-made source and invests it with new meaning by incorporating it into the *Tales* is an accomplishment that deserves its own separate inquiry.

[31] The popularity of such narratives has been asserted as an antidote to the common "boring joke theory" by, among others, Diane Bornstein, "Chaucer's Tale of Melibee as and Example of the Style Clergial," *Chaucer Review* 12 (1978), 236-54. Yet, her assertion of the popularity of such tales seems, at best, merely true. Lawler's argument (*The One and the Many*, 102-8) that the tale is, in any event, central to Chaucer's Christian doctrine, is perhaps the most persuasive resolution of a knotty problem in historical aesthetics.

[32] The standard treatment of Medieval tragedy is Willard Farnham, *The Medieval Heritage of Elizabethan Tragedy* (Berkeley: University of California Press, 1956). The debate over whether it is Chaucer or the Monk who misunderstands Medieval tragedy, and how, is extensive. The most recent contribution is Henry Ansgar Kelly, *Chaucerian Tragedy*, Chaucer Studies 24 (Cambridge: D. S. Brewer, 1997); but see also: Renate Haas, "Chaucer's Monk's Tale: An Ingenious Criticism of Early Humanist Conceptions of Tragedy," *Humanistica Lovaniensia: A Journal of Neo-Latin Studies* 36 (1987), 44-70; Jahan Ramazani, "Chaucer's Monk: The Poetics of Abbreviation, Aggression, and Tragedy," *Chaucer Review* 27 (1993), 260-76.

[33] The disembodied nature of the narrator, undescribed in the "General Prologue," has encouraged critics to see the Nun's Priest's Tale as Chaucer speaking in his own voice. See, *e.g.*, Robert Kilburn Root, *The Poetry of Chaucer* (Boston: Houghton Miflin Company, 1922 [rpt. 1957]), 208. However, no such identification is necessary to appreciate the compassionate satire in the tale.

Chapter Six

[1] Many have pondered, but editors have preseved the sequence.

[2] On the composition of the Canon's Yeoman's Tale seperately from the other *Canterbury Tales*, see Albert E. Hartung, "'Pars Secunda' and the Development of the Canon's Yeoman's Tale," *Chaucer Review* 12 (1977), 111-28. The placement of the Manciple's Tale is so problematic that it led Charles A. Owen to assign it to the putative return to London: "The Plan of the *Canterbury Tales*," *PMLA* 66 (1951), 820-6.

[3] Howard, *Idea*, 305 and Lawler, *The One and the Many*, 145-6 present arguments for the interconnectedness of VIII-X.

[4] Its closest connestion seems to be to the Canon's Yeoman's Tale. See Russell A. Peck, "The Ideas of 'Entente' and Translation in Chaucer's Second Nun's Tale," *Annuale Mediaevale* 8 (1967), 17-37.

[5] It should be noted that many critics have doubted the full recovery of the Yeoman from his isolation and commitment to formbidden knowledge. See, *e.g.*, Howard, *Idea*, 294-8.

[6] See Edgar H. Duncan, "The Literature of Alchemy in Chaucer's Canon's Yeoman's Tale: Framework, Theme, and Character," *Speculum* 43 (1968), 635-8.

[7] Lawler, 146.

[8] Richard M. Trask, "The Manciple's Problem," *Studies in Short Fiction* 14 (1977), 109-16 argues along these lines. Arnold E Davidson, "The Logic of Confusion in Chaucer's Manciple's Tale," *Annuale Mediaevale* 19 (1979), 5-12 and many others object on the grounds that the Manciple is concealing his own failings. In any case there is a moral discontinuity in the tale.

[9] "There is a powerful sense of an ending in this final prologue." Benson, *Riverside Chaucer*, 21.

[10] The Parson cites St. Paul's injunctions against "fables" (1 Tim. 1.4, 4.7; 2 Tim. 4.4) and moral distrust of fiction has been common since Plato. But the Parson cannot avoid the fact that Chaucer has made him a character and a narrator.

[11] Lawler, 154.

[12] Auricular confession had been traditional since, probably, the eighth century. The Council of Trent (1551) rejected the argument that auricular confession (to a priest) had been imposed only as of the Fourth Lateran Council (1215) and affirmed that it was the ancient practice of the Church.

[13] Although precise distinctions of gravity between sins to be confessed were not published until the Council of Trent (1551), the use of the Seven Deadly Sins as a means of spiritual self-analysis was common from the early Church and emphasized in the fourteenth century. The Deadly Sins were substance for meditative prayer; see Thomas H. Bestul, "Chaucer's Parson and the Late Medieval Tradition of Religious Meditation," *Speculum* 64 (1988), 600-19.

[14] Lawler, 148.

[15] See Douglas Wurtele, "The Penitence of Geoffrey Chaucer," *Viator* 11 (1980), 335-59. For a survey of various opinions, see James D. Gordon in *Studies in Medieval Literature in Honor of A. C. Baugh* (Philadelphia: University of Pennsylvania Press, 1961), 81-96; more recently Peter W. Travis, "Deconstructing Chaucer's Retraction," *Exemplaria* 3 (1991), 135-58.

[16] Benson, *Riverside Chaucer*, 22.

Chapter Seven

[1] Even the number of full-length studies is enormous. A few excellent perspectives are provided by Sanford Meech, *Design in Chaucer's Troilus* (Syracuse: University of Syracuse Press, 1959); William Provost, *The Structure of Chaucer's Troilus* (Copenhagen: Rosenkilde and Bagger, 1974); Monica McAlpine, *The Genre of Troilus and Criseyde* (Ithaca: Cornell University Press, 1978); Chauncey Wood, *The Elements of Chaucer's Troilus* (Durham, N.C.: Duke University Press, 1984). Many broader studies, notably Burlin, *Fiction*, include helpful commentary on *Troilus and Criseyde*.

[2] Much has been written on courtly love, but two essays are especially apposite: Carol Heffernan, "Chaucer's Troilus and Criseyde: The Disease of Love and Courtly Love," *Neophilologus* 74 (1990), 294-309 and Adam Brooke Davis, "The Ends of Fiction: Narrative Boundaries and Chaucer's Attitude Towards Courtly Love," *Chaucer Review* 29 (1995), 352-72 (though this latter essay rehabilitates Criseyde a bit too much for my taste.)

[3] See, especially, Kelly, *Chaucerian Tragedy*. Although I am not sure I would go as far as Kelly in identifying Chaucer's notion of tragedy as the basis for subsequent evolution of the genre, the application to *Troilus and Criseyde* is learned and suggestive. A more conventional view is in Robert Graybill, "Aristotelian Tragedy in *Troilus and Criseyde*," *Proceedings of the Medieval Association of the Midwest* (Emporia, KS: Emporia State University, 1993), 90-98.

[4] Kittredge argued that Chaucer thought Lollius was an ancient source on the Trojan War on the basis of a misreading of a reference to a Lollius in the opening lines of Horace's Episle 1.2. Robert W. Pratt showed that this was a common misconception in the fourteenth century: "A Note on Chaucer's Lollius," MLN 65 (1950), 183-7.

[5] For a list of critics themselves overcome by Criseyde, see Gretchen Mieszkowski, "Chaucer's Much Loved Criseyde," *Chaucer Review* 26 (1991), 109-32. Mieszkowski objects to their infatuations.

[6] Ockham's extended treatment of this topic is in his *Tractatus de praedestinatione et de praescientia Dei et de futuris contingentibus*.

Chapter Eight

[1] Lawler, 24-25.

BIBLIOGRAPHY

Archer, John. "The Structure of Anti-Semitism in the *Prioress's Tale*." *Chaucer Review* 25 (1991): 277-84.

Arthur, Ross G. *Medieval Sign Theory and Sir Gawain and the Green Knight*. Toronto: University of Toronto Press, 1987.

Alexander, Philip S. "Madame Eglentyne, Geoffrey Chaucer and the Problem of Medieval Anti-Semitism." *Bulletin of the John Rylands Library of Manchester* 74 (1992): 109-20.

Baum, Paull F. "Chaucer's Puns." *PMLA* 71 (1956): 225-46.

Benson, C. David. *Chaucer's Drama of Style: Poetic Variety and Contrast in the* Canterbury Tales. Chapel Hill: University of North Carolina Press, 1986.

Bennett, J.A.W. *Chaucer's "Book of Fame"*. Oxford: Clarendon Press, 1968.

Bestul, Thomas H. "Chaucer's Parson and the Late Medieval Tradition of Religious Meditation." *Speculum* 64 (1988): 600-19.

- - - . "*The Man of Law's Tale* and the Rhetorical Foundation of Chaucerian Pathos." *Chaucer Review* 9 (1975): 216-26.

Bloomfield, Morton W. "A Tragedy of Victimization and a Christian Comedy." *PMLA* 87 (1972): 384-90.

Bornstein, Diane. "Chaucer's *Tale of Melibee* as an Example of the Style Clergial." *Chaucer Review* 12 (1978): 236-54.

Bowden, Betsy. *Chaucer Aloud: The Varieties of Textual Interpretation*. Philadelphia: University of Pennsylvania Press, 1987.

Bowden, Muriel. *A Commentary on the "General Prologue" to the* Canterbury Tales. London: Macmillan, 1973.

Bowman, Mary R. "Half as Were Mad: Dorigen in the Male World of the *Franklin's Tale*." *Chaucer Review* 27 (1993): 239-51.

Brewer, Derek. *Chaucer: The Poet as Storyteller*. London: Macmillan, 1984.

Bronson, Bertrand H. "In Appreciation of Chaucer's *Parlement of Fowles.*" *University of California Publications in English* 3 (1935): 193-223.

---. *In Search of Chaucer*. Toronto: University of Toronto Press, 1960.

Burlin, Robert B. *Chaucerian Fiction*. Princeton: Princeton University Press, 1977.

Burrow, J.A. *Ricardian Poetry*. London: Routlege & Kegan Paul, 1971.

Chaucer, Geoffrey. *The Riverside Chaucer*, ed. Larry D. Benson. Boston: Houghton Miflin Company, 1987.

Chaucer, Geoffrey. *The Canterbury Tales*, ed. N. F. Blake. London: Arnold, 1980.

Chaucer, Geoffrey. *An Anthology for the Modern Reader*, ed. E. Talbot Donaldson. New York: Ronald Press, 1975

Chaucer at Albany, ed. Rossell Hope Robbins. New York: Burt Franklin and Co., 1975.

Chaucer the Love Poet, ed. Jerome Mitchell and William Provost. Athens: University of Georgia Press, 1973.

Chaucer's Mind and Art, ed. A. C. Cawley. New York: Barnes and Noble, 1970.

Chaucer's Pilgrim Tales, ed. C. David Benson and Elizabeth Robertson. Cambridge: Cambridge University Press, 1990.

Chickering, Howell. "Form and Interpretation in the *Envoy* to the *Clerk's Tale*." *Chaucer Review* 29 (1995): 352-72.

Colish, Marcia L. *The Mirror of Language: A Study in the Medieval Theory of Knowledge*. Lincoln: University of Nebraska Press, 1983.

Cooper, Helen. *The Structure of the* Canterbury Tales. Athens: University of Georgia Press, 1984.

---. *The Canterbury Tales*. Oxford [Eng.]: Clarendon Press, 1989.

Corsa, Helen Storm. *Chaucer, Poet of Mirth and Morality*. Notre Dame: University of Notre Dame Press, 1964.

Davidson, Arnold E. "The Logic of Confusion in Chaucer's *Manciple's Tale*." *Annuale Mediaevale* 19 (1979): 5-12.

Davis, Adam Brooke. "The Ends of Fiction: Narrative Boundaries and Chaucer's Attitude Toward Courtly Love." *Chaucer Review* 28 (1993): 54-66.

Delaney, Sheila. *Chaucer's* House of Fame: *The Poetics of Skeptical Fideism*. Chicago: University of Chicago Press, 1972.

Delasanta, Rodney. "Nominalism and the *Clerk's Tale* Revisited." *Chaucer Review* 31 (1997): 209-231.

Dempster, Germaine. "A Period in the Development of the *Canterbury Tales* Marriage Group and Blocks B^2 and C." *PMLA* 68 (1953) 1142-59.

Donaldson, E. Talbot. "Chaucer the Pilgrim." *PMLA* 69 (1954) 928-36.

- - - . *Speaking of Chaucer*. New York: Norton, 1970.

Duncan, Edgar H. "The Literature of Alchemy in Chaucer's *Canon's Yeoman's Tale*: Framework, Theme, and Character." *Speculum* 43 (1968): 635-8.

Despres, Denise L. "Cultic Anti-Semitism and Chaucer's Litel Clergeon." *Modern Philology* 91 (1994): 413-27.

Elbow, Peter. *Oppositions in Chaucer*. Middletown, CT: Wesleyan University Press, 1975.

Ellis, Roger. *Patterns of Religious Narrative in the* Canterbury Tales. Totowa, NJ: Barnes and Noble, 1986.

Farnham, Willard. *The Medieval Heritage of Elizabethan Tragedy*. Berkeley: University of California Press, 1956.

Farrell, Thomas J. "The 'Envoi de Chaucer' and the *Clerk's Tale*." *Chaucer Review* 24 (1990): 329-36.

Ferster, Judith. *Chaucer on Interpretation*. Cambridge: Cambridge University Press, 1985.

Fletcher, Alan J. "The Preaching of the Pardoner." *Studies in the Age of Chaucer* 11 (1989): 15-35.

Foster, Edward E. "Humor in the *Knight's Tale*." *Chaucer Review* 3 (1968): 88-94.

Frank, Harley Long. "Chaucer's Prioress and the Blessed Virgin." *Chaucer Review* 13 (1979): 346-62.

Frank, Robert Worth, Jr. "Structure and Meaning in the *Parlement of Fowles*." *PMLA* 71 (1956): 530-9.

Frese, Dolores Warwick. *An Ars legendi for Chaucer's* Canterbury Tales: *Re-constructive Reading*. Gainesville: University of Florida Press, 1991.

Fyler, John M. *Chaucer and Ovid*. New Haven: Yale University Press, 1979.

Gallick, Susan. "Styles of Usage in the *Nun's Priest's Tale*." *Chaucer Review* 11 (1977): 232-47.

Ganim, John M. "Carnival Voices and the Envoy to the *Clerk's Tale*." *Chaucer Review* 22 (1987): 112-27.

- - - . *Chaucerian Theatricality*. Princeton: Princeton University Press, 1990.

- - - . *Style and Consciousness in Middle English Narrative*. Princeton: Princeton University Press, 1983.

Garbaty, Thomas J. "Chaucer's Weaving Wife." *Journal of American Folklore* 81 (1968): 342-6.

Gellrich, Jesse M. *The Idea of the Book in the Middle Ages: Language Theory, Mythology, and Fiction*. Ithaca: Cornell University Press, 1985.

Gower, John. "Tale of the Knight Florent." *Confessio Amantis*, ed. Russell A. Peck. New York: Holt, Rinehart and Winston, 1968.

Graybill, Robert. "Aristotelian Tragedy in *Troilus and Criseyde*." *Proceedings of the Medieval Association of the Midwest*. Emporia: Emporia State University, 1993. 90-98.

Grennen, Joseph E. "Hert-huntying in the *Book of the Duchess*." *Modern Language Quarterly* 25 (1964): 131-9.

Haas, Renate. "Chaucer's *Monk's Tale*: An Ingenious Criticism of Early Humanist Conceptions of Tragedy." *Humanistica Lovaniensia: A Journal of Neo-Latin Studies* 36 (1987): 44-70.

Harrington, Norman. "Chaucer's *Merchant's Tale*: Another Swing of the Pendulum." *PMLA* 86 (1971): 25-31.

Hartung, Albert E. "'Pars Secunda' and the Development of the *Canon's Yeoman's Tale*." *Chaucer Review* 12 (1977): 111-28.

Heffernan, Carol. "Chaucer's *Troilus and Criseyde*: The Disease of Love and Courtly Love." *Neophilologus* 74 (1990): 294-309.

Hill, John M. *Chaucerian Belief: The Poetics of Reverence and Delight*. New Haven: Yale University Press, 1991.

Holley, Linda Tarte. *Chaucer's Measuring Eye*. Houston: Rice University Press, 1990.

Howard, Donald Roy. *Chaucer: His Life, His Works, His World*. New York: Dutton, 1987.

- - - . "The Conclusion of the Marriage Group: Chaucer and the Human Condition." *Modern Philology* 57 (1960): 223-32.

- - - . *The Idea of the* Canterbury Tales. Berkeley: University of California Press, 1976.

Huppe, Bernard F., and D.W. Robertson. *Fruyt and Chaf*. Princeton: Princeton University Press, 1963.

The Idea of Medieval Literature: New Essays in Honor of Donald R. Howard, ed. James M. Dean and Christian Zacher. Newark: University of Delaware Press, 1992.

Jauss, Hans Robert. *Toward an Aesthetic of Reception*, tr. Timothy Bahti. Brighton: Harvester Press, 1982.

Jewish Presences in English Literature, ed. Derek Cohen and Deborah Heller. Montreal: McGill-Queen's University Press, 1990.

Jones, Terry. *Chaucer's Knight: The Portrait of a Medieval Mercenary*. London: Weidenfeld and Nicolson, 1980.

Jordan, Robert M. *Chaucer and the Shape of Creation: The Aesthetic Possibilities of Inorganic Structure*. Cambridge: Harvard University Press, 1967.

- - - . *Chaucer's Poetics and the Modern Reader*. Berkeley: University of California Press, 1987. Kellogg, Alfred L. and Louis A. Haselmayer. "Chaucer's Satire of the Pardoner." *Studies in the Age of Chaucer* 11 (1989): 15-35.

Kelly, Henry Ansgar. *Chaucerian Tragedy*. Chaucer Studies 24. Cambridge: D.S. Brewer, 1997.

Kempton, Daniel. "The Nun's Priest's Festive Diction: Al That is Writen . . .". *Essays: Critical Approaches to Medieval and Renaissance Texts* 8 (1995): 101-18.

Kittredge, George Lyman. *Chaucer and His Poetry*. Cambridge: Harvard University Press, 1915.

- - - . "Chaucer's Discussion of Marriage." *Modern Philology* 9 (1912): 435-67.

Knapp, Peggy Ann. *Chaucer and the Social Contest*. New York: Routledge, 1990.

Knight, Stephen. *Ryming Craftily: Meaning in Chaucer's Poetry*. London: Angus and Robertson, 1973.

Koff, Leonard. *Chaucer and the Art of Storytelling*. Berkeley: University of California Press, 1988.

Kökeritz, Helge. "Historical Word-Play in Chaucer." *PMLA* 69 (1954), 951.

Kolve, V. A. *Chaucer and the Imagery of Narrative: The First Five Canterbury Tales*. Stanford: Stanford University Press, 1984.

Koonce, B.G. *Chaucer and the Tradition of Fame: Symbolism in "The House of Fame"*. Princeton: Princeton University Press, 1966.

Koretsky, Allen C. "Dangerous Innocence: Chaucer's Prioress and her Tale." *Jewish Presences in English Literature*. Montreal: McGill-Queens University Press, 1990. 10-24.

Kroger, Steven. "Imagination and the Complex Movement of Chaucer's House of Fame." *Chaucer Review* 28 (1994): 117-34.

Lawler, Traugott. *The One and the Many*. Hamden: E. Archon Books, 1980.

Lee, Brian S. "The Question of Closure in Fragment V of the *Canterbury Tales*." Yearbook of English Studies 22 (1993): 190-200.

Leff, Gordon. *Medieval Thought*. Harmondsworth [Eng.]: Penguin, 1958.

- - - . *William of Ockham: The Metamorphosis of Scholastic Discourse*. Manchester: University of Manchester Press, 1975.

Leicester, H[enry] Marshall, Jr. *The Disenchanted Self: Representing the Subject in the* Canterbury Tales. Berkeley: University of California Press, 1990.

- - - . "The Harmony of Chaucer's *Parlement*: A Dissonant Voice." *Chaucer Review* 9 (1974): 15-34.

Lewis, C[live] S[taples]. *The Allegory of Love*. Oxford: Clarendon Press, 1936.

Literary Nominalism and the Theory of Rereading Late Medieval Texts, ed. Richard J. Utz. Lewiston, NY: Edwin Mellen Press, 1995.

Lumiansky, R.M. "The Character and Performance of Chaucer's Franklin." *University of Toronto Quarterly* 20 (1951): 344-56.

- - - . "Chaucer's *Parlement of Fowles*: A Philosophical Interpretation." *Review of English Studies* 24 (1948): 81-89.

Lynch, Kathryn. "Despoiling Griselda: Chaucer's Walter and the Problem of Knowledge in the *Clerk's Tale*." *Studies in the Age of Chaucer* 10 (1988): 41-70.

- - - . "The Parliament of Fowls and Late Medieval Voluntarism." *Chaucer Review* 25 (1991) 1-16 and 87-95.

Major, John M. "The Personality of Chaucer the Pilgrim." *PMLA* 75 (1960): 160-2.

Manly, John M. *Some New Light on Chaucer*. New York: Henry Holt, 1926.

Mann, Jill. *Chaucer and Medieval Estates Satire: The Literature of Social Classes and the General Prologue to the* Canterbury Tales. Cambridge [Eng.]: Cambridge University Press, 1973.

- - -. *Geoffrey Chaucer*. Atlantic Highlands, NJ: Humanities Press International, 1991.

Matthewson, Effie Jean. "The Illusion of Morality in the Franklin's Tale." *Medium Aevum* 53 (1983): 27-37.

McAlpine, Monica. *The Genre of Troilus and Criseyde*. Ithaca: Cornell University Press, 1978.

McCall, John P. "The Harmony of Chaucer's *Parliament*." *Chaucer Review* 5 (1970): 22-31.

McDonald, Charles. "An Interpretation of Chaucer's *Parlement of Fowles*." *Speculum* 30 (1955): 444-57.

McGregor, Francine. "Whot of Dorigen: Agency and Ambivalence in the *Franklin's Tale*." *Chaucer Review* 31 (1997): 365-78.

Medieval English Studies Presented to George Kane, ed. Ronald Waldron and Joseph Wittig. Woodbridge: D. S. Brewer, 1998.

Medieval Literary Theory and Criticism, c. 1100-c. 1375, ed. A.J. Minnis and A.B. Scott. Oxford: Oxford University Press, 1988.

Medieval Literature and Folklore Studies: Essays in Honor of Marcus Lee Utley, ed. Jerome Mandel and Bruce A. Rosenberg. New Brunswick: Rutgers University Press, 1970.

Medieval Literature: Criticism, Ideology, and History, ed. David Aers. New York: St. Martin's Press, 1986.

Meech, Sanford. *Design in Chaucer's Triolus*. Syracuse: University of Syracuse Press, 1959.

Merrix, Robert P. "Sermon Structure in the Pardoner's Tale." *Chaucer Review* 17 (1983): 235-49.

Mieszkowski, Gretchen. "Chaucer's Much Loved Criseyde." *Chaucer Review* 26 (1991): 109-32.

Miskimin, Alice. *The Renaissance Chaucer*. New Haven: Yale University Press, 1975.

Mitchell, Charles. "The Worthiness of Chaucer's Knight." *Modern Language Quarterly* 25 (1964): 66-75.

Moore, Roger E. "Nominalist Perspectives on Chaucer's 'The Man of Law's Tale'." *Comitatus* 23 (1993): 80-100.

Ockham, William of. *Opera Philosophica*, vol. 1-3. St. Bonaventure, N.Y.: Editiones Instituti Franciscani Universitatis S. Bonaventurae, 1974-(1979).

- - -. *Predestination, God's Foreknowledge, and Future Contingents*, tr. and intro. Marilyn McCord Adams and Norman Kretzmann. New York: Appleton-Century-Crofts, 1969.

- - -. *Ockham's Theory of Terms*, tr. and intro. Michael J. Loux. Notre Dame, IN: Notre Dame University Press, 1974.

Oruch, Jack B. "St. Valentine, Chaucer, and Spring in February." *Speculum* 56 (1981): 534-65.

Owen, Charles A. "The Plan of the *Canterbury Tales*." *PMLA* 66 (1951): 820-6.

Owen, Nancy H. "The Pardoner's Introduction, Prologue, and Tale: Sermon and *Fabliau*." *Journal of English and Germanic Philology* 66 (1967): 541-9.

Owst, Gerald R. *Literature and the Pulpit in Medieval England*. 2nd Ed. New York: Barnes and Noble, 1961.

Page, Barbara. "Concerning the Host." *Chaucer Review* 4 (1969): 1-13.

Patterson, Lee. "For the Wyves Love of Bathe: Feminine Rhetoric and Poetic Resolution in the *Roman de la Rose* and the *Canterbury Tales*." *Speculum* 58 (1983): 656-95.

- - -. *Chaucer and the Subject of History*. Madison: University of Wisconsin Press, 1991.

- - -. *Negotiating the Past: The Historical Understanding of Medieval Literature*. Madison: University of Wisconsin Press, 1987.

Payne, Robert O. *The Key of Remembrance: A Study of Chaucer's Poetics*. New Haven: Yale University Press, 1963.

Pearsall, Derek. *The Canterbury Tales*. London [Eng.]: G. Allen and Unwin, 1985.

Peck, Russell. "Chaucer and the Nominalist Questions." *Speculum* 53 (1978): 745-60.

- - -. "The Ideas of 'Entente' and Translation in Chaucer's *Second Nun's Tale*." *Annuale Mediaevale* 8 (1967): 17-37.

- - -. "St. Paul and the Parson's Tale." *Mediaevalia* 7 (1981), 91-131.

Pichaske, David R., and Laura Sweetland. "Chaucer on Medieval Monarchy: Harry Bailly in the *Canterbury Tales*." *Chaucer Review* 11 (1977): 179-200.

Pratt, Robert W. "A Note on Chaucer's Lollius." *Modern Language Notes* 65 (1950): 183-7.

Provost, William. *The Structure of Chaucer's* Troilus. Copenhagen: Rosenkilde and Bagger, 1974.

Pulham, Carol A. "Promises: Dorigen's Dilemma Revisited." *Chaucer Review* 31 (1996): 76-86.

Ramazani, Jahan. "Chaucer's Monk: The Poetics of Abbreviation, Aggression, and Tragedy." *Chaucer Review* 27 (1993): 260-76.

Robertson, D.W. *A Preface to Chaucer*. Princeton: Princeton University Press, 1962.

Rogers, William Elford. *Upon the Ways: The Structure of the* Canterbury Tales. Victoria [Can.]: University of Victoria Press, 1986.

Root, Robert Kilburn. *The Poetry of Chaucer*. Boston: Houghton Mifflin Company, 1957.

Ross, Thomas Wynne. *Chaucer's Bawdy*. New York: Dutton. 1972.

Ruggiers, Paul. *The Art of the* Canterbury Tales. Madison: University of Wisconsin Press, 1965,

Salter, Elizabeth. *Chaucer's "Knight's Tale" and "Clerk's Tale"*. London [Eng.]: E. Arnold, 1962.

Severs, J. Burke. *The Literary Relationships of Chaucer's "Clerk's Tale"*. New Haven: Yale University Press, 1942.

Shannon, Paul. "The Tongue as Sword: Psalms 56 and 63 and the Pardoner." *Chaucer Review* 27 (1993): 396-400.

Sklute, Larry. "The Inconclusiveness of Form in the *Parlement of Fowles*." *Chaucer Review* 16 (1981): 119-28.

- - -. *Virtue of Necessity: Inconclusiveness and Narrative Form in Chaucer's Poetry*. Columbus: Ohio State University Press, 1984.

Sources and Analogues of Chaucer's Canterbury Tales, ed. William Frank Bryan and Germaine Dempster. New York: Humanities Press, 1958.

Spearing, A.C. *The Gawain-Poet*. Cambridge [Eng.]: Cambridge University Press, 1970.

- - -. *Medieval Dream-Poetry*. Cambridge [Eng.]: Cambridge University Press, 1976.

Steinmetz, Daniel. "Late Medieval Nominalism and the *Clerk's Tale*." *Chaucer Review* 12 (1977): 38-54.

Stepsis, Robert. "*Potentia Absoluta* and the *Clerk's Tale*." *Chaucer Review* 10 (1975): 129-46.

Stilwell, Gardiner. "Unity and Comedy in Chaucer's *Parlement of Fowles*." *Journal of English and Germanic Philology* 49 (1950): 470-495.

Studies in Medieval Literature in Honor of Professor Albert. Croll Baugh ed. MacEdward Leach. Philapelphia: University of Pennsylvania Press, 1961.

Terrell, Katherine H. "Reallocation of Hermeneutic Authority in Chaucer's *House of Fame*." *Chaucer Review* 31 (1997): 279-90.

Thomas, Mary Edith. *Medieval Skepticism and Chaucer: An Evaluation of the Skepticism of the 13th and 14th Centuries, of Geoffrey Chaucer and his Immediate Predecessors*. New York: William-Frederick Press, 1950.

Trask, Richard M. "The Manciple's Problem." *Studies in Short Fiction* 14 (1977): 109-16.

Travis, Peter W. "Deconstructing Chaucer's Retraction." *Exemplaria* 3 (1991): 135-58.

Vaskeerbergen, Bernadette. "Chaucer's House of Fame: A Journey into Skepticism." *Medieval Perspectives* 9 (1994): 279-90.

"The Wedding of Sir Gawain and Dame Ragnell." *Sir Gawain: Eleven Romances and Tales.* Ed. Thomas Hahn, TEAMS. Kalamazoo: Medieval Institute Publications, 1995. 41-80.

Wilhelm, James J. "The Narrator and his Narrative in Chaucer's *Parlement*." *Chaucer Review* 1 (1967): 201-6.

Williams, David. *The* Canterbury Tales: *A Literary Pilgrimage.* Boston: Twayne, 1987.

Williams, George Guion. *A New View of Chaucer.* Durham: Duke University Press, 1965.

Windeatt, Barry A. *Chaucer's Dream Poetry: Sources and Analogues.* Woodbridge, Suffolk: D. S. Brewer, 1982.

Winny, James. *Chaucer's Dream-Poems.* New York: Harper & Row, 1973.

Wood, Chauncey. *The Elements of Chaucer's Troilus.* Durham: Duke University Press, 1984.

Wurtele, Douglas J. "Chaucer's Franklin and the Truth About 'Trouthe'." *English Studies in Canada* 13 (1987): 359-74.

- - - . "The Penitence of Geoffrey Chaucer." *Viator* 11 (1980): 335-59.

Zitter, Emory Stark. "Anti-Semitism in Chaucer's *Prioress's Tale*." *Chaucer Review* 25 (1991): 277-84.

INDEX

A

alchemy, 161, 163, 164, 165, 166, 167, 168, 169
allegory, 2, 7, 9, 10, 12, 40, 44, 88, 89, 103, 105, 109, 143, 144, 155, 159
Alliterative Mort Arthur, 189
ambiguity, 4, 7, 14, 18, 27, 32, 58, 67, 89, 93, 114, 118, 141, 151, 179
analogy, ii, 19, 87, 108
anger, ii, 19, 87, 108
anti-feminism, 22, 81, 99, 112, 118, 152
anti-Semitism, v, 139
Aquinas, 9
astrology, 90
Augustine, 159, 182
Augustinian, 8
authorities, 10, 14, 30, 35, 36, 38, 94, 112, 129, 133, 145, 154, 166
authority, iv, 2, 5, 6, 9, 10, 11, 12, 13, 14, 15, 16, 22, 26, 27, 30, 31, 32, 38, 39, 48, 54, 64, 67, 68, 69, 71, 72, 82, 93, 94, 101, 103, 129, 130, 131, 143, 144, 145, 150, 152, 153, 159, 161, 174, 175, 178, 186, 190, 195, 200, 204, 205

B

beast fable, 150, 155
Boccaccio, 3, 102, 190, 207
Boethius, 9, 79, 186
Bonaventure, 8
Book of the Duchess, 2, 21, 39, 42-54, 59, 60, 204
Bradshaw shift, 91, 129, 181
Burlin, Robert, 6, 207

C

Canterbury Tales, v, 2, 9, 17, 57, 61, 62, 63, 64, 65-183, 185, 189, 201, 204, 207
Canon's Yeoman, 161, 162, 163, 164, 165, 166, 168
Canon's Yeoman's Tale, 161-169
cardinal moral virtues, 154
"Chaucer", 64, 65, 141, 142, 143, 144, 146, 179, 181
chivalry, 21, 22, 24, 71, 72, 73, 80, 85, 142, 205, 207
Clerk, 2, 9, 10, 66, 82, 102, 103, 104, 105, 106, 107, 108, 109, 110, 111, 121, 124, 126, 127
Clerk's Tale, 102-110
commune profit, 9, 10, 20, 24, 53, 56, 59, 103, 104, 105, 108, 110, 118, 127, 131, 145, 161, 178
Confessio Amantis, 207
confession, 92, 95, 100, 102, 164, 173, 176
Cook, 61, 68, 85, 120
Cook's Tale, 85
courtly love, 21, 42, 43, 44, 45, 48, 49, 50, 54, 58, 71, 72, 73, 74, 83, 85, 115, 116, 117, 122, 123, 151, 153, 185, 187, 188, 189, 190, 191, 193, 194, 197, 199, 205

D

damnation, 168, 176
Dante, 54
deadly sins, 145
destiny, 70, 75, 76, 77, 79, 198
Doctor, 66, 67
doctrine, 13, 15, 52, 58, 68, 78, 89, 101, 103, 109, 130, 134, 138, 145, 155, 166, 167, 171, 173, 176, 178, 180, 182, 183, 201
Donaldson, E. Talbot, i, 7, 63, 207
Dream of Scipio, 52, 53, 55
dream vision, v, 16, 25, 39, 51, 58, 59, 70, 72, 203, 205

E

epistemological, 34, 36, 40, 52, 54, 118, 127, 137, 146, 149, 150, 151, 169, 175
epistemology, 38, 39, 42, 141, 177, 203
experience, v, 4, 6, 8, 9, 10, 11, 12, 15, 17, 20, 21, 22, 24, 27, 29, 31, 32, 34, 39, 41, 45, 47, 48, 49, 50, 54, 63, 68, 76, 77, 88, 89, 93, 94, 101, 102, 130, 144, 152, 166, 169, 175, 177, 183, 187, 188, 194, 196, 197, 198, 200, 201, 204

F

fabliau, 23, 81, 111, 113, 114, 115, 117, 205
faith, 1, 5, 7, 8, 10, 13, 16, 18, 19, 22, 88, 124, 139, 157, 158, 159, 160, 169, 175, 177, 178, 179, 198, 199, 205
fate, 51, 75, 100, 152, 153, 186, 197, 205
fiction, ii, iii, v, 1, 2, 3, 4, 6, 7, 13, 15, 16, 17, 18, 19, 20, 23, 26, 27, 31, 33, 39, 40, 41, 42, 46, 47, 48, 64, 65, 67, 68, 69, 72, 86, 87, 90, 92, 100, 109, 117, 124, 140, 141, 142, 165, 167, 168, 169, 170, 172, 173, 174, 178, 186, 189, 199, 200, 201, 205, 207
fideism, 8
foreknowledge, 10, 75, 76, 79, 153, 189, 197, 198
fortitude, 144, 154
Fortune, 35, 38, 44, 50, 51, 55, 56, 72, 73, 74, 75, 76, 77, 79, 81, 89, 103, 106, 107, 116, 117, 131, 148, 149, 185, 193, 195, 196, 197, 200, 205
Franklin, 2, 66, 67, 118, 119, 120, 121, 123, 125, 126, 127
Franklin's Tale, 118-127
free will, 152, 198
Friar, 66, 67, 91, 102

G

Gascoigne, 180
Gellrich, Jesse, 5, 12, 22, 207
General Prologue, 1, 3, 21, 61-70, 79, 80, 82, 93, 102, 118, 120, 130, 132, 134, 137, 139, 140, 147, 150, 155, 157, 170, 174, 179, 180, 181
genre, 23, 24, 71, 81, 111, 127, 137, 140, 151, 178, 186
gentilesse, 24, 54, 91 57, 91, 101, 102, 103, 105, 108, 110, 114, 118, 119, 120, 121, 123, 126, 127, 204
gluttony, 133
Gower, John, 3, 13, 101, 102, 155, 182, 186, 200, 201, 207
grace, 33, 110, 121, 154, 174, 187
greed, 96, 130, 133, 134, 164, 166, 167

H

heresy, 196, 197
hermeneutical, 5, 11, 18, 22
hermeneutics, 5, 11, 18, 22, 205
heuristic, 21, 72, 85, 142, 178, 205
Host, 70, 80, 86, 102, 131, 132, 134, 135, 136, 140, 141, 142, 143, 146, 149, 162, 163, 173
House of Fame, 2, 3, 5, 25-39, 39, 46, 48, 50, 51, 60, 150, 155, 204, 207
Howard, Donald, 207

I

idealism, vi, 73, 79, 80, 84, 85, 89, 90, 111, 113, 115, 118, 191
indeterminacy, v, 7, 39, 58, 95, 102, 121, 167, 170, 203
indeterminate, 2, 24, 186, 197, 205
irony, 1, 4, 5, 7, 18, 66, 77, 101, 111, 112, 116, 158

J

justice, v, 74, 100, 144, 154, 199

K

Knight, vi, 2, 4, 21, 67, 70, 71, 72, 73, 75, 76, 77, 79, 80, 81, 82, 83, 84, 85, 92, 101, 111, 115, 120, 136, 149, 188, 189, 204, 207
Knight's Tale, 74-84

L

lechery, 96, 130, 131, 133, 171
legend, 178
Legend of Good Women, 25
lust, 54, 99, 106, 115, 153, 195

M

Macrobeus, 26, 41, 52
Man of Law, vi, 3, 62, 67, 86, 87, 88, 89, 90, 127, 141, 164, 179, 181, 204
Man of Law's Tale, 86-90
Manciple, 157, 169, 170, 171, 172, 181
Manciple's Tale, 169-173
marriage, 73, 81, 91, 93, 94, 95, 97, 98, 99, 100, 101, 102, 103, 104, 105, 110, 111, 112, 113, 114, 118, 119, 121, 123, 126, 127, 152, 204
marriage group, 91, 118, 127
Melibee, 130, 143, 144, 145, 154, 155, 157, 179, 204
Melibee, Tale of, 143-146
Merchant, 3, 4, 66, 67, 110, 111, 112, 113, 114, 115, 116, 117, 118, 121, 123, 127
Merchant's Tale, 110-118
Miller, vi, 61, 80, 81, 82, 84, 85, 92, 111, 112, 117, 155, 181, 182, 188, 204
Miller's Tale, 80-86

monasticism, 149
Monk, 66, 80, 129, 146, 148, 149, 156
Monk's Tale, 146-149

N

narration, 69, 77, 82, 86, 97, 98
narrative, 2, 4, 6, 7, 16, 17, 18, 22, 23, 25, 27, 28, 29, 42, 46, 49, 63, 64, 67, 70, 71, 72, 80, 81, 82, 86, 87, 88, 89, 100, 102, 103, 104, 107, 108, 109, 111, 114, 117, 118, 121, 125, 130, 131, 132, 153, 154, 155, 159, 171, 179, 185, 186, 187, 188, 191, 200, 201, 203
narrative technique, 2, 6, 7, 16, 17, 72, 102
narrator, 2, 3, 12, 14, 17, 18, 26, 27, 28, 29, 30, 31, 36, 37, 40, 41, 42, 43, 45, 46, 47, 48, 49, 51, 52, 53, 55, 58, 59, 60, 63, 64, 65, 66, 67, 68, 69, 70, 71, 72, 77, 80, 82, 87, 88, 106, 107, 112, 118, 119, 131, 132, 147, 149, 151, 161, 179, 181, 186, 188, 189, 190, 191, 193, 194, 195, 196, 199, 200, 201, 202
nominalism, iv, 9, 10, 11, 12, 13
nominalist, v, 10, 11, 12, 13, 16, 18, 32, 198, 199, 205
Nun's Priest, 2, 9, 10, 129, 150, 151, 153, 154, 155, 156, 157, 168
Nun's Priest's Tale, 150-156

O

Ockham, William of, 10, 11, 175, 198, 203
Ockhamite, 12, 175, 178, 205
Ovid, 25, 27, 28
Ovidian, 28, 196
Ovyde, 28

P

pagan, 53, 87, 88, 149, 163, 200
palinode, 89, 90, 127, 182, 185, 200, 201
parable, 108, 166
paradigm, 21, 22, 45, 48, 50, 83, 99, 185, 191, 194, 195, 197, 205
paradox, 1, 4, 7, 39, 49, 62, 63, 65, 107, 116, 182
Pardoner, 66, 95, 129, 132, 133, 134, 135, 136, 137, 140, 156, 164, 173
Pardoner's Tale, 131-137
Parliament of Fowls, 2, 51, 54-63, 150, 204
Parson, 66, 139, 157, 169, 172, 173, 174, 176, 177, 178, 179, 180, 183, 204
Parson's Tale, 176-184

pedagogy, 133, 144, 155
Penance, 176, 177, 183
Petrarch, 102, 103
Physician, 129, 130, 131, 138
Physician's Tale, 129-131
pilgrim, 3, 17, 63, 65, 66, 67, 70, 80, 87, 102, 108, 114, 132, 133, 134, 135, 136, 139, 140, 141, 142, 144, 152, 155, 161, 163, 165, 167, 174, 178, 179, 181, 182, 204
pilgrimage, 16, 63, 67, 80, 82, 86, 120, 135, 136, 142, 157, 161, 163, 165, 168, 169, 173, 174, 176, 177, 204
Plato, 69
Platonic, 8, 9, 11, 32, 34
Plowman, 66
portraits, 48, 62, 63, 65, 66, 67, 68, 70, 71, 80, 82, 83, 93, 118, 120, 130, 137
preacher, 133
preaching, 137
predestination, 151
pride, 132, 134, 136, 145, 148, 154, 159, 160, 165, 179
priest, 166, 176
Prioress, v, 66, 129, 137, 138, 139, 140, 152, 155, 158
Prioress's Tale, 137-140
prudence, 144, 154, 156
Prudence, Dame, 130, 144, 145, 146, 156

R

realism, vi, 3, 8, 11, 80, 85
reality, ii, 3, 5, 9, 11, 13, 15, 16, 17, 18, 19, 20, 28, 31, 32, 33, 34, 39, 40, 45, 46, 47, 48, 50, 55, 60, 64, 65, 68, 69, 70, 87, 88, 92, 109, 114, 117, 123, 124, 126, 136, 140, 146, 156, 164, 172, 176, 177, 179, 192, 196, 198, 200, 201, 204, 205
reason, 5, 7, 10, 13, 59, 71, 129, 142, 152, 157, 160, 161, 167, 175, 177, 178, 181, 205
Redemption, 154, 158, 172
Reeve, 61, 80, 84, 85
Reeve's Tale, 84-85
Retraction, vi, 2, 89, 157, 180, 181, 182, 184-187, 200, 201
revelation, 1, 11, 35, 36, 37, 39, 44, 47, 59, 108, 158, 159
romance, 3, 14, 42, 70, 81, 115, 116, 117, 120, 142, 144, 153, 185, 186, 189, 190, 191, 192, 197

S

sacrament, 177
salvation, v, 53, 59, 102, 103, 114, 129, 132, 140, 146, 151, 154, 156, 158, 163, 175, 176, 177, 178, 191, 200, 202, 204, 205
Scripture, 11, 94
Second Nun, 157, 158, 160, 168
Second Nun's Tale, 157-161
sermon, 101, 121, 133, 173
Shipman, 181
Sir Gawain and the Green Knight, 4, 189, 207
skepticism, 6, 8, 16, 96, 112
Squire, 120, 121
St. Paul, 13, 53, 155, 174, 182
Stanzaic Morte Arthure, 189
Strode, Ralph, 186, 200
Summoner, 66, 67, 91
symbol, 31, 35, 45, 55, 89, 139, 177

T

Tale of Sir Thopas, 136, 140-143
tavern sins, 133
temperance, 144, 154
Thomistic, 10, 11, 198
Thopas, 136, 142, 143, 179
tragedy, 147, 149, 153, 185, 186, 199
Troilus and Criseyde, v, 2, 4, 17, 21, 89, 182, 185, 189, 190, 192, 194, 201, 205

U

undecideability, iv, v, 56

V

Vergil, 28
Vergilian, 28

W

Wife of Bath, 3, 4, 92, 102, 103, 109, 112, 113, 114, 127, 134, 136, 145, 153, 164
Wife of Bath's Tale, 92-102

STUDIES IN BRITISH LITERATURE

1. Michael E. Allsopp and Michael W. Sundermeier (eds.), **Gerard Manley Hopkins (1844-1889): New Essays on His Life, Writing, and Place in English Literature**
2. Dana Grove, **A Rhetorical Analysis of** *Under the Volcano*: **Malcolm Lowry's Design Governing Postures**
3. Christopher Spencer, **The Genesis of Shakespeare's** *Merchant of Venice*
4. Oscar Wilde, *Vera; or, The Nihilist*, Frances Miriam Reed (ed.)
5. Rob Jackaman, **The Course of English Surrealist Poetry Since the 1930s**
6. Florence Boos, **The Design of William Morris'** *The Earthly Paradise*
7. Gavin Edwards, **George Crabbe's Poetry on Border Land**
8. Martin Green, **A Biography of John Buchan and His Sister Anna: The Personal Background of Their Literary Work**
9. T.H. Howard-Hill (ed.), **The Bridgewater Manuscript of Thomas Middleton's** *A Game at Chess* (1624)
10. Karen Michalson, **Victorian Fantasy Literature: Literary Battles With Church and Empire**
11. Cynthia Marshall, **Essays On C.S. Lewis and George MacDonald: Truth, Fiction, and the Imagination**
12. Kathleen McCormick, *Ulysses*, **"Wandering Rocks," and the Reader: Multiple Pleasures in Reading**
13. Peter Milward, **A Commentary on G.M. Hopkins'** *The Wreck of the Deutschland*
14. David Macaree, **Daniel Defoe: His Political Writings and Literary Devices**
15. Joan M. Walmsley, **John Reynolds, Merchant of Exeter, and His Contribution to the Literary Scene, 1620-1660**
16. Osamu Yamada, Hilda D. Spear and David S. Robb, **The Contribution to Literature of Orcadian Writer George Mackay Brown: An Introduction and a Bibliography**
17. Bouwe Pieter Postmus (ed.), **The Poetry of George Gissing**
18. R.S. White (ed.), **Hazlitt's Criticism of Shakespeare: A Selection**
19. Barry Spurr, **A Literary-Critical Analysis of the Complete Prose Works of Lytton Strachey (1880-1932): A Re-Assessment of His Achievement and Career**
20. Bernard Tucker, **The Poetry of Laetitia Pilkington (1712-1750) and Constantia Grierson (1706-1733)**
21. Brian Taylor, **The Life and Writings of James Owen Hannay (George A. Birmingham) 1865-1950**

22. Rob Jackaman, **A Study of Cultural Centres and Margins in British Poetry Since 1950: Poets and Publishers**
23. Donald Walhout (ed.), **Selected Poems of Gerard Manley Hopkins with English Paraphrases**
24. D.B.D. Asker, **The Modern Bestiary--Animals in English Fiction 1880-1945**
25. Lynne Marie DeCicco, **Women and Lawyers in the Mid-Nineteenth Century English Novel: Uneasy Alliances and Narrative Misrepresentation**
26. Elizabeth J. Deis (ed.), **George Meredith's 1895 Collection of Three Stories: Explorations of Gender and Power**
27. Manju Jaidka, **T.S. Eliot's Use of Popular Sources**
28. Graeme Davis, **The Word-Order of Ælfric**
29. Julian Stannard, **Fleur Adcock in Context: From Movement to Martians**
30. Thomas Price, **Critical Edition of** *The Jealous Wife* **and** *Polly Honeycombe* **by George Colman the Elder (1732-1794)**
31. Richard A. Cardwell (ed.), **Lord Byron the European: Essays From The International Byron Society**
32. Patricia Gately, Dennis Leavens, D.Cole Woodcox (eds.), **Perspectives on Self and Community in George Eliot: Dorothea's Window**
33. Sandra J. Pyle, **Mirth and Morality of Shakespeare's Holy Fools**
34. Richard M. Dunn, **Geoffrey Scott and the Berenson Circle: Literary and Aesthetic Life in the Early 20th Century**
35. Gary Gautier, **Landed Patriarchy in Fielding's Novels: Fictional Landscapes, Fictional Genders**
36. John Delli-Carpini, **Prayer and Piety in the Poems of Gerard Manley Hopkins: The Landscape of a Soul**
37. Kevin Alexander Boon, **An Interpretive Reading of Virginia Woolf's** *The Waves*
38. John Coates, **Social Discontinuity in the Novels of Elizabeth Bowen: The Conservative Quest**
39. Joan H. Pittock, **Henry Birkhead, Founder of the Oxford Chair of Poetry: Poetry and the Redemption of History**
40. Peter Heaney (ed.), **Selected Writings of the Laureate Dunces, Nahum Tate (Laureate 1692-1715), Laurence Eusden (1718-1730), and Colley Cibber (1730-1757**
41. Edward E. Foster, **Understanding Chaucer's Intellectual and Interpretative World: Nominalist Fiction**